LETTERS *of* MEDIEVAL WOMEN

EDITED BY
ANNE CRAWFORD

SUTTON PUBLISHING

First published in the United Kingdom in 2002 by
Sutton Publishing Limited · Phoenix Mill
Thrupp · Stroud · Gloucestershire · GL5 2BU

British Library Cataloguing in Publication Data
A catalogue record for this book is available from the British Library.

ISBN 0-7509-2798-4

Typeset in 11/14.5pt Sabon.
Typesetting and origination by
Sutton Publishing Limited.
Printed and bound in England by
J.H. Haynes & Co. Ltd, Sparkford.

Contents

Acknowledgements

My greatest debt in compiling this book is to those historians who have gone before me in editing the letters of medieval women. My thanks are also due to Paul Johnson and Marc Morris for their translations from the French and Latin.

List of Letters

Alice Crane to Margaret Paston, 29 June (*c.* 1455)
Elizabeth Mountford to John Paston, *c.* 1460–6
Elizabeth Poynings to Sir John Paston, 15 December (?1468)
Dame Elizabeth Browne to John Paston, 23 September 1485
Margery Hampden to Thomas Stonor, *c.* 1465
Margery Hampden to William Stonor, *c.* 1477
Margaret Stephen to Thomas Perrott, 27 October (*c.* 1468)
Dame Katherine Arundell to Thomas Stonor, 27 January (?1473)
Lucy Prynce to Thomas Clifford, *c.* 1474
Dame Agnes Plumpton to Thomas Everingham, 15 January
    1503

Chapter 6: *Women and their patrons, friends and servants*
Letters from patrons to clients:
Eleanor, Duchess of Brittany, to her subjects in Brittany, 27 May
    1208
Eleanor Despenser to John Inge, Sheriff of Glamorgan, 6 March
    1322
Eleanor Despenser to John Stonor, 7 February (*c.* 1323–6)
Margaret, Countess of Devon, to Edmund Stonor, 13 January 1380
Elizabeth, Lady Zouche, to John Bore, 18 March and 31 August
    1402
Elizabeth, Countess of Oxford, to John Paston, 7 August,
    1 February and 13 April (?1454)
Eleanor, Duchess of Norfolk, to John Paston, 8 June 1455
Margaret Paston to Sir James Gloys, 18 January 1473
Alice, Duchess of Suffolk, to William Stonor, 5 March (?1475)
Elizabeth, Duchess of Suffolk, to John Paston, ?1483
Margaret, Countess of Oxford, to John Paston, 19 May 1486 and
    15 January (*c.* 1494–8)
Elizabeth, Duchess of Norfolk, to Sir William Knyvet, Sir John
    Paston and others, 14 September (?1496)
Elizabeth, Duchess of Norfolk, to Sir John Paston, 28 February
    1497
Margaret, Countess of Richmond, to (?Sir John Paston) 10 February
    (*c.* 1497–1503)

Letters to equals:

Agatha de Mortimer to Walter de Merton, Chancellor, *c.* 1272–4

Aline, Countess of Norfolk, to Walter de Merton, Chancellor,
    c. 1272–4

Eleanor and Joan of England to John de Kirkby, Bishop of Ely,
    1286

Margaret d'Umfreville to Henry de Clyf, 1331

Marie, Countess of Pembroke, to Henry Burghersh, Bishop of
    Lincoln, Chancellor, 1329

Joan Armburgh to John Horell, *c.* 1429–30

Alice, Lady Sudeley, to Thomas Stonor, 4 April (*c.* 1420s)

Eleanor Chamber to William Paston, November *c.* 1442

Dame Alice Ogard to John Paston, 30 March 1456

Elizabeth, Countess of Surrey, to John Paston 3 October 1485

Alice, Lady Fitzhugh, to John Paston, 24 February (?1486)

Joan Trowe to John Porter, *c.* 1495

Dame Elizabeth de la Pole to Sir Robert Plumpton, 26 November
    1501 and 10 July (?1504)

Maud Roos to Sir Robert Plumpton, ?1504

Letters from clients to lords and patrons:

Maud, Marshal of England and Countess of Norfolk and Warenne,
    to Henry III, 1248

Cecily de Beauchamp to Edward I, 24 August 1295

Matilda Mortimer to Edward I, 1297

Ela, Countess of Warwick, to Edward I, *c.* 1272–98

Matilda de Bokeshull to Robert Baldock, Chancellor, 1325

Marie, Countess of Pembroke, to Edward III, 1335 and 1353

Maud to John, Duke of Lancaster, 1376

Constance, Lady Husee, to Henry VI, 1441

Joan Maryot to William Paston, *c.* 1442 (two letters)

Cecily, Duchess of York, to Queen Margaret of Anjou, 1453

Elizabeth Greene to Sir Robert Plumpton, November 1487

Joanna de Kynnesley to Henry IV, *c.* 1405

Joanna Conway to Cecily, Duchess of York, *c.* 1450–76

Chapter 7: Women of religion

The nuns of St Marys, Chester, to Queen Eleanor of Provence,
  c. 1253–4

Matilda, Prioress of Barking Abbey, to Henry III, 3 December 1258

Mabel de Tichborne, Abbess of Wherwell, to Walter de Merton,
  Chancellor, 1263

Alice 'the convert' of Winchester, to Edward I, 1289

Clemence de Balliol, Abbess of Elstow, to William Hamilton,
  Chancellor, 1306

The Prioress of Rowney to Henry IV, 12 November 1400

Joan Keteryche, Abbess of Denny, to John Paston, 31 January 1462

Note on dating

? 1479 = date not given, but almost certain.

c. 1479 = date not given, but best guess from internal or other
  evidence.

c. 1460–66 = date not given, covering dates are most likely period.

Any of the above enclosed in brackets = dd/mm known but not the
  year, for example 12 January (?1479).

The English of the letters has been updated to make it more
accessible to the modern reader.

Introduction

Many editions of letters written by English correspondents in the Middle Ages have been published in the last two centuries, and more recently a number of works devoted to original records relating to medieval women have appeared. In both categories the documents printed have been largely written by men. Most surviving records from the period are business or legal in nature and formal and factual in content. They give little indication of the negotiations, emotions or relationships behind the documents. This volume is devoted solely to letters written by women, where their own views and thoughts are expressed; and while most of them were dictated and are businesslike in tone, sometimes the writer's feelings are apparent. The majority of the letters have appeared in print before, the earlier ones often in nineteenth-century editions, which are now difficult to obtain except from specialist libraries, and many of the later ones in editions of the three great family collections of the fifteenth century, the Pastons, the Stonors and the Plumptons. A minority of the letters have never appeared in print before and come from the large archive of correspondence sent to the royal chancery, now in the Public Record Office. Others have been printed in Latin and French but not in English. This edition is not intended to be exhaustive and other letters by medieval women remain unpublished in libraries and archives.

In publications of medieval letters the contents are often arranged by date or by subject, but the former is a sterile arrangement and the latter perplexing, since so many of the letters cover a range of issues: some business, some personal. Here, therefore, an attempt has been made to illuminate the condition of medieval women by categorising the letters as they themselves might have done, by the identity of the recipient. This creates a series of ever-widening circles, beginning with members of their family, parents, husbands and children and then extending to take in kin, relatives by blood or marriage, before widening again to take in friends and acquaintances and finally moving to an outer group of recipients whom they did not know personally and to whom they were often supplicants. The exception to this pattern is religious women, whose experience was somewhat different and who have been given a chapter to themselves. Within each section the letters are arranged generally in a chronological order, while allowing letters written by one woman to be grouped together. Some women have examples of their letters in more than one section and these are cross-referenced. In the fifteenth century the women of the Paston, Stonor and Plumpton families wrote large numbers of letters, and in order not to unbalance the book, the letters from any one woman have been limited to a maximum of half a dozen. The earliest letter, written by Adela, Countess of Blois, daughter of William the Conqueror, dates from 1130, though there is then a gap of nearly a century until the next; the most recent letters are several from the Plumpton women written in 1506. Two of the correspondents, Adela of Blois and Marie de St Pol, Countess of Pembroke, were not English born, but have been included because the role of Adela and her sons is of significance to English history, and because Marie chose to spend most of her very long life in England. While it is to be expected that the greatest number date from the fifteenth century it is more surprising to find that a greater number of letters have survived that were written in the thirteenth century than in the fourteenth. This span of 400 years covers a period of great social change, most marked from the second half of the fourteenth century onwards, which affected women quite as much as men.

At the beginning of the period, in the early twelfth century, English society was divided very clearly into three groups, a division which was echoed in most societies around the world. There was a knightly or military caste, a clerical or priestly one, and a labouring one whose toil supported the other two. England was a rural society, with independent towns forming tiny islands in a sea of feudal landholding, their markets largely dependent on the immediate hinterland and where only a very few towns, mostly ports, had trade routes more than a few miles long. Thus, there were only a very few urban dwellers who did not fall easily into one of the three categories. By 1500, society was much more complex. The growth of trade and craftsmanship in the towns, the Black Death, which significantly altered the condition of the labouring classes, the growth of lay literacy, which broke the clerical stranglehold on bureaucracy and administration, the new forms of taxation necessitated by the Hundred Years' War with France and the administration they gave rise to, and finally the expansion of the common law and lawyers to service it, all led to a much greater variety of ways to earn a living and perhaps accumulate wealth. Having said that, landholding was still the measure of a man's standing in society, and most successful merchants, lawyers and administrators acquired land when and where they could. The use of the term 'man' in this context has been deliberate. Women in this period were defined by whose daughter, wife or widow they were. Almost everybody, other than those who followed a religious calling, expected to marry, and before or during her marriage a woman's position in society was marked by whether she laboured with her hands or supervised the labour of others. If the latter, she was of gentle or equivalent status, and this determined how she spent her time and the people she mixed with both before and after marriage.

The women whose letters have survived come almost exclusively from the first of the three classes, which by the mid-fourteenth century can better be described as the aristocracy and gentry. Only a handful of the letters come from women who probably came from somewhat lower levels of society. This is not really surprising. The urban classes tended to live close to their relatives, friends and business contacts, and the same was even more true of the labouring classes, who had no reason to send letters. While other records, such as wills and those created by the courts, particularly church courts, do much to illuminate the lives of women of other social classes, letters show the reality of lives lived by women of the upper or 'gentle' classes. In the Middle Ages the term 'gentle' did not carry the modern meaning of soft or kind, but implied a code of behaviour encompassing refinement, education, good manners and honourable dealings which informed a whole way of life and which was instilled in children at an early age. The word 'noble' had a similar meaning and was not applied purely to the peerage. The term 'gentleman', increasingly used in the fifteenth century, was the equivalent of 'esquire', common in earlier centuries; both were applied to the strata of society immediately below knights. Gentle, or noble, society can be defined as families who owed their wealth and authority to the holding of land. While this covered a wide range of income and social position, from families whose life was based on a single manor, worth at most £50 a year, to aristocrats whose estates ranged over a number of counties and brought in revenue of several thousand pounds a year, it also implied a common culture. This was based on concern for the family and its status, interest in maintaining and extending landholdings, and the practice of social conventions, which included religious observance, artistic patronage and conspicuous consumption.

In the period 1200–1500 there were at any one time about sixty peers, while in the average county there were about sixty to seventy significant landholders, many of them knights, who provided the personnel for county officialdom: becoming MPs, sheriffs, JPs, escheators, and who were often retainers of local peers. Below these county or 'upper' gentry were perhaps three times their number of 'parish' or lower gentry, whose influence spread no wider than their immediate locale. This county society was tight knit, where a policy of intermarriage was fiercely pursued, but while it was tightly knit, it was by no means static. Families at the top died out in the male line, to be replaced in the peerage by men from the rank below, who had married their heiresses or who had prospered in royal service. The gentry was constantly being reinforced from below by successful lawyers or merchants who bought or married land, or by yeomen (who owned their own land but tilled it themselves) who had accumulated enough land to join the class above. The different strands of this society were linked together by the concept of service and the relationship between master and man, which began at the top with the king and the nobles who served him directly and ran down to the holder of a single manor and the yeomen whose younger sons might be members of his household. An esquire or gentleman in a lord's service might find himself acting as the lord's steward or receiver, attending him in his household, sitting on his council, raising troops for him in time of war, and acting in his interests locally. In return the lord would use his influence to obtain local offices for his servants, good marriages, grants of land or fees, and would see that their lawsuits prospered. A lord who looked after his servants' interests was regarded as a 'good lord'. Both sides gained equally from service, and each man was probably both a servant to one above him and a lord to one below. It was perfectly possible to serve more than one master, though it was recognised that one 'especial good lord' had first call on those services. Women's networks of service were less formal, but a girl who served in a lady's household might continue to act as her client throughout her lifetime, even if her husband had a service relationship with a quite different family. All connections with people of influence were useful in the important business of family advancement.

Almost all existing letters by medieval men or women concern business of one sort or another, which is why they were preserved in the first place, and so rather than wonder at the paucity of love letters, we should give thanks that even a handful have survived. In many examples, of course, the personal and the practical can be found in the same letter. Some of the letters are no more than a few lines long, perhaps naming the messenger who was expected to deliver a longer, verbal account of the business in hand, others cover pages ranging over a broad spectrum of subjects. Throughout the Middle Ages, gentlewomen, like their husbands, used a clerk to write their letters, rarely even signing their own names. This does not mean that the views expressed are not their own, any more than would be the case for a modern business person dictating to a secretary, nor does dictation seem to have inhibited the expression of their views or feelings. Literacy is a difficult accomplishment to measure, but in the early part of our period it was confined largely to the clerical class. Aristocratic society in the twelfth and thirteenth centuries might be able to read French and possibly a little Latin, but they seldom wrote, for they had no need to do so. In the second half of the Middle Ages there is plenty of evidence that both aristocratic men and women could read and write, while slightly lower down the social scale, many gently born women fell into the category of reading but not writing. Evidence from women's wills shows that book-owning was widespread before the introduction of printing and while many may have been treasured more for their illuminations and fine bindings than their content, their bequests in wills show them as family heirlooms. Most of those bequeathed were devotional works of one kind or another, but this may be just because they were intrinsically the most valuable, and there are sometimes references to French books or romances. Even when gentlewomen were able to write, it was often poorly and they generally used a clerk; it is evident that Margery Paston could write, but, nevertheless, she had even her love letters written for her. The more prolific writers used a variety of scribes; Agnes Paston, for example, apologised for the handwriting in one of her letters, because the matter was too urgent for her to wait for a 'good secretary'. The note that Elizabeth, Duchess of Suffolk, sent to John Paston, so urgent that she wrote the whole thing herself, is a rarity for a noble or gentle woman in the mid-fifteenth century. It is interesting that one of the other few holograph letters in the collection is from Elizabeth Stonor, who came from a wealthy merchant family rather than a gentle one.

Letter-writing was a serious business and not easily undertaken. It is seldom possible to tell when a letter was closely dictated or when it was written by a clerk on the basis of instructions: the latter is more likely if the letter was short and concerned purely with business. Correspondents were often uneasy at entrusting their secrets to paper and a letter often served only as a brief introduction to a confidential messenger who carried it. In other cases they asked the recipient to burn the letter. Most people found it difficult to express their thoughts on paper, and there are passages in many of the letters where it is difficult to tease out the writer's meaning. Many letters survive only in draft, full of amendments and interlineations, to be copied later by a clerk. Yet all gentry families, as well as those of the aristocracy, kept accounts, wrote business letters, received written bills from merchants and shopkeepers, and almost certainly owned at least a book or two. This meant that their senior servants, the stewards, and bailiffs, born into the rank below them were also literate. The letters are written in one of three languages, Latin, French or English; those in Latin and French are identified as such in the text. In the early years after the Conquest, when only the clergy could write, all letters were in Latin. The spoken language of the Norman aristocracy was, of course, French, and as late as the early fourteenth century English children who received schooling were taught in French, which remained the language of gentility. As lay literacy began to spread among the aristocratic and knightly classes, they wrote in the language that they spoke, that is, French, but Latin remained the language of the courts and the royal chancery, so that thirteenth- and fourteenth-century letters could be in either language. It is not until the the last quarter of the fourteenth century that English, always spoken by the lower classes and probably learnt by the upper classes in earlier centuries from their nurses and childhood servants, became the spoken and written language of everyday life for all Englishmen. Latin, however, continued to be the language of legal documents.

The common form of the letters was to begin straight away with the salutation, suitably couched according to the rank of the addressee as either inferior or superior to the writer, and then to press on with the matter until the end, without breaking it into paragraphs, and then follow with an indication of the date and place at which it was written. Whatever the relationship between writer and recipient, the salutation was almost invariably formal, and a child would write 'my right worshipful father' and not 'dear father' and there was no place for endearments or even Christian names. An exception which proves the rule is Margery Paston: in one letter she addresses her husband John as 'Right reverend and worshipful sir', but ends with a postscript, 'Sir, I pray you, if you tarry long in London, that it will please you to send for me, for I think it long since I lay in your arms', and in a letter probably written only a few days later, she begins 'Mine own sweet heart'. Other women sometimes addressed their husbands as 'cousin'. This and other terms such as 'brother' and 'son', which to modern eyes imply a specific blood relationship, were much more loosely used in the Middle Ages. 'Brother' might be used not only for a sibling but also a close friend or associate, while two of our correspondents, the Countess of Oxford and Lady Fitzhugh, either call John Paston 'son' or refer to themselves as his 'mother'. In this case it was an acknowledgement of the close patron/client relationship they had with him.

The dating of letters was rarely precise. Dates were often given by reference to the nearest saint's day, and if the year was given at all, it was only the regnal year, that is, by the number of years the king had been on the throne. This means that most of the letters have to be dated from internal evidence. The physical nature of the letters changes substantially in the course of the Middle Ages. In the earlier part, letters were written on parchment, usually a long thin strip in 'landscape' shape with a tag on which a seal could be affixed. The change to the letter form similar to that still in use today, that is, on paper and in 'portrait' shape, came at much the same time as the change in the language from French to English. In the fifteenth century, the paper which was available in English towns came from France or northern Italy. It was strong, handmade and varied in quality from a fine, smooth surface to coarse, thick paper with a rough surface. The first English paper mill was established at Hertford in 1494. Sheets of paper varied a little in size but were usually 10–12 inches wide and 16–18 inches long. This was a large area to fill, so most correspondents would simply cut off the rest when they came to the end of their letter. The paper letter could then be folded into a small oblong packet and fastened by passing a thread or strip of paper through the folded thicknesses and sealing the ends. The letter was then superscribed with the recipient's name and location, a style which remained in use until the introduction of envelopes in the nineteenth century.

Seals played an important part in authenticating a letter. The use of heraldry on seals from the late twelfth century onwards reflected the increasingly hereditary nature of coats of arms and the family honour they portrayed. Most noblewomen's seals were a double-pointed oval in shape, and a common early design was to show a figure of a lady often holding a lily (the sign of the Virgin Mary) or with a hawk or dog (a sign of high social standing), with a coat of arms on the reverse. Later designs often depict the lady carrying shields bearing the relevant arms or with the arms incorporated into the design of her gown. While it was customary for wives and widows to bear their husband's arms on their seal, the women must have played a dominant part in the design of their own seals, because these often also carried their father's arms, and it was not unknown to display their mother's as well. It reminded the world of their illustrious kin, just as the husband or son of an heiress might adopt her family's arms. The custom of ladies designing and using their own seals was for high-born women, lesser ones simply used their husband's seal. There was, of course, no postal service. Letter delivery was dependent on either personal delivery by a servant of the writer, or if it was going far afield, on a friend, neighbour or acquaintance who happened to be travelling in roughly the right direction, and who could then pass it on for another stage in its journey. If a messenger of one sort or another could not be found, the letter remained unwritten. If a messenger turned up unexpectedly, a brief note was often despatched, telling the recipient that the messenger could be trusted to explain matters further.

* * *

Despite the fact that a medieval woman's identity was dependent upon her father and husband, and that both under the law and in the eyes of the Church she occupied a subordinate position, it would be quite wrong not to attempt to appreciate the difference between theory and practice. In theory women were expected to demonstate meekness, humility and obedience; in practice many of them found that the qualities that served them best were forcefulness, practicality and guile. Women could not become priests or MPs, go to university or practice law, but they could and did administer estates, hire and fire men, sue at law in their own name and, if so inclined, exert a powerful influence over their male relations. As widows they were expected to fulfill the same military obligations to the Crown for their lands as their husbands had done, and in theory they could, by royal commission, be appointed as justices of the peace; in practice they very rarely were. Ela, widowed Countess of Salisbury and Wiltshire, was sheriff of Wiltshire for a number of years in the late 1220s and early 1230s, but an example like this is the exception which proves the rule that women did not hold public office. While all the goods a wife brought to the marriage became the property of her husband, and technically the same was true for any land she owned, there were in practice limits on his freedom to do what he willed with her land, even if the income from it was at his disposal. After his death, the law granted every widow her rightful share, commonly one third, of her husband's estate, both in lands and goods, for the duration of her lifetime, whether or not she remarried. This state of affairs existed throughout most of the period, during which the use of certain technical terms, such as marriage portion, jointure and dower, was common, and should therefore be explained.

Marriage in the Middle Ages, particularly among the landowning classes, was a matter of family policy and women often played an important part in the discussions leading up to formal marriage negotiations. Their informal networks and knowledge of local families suggested eligible parties for their children, or they urged their menfolk to look about them for matches for a specific child. An agreement to marry in the future, technically called a pre-contract, was more important than a modern engagement, and if followed by consummation, constituted a valid marriage in the eyes of the Church. Equally, even if a church ceremony had taken place, it was not a true marriage until after consummation. Whatever part kinsmen and friends played in arranging a marriage, as far as the Church was concerned, consent between the partners was essential and if one of the parties could later prove coercion, then church law held the marriage to be null and void. Age at first marriage in general depended on the ability of a couple, or a couple's family, to provide for a separate household for them and their future children.

For the gentle classes this was generally earlier than for those in the lower social classes, whose age at first marriage was much more dependent on economic factors. While children could be betrothed at any age, canon law did not allow marriage below the age of seven, and those that took place before the age of puberty (twelve for a girl, fourteen for a boy) had to be reviewed then and confirmed as agreeable to the pair, or publicly rejected. On the whole, child marriages only occurred among aristocratic families and usually involved substantial heirs or heiresses. When they did take place, it was usual to specify at the time of the marriage the age at which the couple would first start to live together as man and wife; in the intervening period the two children were likely to be brought up in the same household. Where possible, parents usually aimed for a match with a person of a similar age to their child, thus arranging a 'companionate marriage'. It was very rare for a member of the gentle classes not to marry at all unless they had a religious vocation; among the labouring classes it was more common, and it has been estimated that approximately 10 per cent remained single. Marrying children off while they were in their teens had several practical advantages. For a male heir it increased the chances of him having a son and thus securing the succession before his father died, and it also meant that if his father died while he was still under age (less than twenty-one), then as a married man he was not placed in the wardship, or guardianship, of the king or a senior landowner; marriage for younger sons was less of a priority and tended to happen in their mid to late twenties. For all daughters, marriage in their later teens meant that they were less likely to have the time or opportunity to choose someone unsuitable for themselves. For a girl to marry without parental consent or against parental wishes was to forfeit her place in society and be permanently estranged from her family and peers. Parental choice, made with the good of the larger family unit in mind, was what mattered, but while parental pressure on young people was accepted, actual coercion was frowned on both by society and the church.

Medieval law accepted that where there was a failure of male heirs, land could pass to a female on her marriage. From the time of

Henry I, if there were no sons, but more than one daughter, then the lands were divided between all the daughters. In the cases of major landholders or peers, the Crown might intervene to ensure that the title or bulk of the land went to the eldest daughter. It was still possible for a family to keep an heiress's inheritance intact, rather than have it subsumed into a future husband's holdings, by marrying her to a younger son, or to a widower with a son to inherit his own land. The increasing use of entails in the fourteenth and fifteenth centuries, which limited the succession of estates to male heirs, deprived some daughters of their right to land in favour of uncles, cousins or nephews, though this seems to have been a policy pursued more vigorously in the north than in the south. The marriage of a daughter who was not an heiress nonetheless played an important role in extending her family's social and political links. Having chosen a prospective husband with these factors in mind, her parents were prepared to contribute to her future well-being by payment to her bridegroom's family, but they also wanted to be sure that she would be well-provided for by his family in return. It was striking the balance between these two factors that the marriage contract was all about. Once a candidate had been identified, and the agreement of his family gained in principle, then serious bargaining could begin. During the negotiations leading to a formal marriage contract (of which several hundred survive), conducted, for the sake of argument, by the fathers of the two young people involved, the father of the bride was required to state what her marriage portion was to be; the term more commonly used in later periods was dowry. This could be land, money or goods, depending on the status or degree of her father; in the earlier part of the period it was more likely to be land, which was frequently then earmarked by her new family for the use of her daughters or younger sons. By the second half of the period, money was much more common than land. When land was given as the maritagium or dowry, it went to the young couple, while a cash dowry went to the groom's father, who had consequently to provide all the land to support the couple himself; he could, however, use the money to fund marriage portions for his own daughters. The large sum required for a dowry could rarely be found immediately and was frequently paid in instalments to the groom's father over a set number of years, backed up with guarantees for payment, often by pledging land worth a specific amount per annum. In addition to her dowry, a bride had to be provided with jewels and clothes which reflected well upon her family. However, if the bride died childless, a significant part of her portion, often half of it, reverted to her father or his heir. Despite the financial outlay involved, fathers were not anxious to leave daughters unmarried because this was to waste assets in the local network of families. While eldest sons and heiresses tended to marry up, younger sons and daughters married down, which meant that all but the greatest magnates married children into the gentry; this was a significant factor in the cohesiveness of society.

In return for the marriage portion paid by the father of the bride, the father of the groom had to show how he intended to provide for the support for the couple, until the time of his own death, when it was presumed that the groom would come into his inheritance; this was done either by giving the young couple some land or financing career training for his son. If the bride was an heiress (or with her sisters, a co-heiress), then the corresponding provision made by the groom's father would have to be higher to take account of this. During the course of the marriage, both parties might severally inherit more than was specified in the marriage negotiations. On the death of the husband, his wife was legally entitled to a portion of the lands and other possessions he held at the time of his death to support her in her widowhood. A widow's holding was referred to as her dower, hence the term dowager. In the early Middle Ages a husband often specified at the church door at the time of his marriage the amount of dower it was agreed his new wife should have as a widow, or it could be an endowment of one third of the land which the husband held at the time of the marriage. As this was often much less than the amount of land he died possessing, a widow's entitlement gradually came to be one third of the lands and possessions he held at the time of his death. The exception to this rule was under the form of tenure known as 'gavelkind', particularly prevalent in Kent, which specified a half of the husband's holdings, but would be surrendered upon remarriage. However, no wife had any independent control over land as long as the marriage lasted, and once widowed she had no right to specific lands outside a jointure or her own inheritance; her dower lands were assigned her by the heir and were of his choosing, provided they were of the appropriate value, unless particular lands were nominated as the dower at the time of her marriage.

The marriage of heiresses was usually to men who would be heirs in their turn, so in many cases the groom's father settled enough of his own land on his son and his new wife to match what she had inherited. The couple would then hold all that land jointly during their lives with reversion to the survivor and their children; this agreed endowment at marriage was called the jointure. It developed in response to the growing custom of granting land to feoffees to use as directed by the grantor (in other words, setting up a trust) which enabled a man to dispose of his land as he wished after death, since land could not be disposed of by will. Land which was held by feoffees could not be claimed as dower because the husband did not hold it and the widow was left much more poorly provided for than she should have been. An appropriate jointure agreed at the time of her marriage protected her from this situation. The more desirable the bride was in terms of her inheritance, the more her family would require the groom's father to provide as his share of the jointure, thus depleting his own holdings during his lifetime. Jointure also protected the bride if her new husband died before coming into his patrimony, since it would be larger than any widow's holding she would be due. If she had the benefit of a jointure dating from the time of her marriage, her widow's third, or dower, would be taken from all her husband's lands outside those jointly owned. If she was also an heiress, then she had the right to hold the lands of her own inheritance during her widowhood. She might therefore end up with considerably more land than the third of her late husband's estates which was her dower, all of which she retained until her death, whether or not she remarried. The legal right of a widow to dower applied to every widow in the country, whatever her rank, and meant that at any one time a significant proportion of the wealth of the country was in the hands of women, which had a considerable effect on the structure of landed society.

Dower was a family affair and as such, subject to all the emotions pertaining to any family business: misunderstandings, anger, jealousy, trust and affection. Even the most loving of sons might mildly resent that a minimum of one third of his inheritance, and often a great deal more, was held by his mother, who might live for many years or carry it off to a new husband. If the widow was a young second or subsequent wife, who remarried, then the heir, often her stepson, had even more reason to feel aggrieved. Almost all litigation relating to dower was between people related by blood or marriage. A man's financial standing could be substantially depleted if his family had the misfortune to have dowagers from more than one generation at a single time, or worse still, dowagers from the same generation, perhaps where two brothers had died in quick succession. If a widow, particularly an older one, chose not to remarry, she might prove willing to hand over her dower lands to the heir in exchange for an annuity, thus maintaining family harmony, and it was not unknown, particularly among the smaller landowners, for a widow to forego her dower to the benefit of her son in return for a home and support by him. On the other hand, the holding of estates in dower or jointure could be of benefit to a family. It retained in the family possession some part of its lands during a minority, when the wardship of the heir, if he held land directly from the Crown, would be granted to a guardian who might milk the remaining estates for all he could get out of them, seriously depleting their value for years to come. It also offered some form of protection in the event of a political disaster, since after 1388 jointure, but not dower, lands were technically exempt from confiscation by the Crown if the landowner was dead and had been attainted for treason. In this eventuality, however, a vulnerable widow might find all sorts of legal attacks were made on her property by men on the make who were aiming to take advantage of her weak position, and one or two of the letters illustrate this. The widow of a traitor without jointure had no choice but to cast herself on the mercy of the king, and was usually granted a small annuity in lieu of dower, and the same was true for the wife of a traitor who had escaped abroad. The only other occasion when a widow could legally be deprived of dower was if she had left home in the course of an adulterous affair. If she was forgiven and kept by her husband, then she maintained her right to dower. In the Anglo-Norman period widows were regarded as profitable assets of the Crown. Women had to pay a fine to enter their dower, and those who did not wish to remarry had to pay another fine for the privilege of remaining single. As the levels of such fines rose, a woman might end up having to sell most of her dower lands to pay them. One of the key clauses of Magna Carta was that widows did not have to pay for their dower and they were not to be compelled to remarry.

The economics of marriage was of vital concern to the landholding classes, since it was primarily designed to cement family alliances and consolidate and extend estates. Marriage also played a formative role in the formation of a cohesive group and identity, whether among the baronage or a county community. Control of the choice of marriage partners tended to exclude outsiders, retain land within the approved group and helped to solve problems posed by inheritance. For instance, it was not uncommon for siblings to marry siblings, which increased the chance of inheritance or at worst, kept everything within the orbit of two families. It was not possible to control the pattern of inheritance, for who knew when a woman might end up as the ultimate heiress of an estate, but a careful set of marriages could reunite divided inheritances sometimes two or three generations on. In the period following the Black Death it has been estimated that about 40 per cent of daughters became heiresses in preference to the collateral male heir. Women who were already heiresses at the time of their marriage were almost invariably married to men who were heirs in their turn because of the high jointure cost of such a marriage. If the heiress was intended for a younger son, which tended to happen in the higher ranks of society, then the jointure settlement would mean that his eldest brother would suffer from a depleted inheritance. The financial sacrifices made to get an heiress often failed to pay off when she died childless, despite the safeguards for such an eventuality which were usually written into the contract. Under the laws of inheritance, a man could retain his deceased wife's inheritance for his lifetime only if she had borne him a living child (whether or not that child was still alive at the time of her death); if not, then on her death the inheritance reverted to her own family heirs. Heiresses were often seen as a means of raising the social status of *nouveau riche* families, who were therefore willing to gamble on the possibility of a childless marriage and able to pay for a large jointure. In many cases wives unexpectedly became heiresses after they had married; nor were heiresses just daughters, they could be granddaughters, sisters, aunts or nieces. Such women were likely to have married lower, and their husband's family had cause to be thankful for their good fortune. Very few marriage contracts made provision for subsequent changes to their terms if the bride unexpectedly inherited. In the early Middle Ages feudal lords also had the right to sanction heiress marriages and the second marriage of widows, but by about 1300 this right seems to have been reserved to the Crown and only related to families which held their lands directly of the king. This right provided an extremely useful form of patronage for the Crown, which tended not to marry heiresses or widows to equals unless they came from the aristocracy, but to royal servants deserving of reward. In the case of the greatest heiresses, marriage to the king's own younger sons often enabled the Crown to provide for a cadet line without depleting its own coffers to any great degree.

While marriage was seen as a means of social advancement and family aggrandisement, it was also a sacrament and subject to canon law. By the early twelfth century, the Church was tightening its grip on marriage and its courts were becoming the sole arbiter in cases of dispute. This was accepted by feudal society because of the need to define legitimate hereditary succession. For a valid, indissoluble marriage the Church insisted that there should be no impediment of consanguinity, or blood relationship, between the contracting parties, who should be free to marry and genuinely gave their consent. If these conditions were fulfilled, then marriages contracted in secrecy, with solemn vows, were as valid as those contracted

17

publicly in the presence of a priest and other witnesses. Secret marriages were not uncommon and were contracted at all levels of society, and in many cases were supported in the Church courts. The major impediment to a valid marriage was consanguinity. In 1215 the Church reduced the degrees of relationship which barred marriage from seven to four; in other words, a couple could not marry if they had a great-great-grandparent in common. At the time of a proposed marriage, it was therefore essential to know if the parties were within the prohibited degrees, and it was here that women, as keepers of the tribal memory, played an important role. However, what the Church forbade, it could also give consent to, and after the proper application and fees, couples within the prohibited relationships were able to obtain a dispensation to marry. It was not unknown, particularly in the peerage, where male heirs were essential and where most members of the class were distantly related, for marriages to be contracted without dispensation, so that if the marriage proved infertile, it could be dissolved on the grounds of consanguinity. A woman whose marriage was annulled on the grounds of consanguinity was not entitled to dower on the death of her former husband, even if she had borne children in the marriage. Infertility was not accepted as a justification for ending a marriage, but impotence and lack of consummation were. Divorce was unknown in the Middle Ages, and marriage could be ended only by annulment or by separation. This was handled by a Church court, and in the first case it would rule that the marriage had never been valid and the couple were free to remarry, and in the second it accepted the validity of the marriage and the legitimacy of any children from it, but allowed the couple to live apart but not to remarry; the main reasons cited were adultery, heresy and above all, cruelty. Consanguinity was not an issue which arose very frequently in the courts, much more time was spent on cases involving bigamy or pre-contract. The former were often the result of clandestine marriages which gave rise to confusion about their legitimacy, and pre-contract was a formal agreement to marry someone else entered into before the disputed marriage and thus invalidating it. Pre-contract, real or fictional, was, like consanguinity, used to end unwanted marriages. On the whole, Church courts seem to have been even-handed in dealing with matrimonial disputes and there was no obvious bias towards men.

Couples married when their families could provide a separate establishment, so nuclear families rather than extended co-resident ones were the norm, though elite families with more space did sometimes provide accommodation for in-laws and other relatives. Once married and established in her new home, it was a woman's duty to bear children, preferably sons. Though medical textbooks did not automatically blame women for infertility, the misogyny that was so deeply rooted in the medieval mind did not generally acknowledge the responsibility of men in the fertility of a marriage. If a woman bore no children, she was condemned as a barren wife, and if she bore only girls, then that, too, was her responsibility. Male eyes and minds were largely closed to the obvious examples at all levels of society where women barren in one marriage were fruitful in a subsequent one, or bore daughters to one husband and sons to another. While wealth and status remained rooted in the possession of land and at least nominally the holding of land entailed military obligations, it was inevitable that both men and women wished for sons to inherit. The English system of primogeniture emphasised the importance of lineage rather than the broader clan system, and was inclined to lead to family tensions between the heir and his younger brothers, to fathers looking over their shoulders at sons eager to inherit and to sons grudging the amount of land still held by a widowed mother as her dower. But if male heirs were eagerly awaited, it would be wrong to infer that girls were not valued. They were immensely important players in the network of blood ties, friendship and patronage which supported local, county and national life.

Women of various classes played a role in the upbringing and education of gently-born girls. The gentry household would employ a nurse, who was likely to be from the trade or craft level of society, while in aristocratic households there would be a governess in charge of the nursery who was a gentlewoman and who supervised the nursery staff, taught her small charges good manners and probably their first letters. Once a girl had survived the dangers of early childhood, then she had to be suitably educated so that she might in future be able to carry out her responsibilities. Very little is known for certain about the education of girls, since it was largely informal and took place within the home. In all but the highest households, a girl's education began at her mother's hands probably when she was quite young, before she was seven and had left the nursery. The image of St Anne teaching the Virgin to read was a very popular one, and almost certainly reflected common practice in gentry households. A surprising number of girls from gentry families were sent to a local nunnery to be educated, where the fees their parents paid formed an essential part of the income of many small religious houses. It was not impossible for girls to receive formal schooling, as is illustrated by a statute of 1406, which stated that 'any man or woman, of whatever estate or condition, be free to put his son or daughter to learn letters at any school in the kingdom'. This was provided, of course, that they or a patron could furnish the school fees, but it was inevitable that educational opportunities for girls were much more limited than for boys. Latin grammar, for instance, had no place in their curriculum, and while many women would have picked up enough to follow services in their missals, they would have been denied the chance to read other devotional literature until these works began to be translated, or written in English, in the fifteenth century. Wherever it took place, education for girls included being taught to read, and in the later period, to write, to receive religious instruction, to learn French, music and dancing, needlework, spinning and good manners and modest deportment, including how to behave towards a social superior. In their early teens girls were frequently sent to complete their education in the service of a local lady, in much the same way as their brothers served local lords. In many ways, the most important part of a girl's education was probably acquired simply by watching her parents, or the lady with whom she was in service, fulfil their duties, and by absorbing an understanding of the roles and responsibilites of members of the household around her. Above all, a girl's education was designed to teach her how to run a household, to be a credit to her parents and a useful partner of her future husband, and thus fulfil her role in society.

From a girl's early teens and sometimes earlier, her family and friends were on the lookout for a suitable husband for her. Suitable almost invariably meant someone from the same social circles as her parents. He was likely to be the son of someone with whom her father did business, whose lands lay nearby, or who was a fellow JP, or a fellow retainer of the local lord. In some cases a number of preliminary enquires would be carried out before a suitable match was found, that is, one where both families could agree upon the financial arrangements. Once married, most ladies would certainly not have lived the proverbial life of leisure. Part of a girl's education was devoted to the running of a household, but once married her duties were not purely domestic. The wife of a landowner would be expected to play a part in the administration of his estates as and when the need arose. A man of standing would spend time away from his chief residence for a number of reasons: visiting his other estates, sitting as a JP or MP, pursuing legal affairs in London or attending his lord in peace or war. Such a man would expect his wife to manage his affairs in his absence, dealing with his steward, bailiffs and lawyers as he would himself. She could seek his advice by letter, but as we have seen, this was not always easy, and in many cases she would have to take significant decisions herself, in addition to the more routine business of rent-collecting, accounting, counselling and bargaining entailed by the ownership of property. At all levels of society, but none more so than in its upper reaches, medieval marriage was a partnership in the business of maintaining and expanding estates, as well as in familial affairs; and what in theory looked like total dependence of a woman on her husband, when examined closely begins to look much more like inter-dependence. In bad times, some women, like Margaret Paston, could find themselves physically defending family property, or like two successive Plumpton wives, engaged in the hopeless task of trying to raise money for the lawsuits pursued by their feckless husband, Sir Robert. Much of the evidence for the role of women in running landed estates comes from the fifteenth century, where surviving letters give some indication of what was really going on behind the legal fiction that business was conducted solely in the name of the man, but there is no reason to believe that matters were much different in earlier centuries; if the husband was away from home, then the chances are that instructions were issued by his wife. While it is impossible to assess how much the success in running particular estates was due to the management of the landowner and how much to the abilities of his officials, it is generally accepted that, as in any business, success springs from good direction from above. While she was married, a wife's skills and commitment were hidden behind her husband, but once she was a widow, her abilities were revealed, and there are plenty of examples of dowagers effectively running large estates.

When widowed, a woman whose dower included estates was thus well trained to run them efficiently by herself. Widowhood was a highly significant part of the experience of medieval womanhood, and many women experienced it more than once. It has been conservatively estimated that in medieval England at least 10 per cent of households were headed by widows. Any woman in control of property needed more than a passing aquaintance with the law, and never more so than over the issue of her dower. Many new widows had to resort to the law to obtain their rights, or fend off claims to parts of their dower lands from other litigants. Unlike other major civil pleas, where property cases were brought before the king's justices, dower cases required the woman to be the plaintiff, although if she had remarried, her new husband could be joined with her in the case. Thousands of cases on the plea rolls show the difficulty many widows had in obtaining their legal dower entitlements, particularly if they had no son, when their husband's heir, perhaps a son by another marriage, a brother or a cousin, resented the diminution of their inheritance and attempted to find ways around handing it over. Even sons were known to battle with their mothers over the issue. Widows of landowners had the same responsibilities as their husbands to fulfil the obligations of their holdings, providing men and supplies for military campaigns and attending the king's courts to hear pleas, although usually they sent a male deputy in their place. It was thus a good career move for an ambitious man to serve a widow. At a more local level, although widows could not hold public office they held all the manorial rights formerly belonging to their husband. Manorial courts had to be held by a steward with legal training, but the court was held in her name and any difficult matters were referred to the lady and her council. All landowners, men and women alike, had councils to advise them, usually consisting of their senior estate and household officials, and retained lawyers to join the council when necessary. One of the most striking features of the letters are the number of references to lawsuits over property. In the days before the registration of title of freehold property, proof of ownership depended on the safe keeping of title deeds, and on local memory, and there are several references in the letters to the care of deeds, while Joan Trowe's letter to her legal adviser, setting out the history of the ownership of a house, illustrates the importance of knowing the descent of a legal title. Where ownership was shared, the opportunites for mistakes and deceptions multiplied. Someone with a weak title but powerful friends could often triumph over a rival with a stronger title but less influential allies.

As a widow, often the first task a women had to perform was the execution of her husband's will. A very high proportion of men appointed their wives as their executrix, in many cases as sole executor, which is a good indication of the trust placed in them and of complete faith in their ability to handle such business. Nor were wives the only women so appointed. Daughters, mothers, sisters and even on some occasions unrelated women of status and influence were asked to be an executrix. In the ecclesiastical courts responsible for handling testamentary affairs, men and women enjoyed equal standing as well as equal responsibility for the discharge of the duties enjoined on them by the testator, and in some cases these were many and burdensome. One of the most common was the discharge of his debts. Widowhood was the time of greatest independence for a medieval woman. Legally she was a 'femme sole', subject to no man, be he father or husband, and could answer for herself in the courts or initiate a lawsuit in her own name. She could choose whether or not she remarried, though if she were young and/or rich, she might be subject to pressure from her family, or lord, to do so. Some widows chose to take a vow of celibacy, thus removing any pressure to remarry, and were then known as vowesses. There are many examples of widows swiftly remarrying a senior official of their late husband's, which suggests either a liaison during the latter's lifetime or a means of retaining the services of a known and valued colleague. If a widow was older, she could choose whether or not to retain her dower lands or to hand them over to her son or her husband's male heir in return for an annuity, which would enable her to live comfortably but without the burden of running estates. Many widows chose to leave country manors and take a house in the local county town, where they could more easily see their friends and shop. Some in the early part of the Middle Ages chose to take the veil and retire to the contemplative life, but in the later period pious women on the whole preferred to lodge in a nunnery and take part in the religious life in the company of like-minded women, but to remain secular. Their payment for board and lodging was a useful supplement to the income of the nunnery, few of which were well endowed. It also offered the nunnery the prospect of a future bequest under the will of the resident widow.

Managing a medieval household, even for the lower gentry living locally on a single manor, would have entailed the support of about a dozen people outside the immediate family, the great majority of them men. Further up the social scale the numbers could rise to approximately a hundred, of whom only about a tenth would be women. Servants in a gentle household were male and mostly single; conversely, servants in urban households tended to be female because their brothers were tradesmen and artisans. On country estates, women were employed only in the nursery and the laundry and tended to be married to men in the household. The mistress of the household might also have a waiting gentlewoman, (or more if she was aristocratic), probably also married to a senior man in the household, or she might receive into the household one or two gently-born girls for training. In the highest aristocratic circles there would in effect be two households; the lady was responsible for her own household all of the time and her husband's when he himself was away. Whatever the size of the household, it had to be fed, clothed, doctored, and managed, chiefly by the lady of the house. If husband and wife were both away, then arrangements had to be made not just for the main body of the household that remained, but the smaller one which travelled with them. Heads of households, be they men or women, travelled to supervise their estates, pursue business opportunities, visit those to whom they were patrons, or their own lords, go on pilgrimage and visit family and friends. Even for members of the gentry the travelling household was likely to include about half a dozen people. Travelling was therefore expensive and carriages and good horses were a status symbol, but hiring horses for travelling was another practical alternative.

The family and its household functioned as a community, living, eating, working and worshipping together, and this formed a woman's primary circle. Ensuring that the household was properly supplied at every level was not just a domestic matter. All aspects of life in the household were expected to reflect the honour of the householder, the quality and quantity of food served at table, the plate and jewels displayed, the livery and gowns worn by its members, the entertainment provided, the furniture and books owned, the piety observed and the charity practised and the style in which travelling was undertaken. Hospitality was an immensely important part of medieval life. A family was judged by its ability to provide good food and wine for visitors and entertain widely. If it could not so provide, its standing fell proportionately, and its declining 'worship' (a word widely used and meaning standing or status) meant an inability to arrange good marriages, raise loans and attract offices, and the start of a spiral of decline like that suffered by the Plumptons. While families were judged by the conspicuous consumption they displayed, there was also a practical side to the purchase of valuable items such as plate, jewels and books; in the days before banks they were a simple way of investing during good times in articles which could easily be pledged as security for a loan or converted into cash in bad times or later refashioned to keep up with new styles. There are occasional references in the letters to the purchase of luxuries like these. Hospitality was greater in the winter season, since the demands of farming took more time in the summer. From the guest lists that have survived it is clear that the housewife was providing for a regular mix of estate officials and workers, visiting clergy and social peers including family and close friends. Nor did this hospitality cease on widowhood. Widowed gentlewomen often had the wealth, authority and social connections to continue to command respect among their male peers and to play an important networking role by providing objective advice and views and a neutral meeting place, since they themselves were likely to be slightly removed from the dynastic manoeuvrings or business schemes taking place in their locale. Women throughout their lives were as active as their husbands in expanding and consolidating their network of kin, friends and allies by the exchange of hospitality, favours and news and as keen to use those networks to secure offices, marriages and favours, for their own relatives and dependents as well as for those of their husband.

One of the main tasks in running a medieval household lay in ensuring adequate supplies of provisions, and this involved a considerable amount of long-term planning. Food came from a range of sources; most manors retained some desmesne land for the use of the lord, even in the later Middle Ages when much land was leased out, so that he could keep his own animals and grow his own crops. Well-stocked fish ponds played another essential part in provisioning the household because taking Lent and fast days (the standard pattern was abstinence from meat on Wednesdays, Fridays and Saturdays) into account, meat was only eaten on about half the days in the year. When impressing important guests, more exotic meats such as swan, heron, cony (rabbit), pheasant or shellfish might be served, and these, like other supplies which were not produced at home, were purchased locally. Luxuries, including sugar and the spices essential for medieval cooking, came from large towns and above all, from London. Sea fish were widely purchased by those living near the coast, and even for those further inland, salt cod provided a change from freshwater fish. Likewise, cloth for the household was likely to be spun at home or purchased locally to be made up at home, while fine cloth for the lord and lady might well have come from London. The provision of summer and winter liveries for the household was a major expenditure each year. This pattern also applied to drink: ale was brewed at home, supplemented perhaps by local purchases, but wine came either from its port of entry or from the capital. Every house of any standing had its own brewhouse, bakehouse and dairy, and within the house a pantry for the distribution of bread and similar things, a buttery for the distribution of ale and wine (hence the term butler) and a larder for fish and meat, separate in big houses, combined in smaller ones. The management of each of these domestic departments was the responsibility of a senior member of the household, under the close supervision of the lady.

Pastimes are rarely mentioned in anything as serious as a letter, but from other evidence it is possible to create a picture of how the leisure time of a medieval lady might be spent. Aristocratic women were expected to be patrons of writers and musicians because it redounded to the honour and credit of the family, and failure to at least make a gesture in this direction threw doubt upon the family's gentility. In the early part of the period a woman's chamber, or solar, was the cultural centre of the household, and would be furnished with fine hangings on her bed and upon the walls. Visitors, both women and men, would be welcomed there with fine wine, good music and civilised conversation. A gentle household almost certainly included among its members someone with musical abilities, but travelling minstrels and harpers could usually be sure of a welcome at any manor house to raise the tone of the entertainment. At quieter times, reading books aloud, be they religious or romances or the very popular courtesy books (which detailed the behaviour and attitudes considered essential to a gentle person), was a way of allowing women to be instructed or entertained while continuing with the essential task of sewing. The best known of all the courtesy books originated in France in about 1370, by Geoffroi de la Tour Landry as advice to his daughters, and was already very popular when Caxton chose it to be published in English in 1483, describing it as 'necessary to every gentlewoman of

27

what estate she be'. While the courtesy books emphasised the respect in which children should hold their parents, they make no reference to other family relationships such as siblings, let alone more distant relatives such as uncles, aunts or cousins. At a time when an oral tradition was still strong, the telling of stories, recounting of genealogies and good old gossip also enabled tongues and hands to be busy at the same time. It is also highly likely at these sessions among female friends, with their knowledge of the family ramifications of their acquaintances, that potential alliances were discussed. Most medieval men and women enjoyed chess and 'tables', an early form of backgammon, and were frequent gamblers. Women also found hunting and hawking an agreeable form of outdoor exercise, and to partake of these was another indication of status.

The experience of a woman who headed a nunnery was similar in many practical ways to that of a widowed landowner. They each had estates which had to be efficiently administered to provide what was needed for the support of the households for which they were responsible. They were both managing sizable groups of men and women, with all the problems that was likely to entail, and while the head of a convent had much greater spiritual duties, a lady was also expected to give a devotional lead, ensuring that her household fulfilled its religious observances. The amount of time a lady spent at her devotions clearly varied according to the level of her piety. If she was very pious, most of her days could be spent at her prayers, interspersed with services and the reading of holy texts. This was particularly true of widows, some of whom (Cecily Neville, Duchess of York, and Margaret Beaufort, Countess of Richmond, were particularly noted examples) led households devoted to God which were in many ways the lay equivalent of religious houses. More worldly ladies were still expected to take their charitable responsibilities seriously, giving alms, visiting the sick and providing a lead to both their household and their community. Men and women founded charities for each other's souls, provided candles for shrines and went on pilgrimages, but there is some evidence that women were, and were expected to be, the more pious and charitable sex. All the earliest known books of hours, which were small, easily carried, devotional aids, were produced for women. Many of them were illustrated, so by commissioning one, a woman could fulfil her artistic patronage as well as showing her piety.

Letters enable the experience of medieval women from landed society to reach us in their own words far more clearly than any other type of surviving record. They reveal the important role that a lady played in maintaining the 'worship' of her family in local society. She may not have held office as her father, husband and brother did, but she was equally active in arranging marriages, supporting tenants and clients for whom her husband was 'lord', participating in lawsuits and providing hospitality to create and maintain good relations with neighbours, and where necessary intervening in disputes as a peacemaker. The style with which she ran her household, clothed and fed it and offered hospitality, was as important in displaying the status of her family as her husband's retinue when he rode from home. Whenever he was absent, she acted in his stead, providing the seamless replacement required for running the family business of estate management. The rearing of her children was generally done with love and discipline, to ensure that they were equipped to survive in a harsh world by providing the education, training and social skills, and contacts required to launch them into it. The custom of sending them away from home into service evolved not from a lack of care or concern but as a way of involving the local community in that training. The picture that emerges from these letters is not one of married women dependent on their husbands and confined to the purely domestic sphere, but of interdependent couples running their family and estate business together as a unit. As abbesses or prioresses running nunneries, or more commonly, as widows with dower lands, medieval gentlewomen could prove as competent as male landowners, and that their menfolk knew this is demonstated by the countless wills appointing them as executor.

ONE

'Dear and wellbeloved father':
Women and their parents

The birth of a child has always been a matter for rejoicing. In the Middle Ages both the child's baptism and the 'churching' of the mother a month later were social occasions. Childbirth was a communal experience, the responsibility of a midwife and the women of the household, but it did not exclude men and occasionally a male doctor was present, more frequently a priest. It seems that whenever possible, a woman's own mother was present at the birth, particularly that of a first child. The presence of other women bore witness to the birth, and there are many examples, particularly in Church courts, which dealt with family matters, of women giving evidence based on their attendance at a birth. Because of the uncertainty of life, the infant was usually baptised within a day or so of its birth, and its godparents were likely to be men or women of local importance, either lay or ecclesiastical, who could attend at short notice. Most children were given the name of a saint, a godparent or a relative, which accounts for the relatively small number of christian names in circulation. The mother was not present at the baptism even if she was fit, because until she had been churched she was regarded as unclean and was therefore not seen in public. Her churching, on the other hand, was an indication that she had survived the hazardous business of childbirth and was usually a joyful feast. Children born into the social strata from which most of our letters come, the nobility and gentry, were generally wet-nursed, though there are documented cases of even queens breastfeeding their children. Breastfeeding was recognised as a form of contraception and women lower down the social scale tended to breastfeed for two years. Gentlewomen using wet nurses, on the other hand, were able to have children more frequently. Children were brought up in the family household by women for the first few years of their lives. Their mothers, except in the smaller households, had nothing to do with the physical care of their children, which was the responsibility of a nurse. The Middle Ages regarded the first seven years of a child's life as its infancy, the next seven as its childhood. Thus, at the age of about seven, boys passed into male care, but girls continued to be looked after by women and their upbringing was supervised by their mother.

The evidence for the education of girls is sparse. It was less formal than that of their brothers, but they were usually taught to read, and sometimes to write, either by their mother, or in an aristocratic household by the governess or the family chaplain. Evidence from wills shows that many women owned and treasured books. Girls would also receive religious instruction and many would learn French, all would learn spinning, needlework, music, dancing, riding and how to run a household. Managing the household of a noble or substantial gentry family was akin to managing a business, with large numbers of people to be fed, housed, clothed, doctored and used productively. Many wives also found that they were left for long periods to manage the family estates while their husbands were at court, away on business or on campaigns overseas. This required a basic knowledge of estate management and often of the law, so that they could direct their officials, but these were skills a woman was more likely to learn after she was married than before. Some girls would have been sent while younger to a local nunnery to be educated, while many adolescent girls, like their brothers, also spent some time in another household, usually that of a woman from a slightly higher level, learning social skills and making useful contacts. In short, the upbringing of noble children was set in a pattern in the Middle Ages that would still have been in many ways recognisable to their counterparts in the early twentieth century. Although this pattern was the norm, individual circumstance might alter it. On the death of their father, a child who was an heir or heiress would move to the household of the person who acquired their wardship, no matter how young they were. While lower down the social scale, the mother or other close relative would customarily be granted wardship, this was not the case among the nobility or in any gentry family whose lands were held directly from the Crown, where the wardship was in the king's gift. In the case of a child marriage, the bride would be sent to her new husband's family, to be brought up with him. Younger children, particularly girls, were generally left in their mother's care.

A commonly held view is that medieval parents treated their children harshly, that love, if it existed, was rarely displayed, and that they regarded them as little more than chattels to be disposed of in a way most advantageous to the family concerns. There are certainly elements of truth in this, but it should certainly not be regarded as the whole picture. As head of the family, and as a reflection of feudal society, the father had absolute rights over its members, and the fear and respect which was his due was enforced even after his children had grown up and left home. Wife-beating was sanctioned by society as long as it was not excessive, and children were routinely beaten to ensure their obedience, yet there is also evidence of fatherly indulgence and affection. The reverence shown by medieval children to their father is also there in their relationship with their mother. While there is evidence that mothers could be as harsh as fathers with their children, it was often the case that they acted as an intermediary, mitigating the worst paternal excesses. In general it would seem that women had a practical and unsentimental approach to their children's upbringing, and that in sending them away from home, they did so, not out of a lack of love, but in the sincere belief that it was in the children's best interests. Since a number of the letters here deal with the custom of service in another household, we should look at it in a little more detail. It seems to have been peculiar to England (and was remarked upon by foreign visitors) and common among the nobility and gentry but not among the merchant class, where it was replaced by the more formal system of apprenticeship. Service did not mean subservience, nor the pursuit of menial tasks, but position and social advancement not just for the child who served but by association for

33

the whole family. It was viewed in a practical way by both sides, and the lord/client relationship was the most important one in the social structure of the Middle Ages. Service was a way of ensuring that both boys and girls learnt self-reliance, social graces and how to make useful contacts. Secure in the knowledge that their children were mixing with people of their own class, if any met a potential marriage partner, parents might well agree to the match providing that the financial and family details could be worked out. To medieval parents, service also had other, less obvious advantages: with adolescent children subject to outside discipline, it lessened inevitable tensions at home, and it also reduced the likelihood of more than one child succumbing to the same illness. While it is clear that some girls were unhappy in their new households, or were at least homesick, it is also clear that they felt free to complain of their unhappiness to their parents, with the hope that something might be done about it. The girls would attend upon the lady of the household, run errands, sew and embroider, make music and conversation, but most importantly, learn by watching their lady perform her duties. Despite early marriages, often following a period away from home, there is plenty of evidence that shows strong attachments by women to their natal families and their continuing identity with them. This is particularly true for heiresses, who might choose, often decades later, to be buried with their parents or at the church of their family home, rather than with their husbands, or who continued to patronise religious foundations or charities favoured by their parents and encouraged their children, particularly their daughters, to do likewise.

The letters in this chapter are both from women to their parents and from mothers to their daughters.

WOMEN AND THEIR FATHERS

Early letters between women and their parents are almost exclusively restricted to women in the royal family. It is not until the fifteenth century, with its collections of gentry letters, that evidence survives of the relationship between more ordinary women and their parents.

Thirteenth-century letters are from daughters of the king to their father. Henry III and his wife, Eleanor of Provence, had a happy and, for the most part, harmonious marriage, and their children grew up in a close and loving circle. Eleanor was a prolific letter writer and had a chatty, informal style that is curiously modern. Her daughters followed her example. Although Eleanor bore Henry nine children, only four survived to adulthood, the future Edward I, Edmund, Earl of Lancaster and two daughters, Margaret and Beatrice. Beatrice, who was born in Bordeaux in 1242, married John de Dreux, son and heir of the Duke of Brittany, when she was eighteen. The marriage was arranged by Queen Eleanor and her sister Margaret, Queen of France, who had initiated the proposals. This type of female networking on the international stage is often overlooked, but it was almost certainly more widespread than the surviving evidence suggests and was echoed further down the social scale. The young couple visited England on a number of occasions, and when Beatrice accompanied her husband on a crusade in 1270, she left some of her children in the care of her own mother at Westminster. She was also on good and affectionate terms with her mother-in-law, the Duchess Blanche. In 1268, Henry bestowed on John the honour of Richmond in Yorkshire, to which the Dukes of Brittany had an hereditary claim. Beatrice died in 1275 during a visit to London and was buried in the Franciscan priory church there, where her mother's heart was later to be buried. Her grieving husband chose never to remarry and was very generous to the Franciscan priory in her memory. The cause of her death is not known, but while she did not apparently die in childbed, her death may have been linked to the birth of her last child, Eleanor (see below). When she was at home in Brittany, Beatrice corresponded frequently with her parents; in a letter to the duke and his son about revenues from the honour of Richmond, Henry included a request for Beatrice to write to him immediately with news of herself, because he was anxious to hear. Both letters by Beatrice are short and informal, the first, written soon after her marriage, concerns her father's half-sister, one of the children of Queen Isabella of Angoulême's second marriage. Like many of her family, the Lady de Croun saw Henry III as a soft touch and made frequent visits to the English court, where she was rewarded with an annual pension. When this dried up due to the impoverished state of her brother's Exchequer, it was a shrewd move on her part to enlist Beatrice's help, because her loving father was unlikely to refuse her the boon.

Beatrice of Brittany to Henry III, 1262

To the high lord and her very dear father, if it pleaseth him, Henry by the grace of God, King of England, Lord of Ireland and Duke of Aquitaine, Beatrice his devoted daughter, wife to my lord John of Brittany, health and love as to her dear lord, with willingness to do his pleasure in all things.

I give you to know, sire, that my aunt, the Lady of Croun, has come to see me, and has begged me to pray you that you would give her a debt which you owe her. And know, sire, that she has great need of it, for a daughter of hers who is married. Wherefore, I pray you, sire, that you, if you please, grant her this debt, and that you so act in this affair that she may perceive that my prayers have availed for her.

(Everett-Green, Lives of the Princesses, *vol. 2, p. 243; Latin)*

Beatrice's second letter is even shorter, and it accompanied a letter from her husband to her father, offering military aid if required. Although undated, it probably comes from the mid-1260s, when her parents were fighting the Barons' War and her mother was raising money and troops in France.

Beatrice of Brittany to Henry III, c. 1260–8

To the most excellent lord and father, if it pleases, to the venerable lord Henry, by the grace of God, illustrious King of England, Lord of Ireland and Duke of Aquitaine, his most faithful daughter Beatrice, consort of the Lord John, heir of the Duke of Brittany, sends greetings with all reverence and honour.

We rejoice to hear of your successes, of which your letters brought news and we report that our lady Duchess is in flourishing health, by divine favour, and because we always desire, with our whole heart, to know about you, we beg that you will frequently tell us how you are, let it be successful and pleasing, in order to increase our happiness. Be always strong in the Lord.

(*Royal Letters Illustrative of the Reign of Henry III, no. DCLXIII;*
Latin)

When she was widowed in 1272, Henry III's queen, Eleanor of Provence, retired to the convent of Amesbury in Wiltshire, and later begged her son, Edward I, to allow one of her granddaughters to be entered as a child to the convent as a companion. Mary was the fourth of Edward's five surviving daughters, which meant that he had a sufficient number of girls available for diplomatic marriage purposes to permit him to dedicate one to the Church to please his mother. Mary's mother, Eleanor of Castile, was less enthusiastic about losing her daughter at such a young age, but reluctantly gave her consent, so in 1285, at seven years old, Mary became a novice at Amesbury, joining her cousin, Eleanor, youngest daughter of Beatrice of Brittany (see above) and thus another granddaughter of Queen Eleanor. Amesbury was a daughter house of the great Plantagenet foundation of Fontevrault in France, where Henry II, Eleanor of Aquitaine, and some of their children were buried. It was among the richest and most fashionable of English convents and Mary's dowry brought it an income of 50 marks per annum. Mary herself, meanwhile, was granted £100 per annum for life by her father, despite a nominal vow of poverty, and spent it, if not on clothes, then certainly on food, horses and gambling. She clearly did not have a vocation, and visited the court whenever she could, taking several nuns with her on each occasion to enjoy the treats of secular life. On the death of their grandmother in 1291, Eleanor of Brittany moved to the mother house at Fontevrault, but Mary had no intention of going with her, nor would her father countenance such a move out of England (see also chapter 2). Edward doubled her income and ordered an annual dispatch of wine from Southampton to her. Despite her allowance, she fell into debt, which her father paid, and then he gave her several manors. Nominally, income from them was to be used for charitable purposes, but there is no evidence she used it for anything other than her own comfort. This evidence of fatherly indulgence is in striking contrast to Edward's strength and ruthlessness as king. The escheators Mary refers to in her letter were the king's officers in the counties responsible for taking into custody lands held by tenants of the Crown on their death while determining who was the heir to them. In this case they had been taken by the escheators in error, because the dead man was a convent tenant and did not hold directly from the Crown. The Earl of Gloucester she refers to was Edward's son-in-law, Gilbert de Clare, who was married to Mary's elder sister, Joan of Acre.

Mary, nun of Amesbury, to Edward I, 1293

To the most high and noble prince, and her dearest and most beloved lord and father, my lord, by the grace of God, King of England, his devoted nun, Mary, wishes health, with all honour and reverence.

Dearest sire, we understand that your escheators have seized and placed in your hands the manors of Leighton and of la Grave, with all their appurtenances, on account of the death of a guardian of the said places. And because you know that your ancestors gave them in perpetual alms to the convent of Fontevraud, we beg you, dearest sire, for God's sake and your soul's, that you will place the said manors out of all seisin, if you please, and command the escheators to go away without taking anything.

And whereas my lord the Earl of Gloucester has also, for the same reason, seized the manor of Stanvele [Staveley?], may it please you to command the Earl and his people that they make take away their hands from the goods of my lady the Abbess, freely and without damage done. Do as much, most sweet father, for the love of me, that my lady the Abbess of Fontevraud may perceive in all things that I am a good attorney for her in this country. I commend to Jesus Christ the body and soul of you.

(SC 1/19/110; Everett-Green, Lives of the Princesses, *vol. 2,*
pp. 418–19; French)

Following the thirteenth-century royal letters there is a gap for the whole of the fourteenth century before the riches of the fifteenth-century gentry letters become available. The first is the only example of a letter to a step-parent; this is surprising, given the number of second, third and even fourth marriages that took place in the Middle Ages. Margaret was almost certainly the daughter of Philip Kedington and Joan, later the wife of Robert Armburgh. She married William Walkerne in 1428/9 and was expecting her first child at the time of writing. Her letter throws an interesting light on the customs of childbirth. As soon as the mother was recovered and had been churched, she could expect a round of visits, not only from her own friends, but from her mother's as well, indicating that she was expecting her mother to be present for her lying-in. Her anxiety to put on a good display for the sake of her family honour is an indication that a desire for status and keeping up with the neighbours has been with us for a long while; in the Middle Ages the term used was 'worship' and implies both status and self-respect. Her husband, newly come into his estates and as yet without income from them, and with other important calls on his money, was, according to his wife, not able to provide the extra cash, hence the plea to her stepfather for a loan. Whether or not Robert Armburgh was able to oblige is not vouchsafed, but he and her mother were already in serious financial difficulties over a legal case and the expenses of Margaret's wedding, so she may have had to put a brave face on it and receive her visitors with what she had.

Margaret Walkerne to her stepfather, Robert Armburgh, c. 1430

My dear and well beloved father, I commend me to you, doing you to wit that I have but a little while to go and am like within a short time with the grace of God to be delivered of child. And for as much as ladies and gentlewomen and other friends of my mother's and mine are like to visit me while I lie in child bed and I am not purveyed of honest bedding without the which my husband's honest [honour?] and mine may not be saved, and also my friends have been put to so grievous costs and importable charges through entangling of their adversaries, and my husband is new come into his lands and is but bare and as yet hath little profit taken thereof and hath laid great cost on his husbandry that they may not acquit them to me as they would [wish], therefore I would beseech you of your good fatherhood that you would vouchsafe in saving of mine husband's worship and mine to lend me two marks [13*s* 4*d*] or twenty shillings unto the next term [rent] day that my husband's farm comes in, and then with the grace of God you shall be well and truly paid again. I can no more at this time.

(*Chetham Mun. E.6.10(4); The Armburgh Papers, pp. 126–7*)

The next letter takes us to the widespread custom of placing adolescent boys and girls in other households as part of their general education. Dorothy was the fourth of the five daughters of Sir Robert Plumpton and his wife, Dame Agnes, and she had one brother, William, who was born in 1484. We do not know Dorothy's age when she wrote this letter, but she was probably in her late teens or early twenties. Her mother had died two years previously in 1504 and her father had promptly married Isabel, daughter of Ralph, Lord Neville, a girl probably younger than Dorothy. It was a very good match for the impoverished Plumptons because Isabel's brother had succeeded their grandfather as Earl of Westmorland. At some point, either before or after her father's remarriage, Dorothy entered the household of Isabel's mother, the former Lady Neville, who was then married to Thomas, Lord Darcy. It may well have been because of some friction between her and her new mistress that Dorothy's letter expresses considerable unhappiness. She wanted to come home, and in previous letters had begged her father to send for her but had received no reply from him, allowing ill-natured persons in the household to claim Sir Robert had little concern for her. She does not say why she was unhappy, but the news of her wishing to leave the Hirst had reached Lady Darcy, presumably via her daughter, and shamed her slightly, so she had begun to treat Dorothy rather better, even offering to help her find another situation. Whether or not Dorothy's despair at her father's neglect ended with a summons home or even a gift of the desired hat and cloth, we do not know, but she subsequently married Henry Arthington.

Dorothy Plumpton to Sir Robert Plumpton, 18 May (?1506)

Right worshipful father, in the most humble manner I can, I recommend me unto you, and to my lady mother, and to all my brethren and sistren, whom I beseech Almighty God to maintain and preserve in prosperous health and increase of worship, entirely requiring you of your daily blessing. Letting you know that I sent you message by Whyghame of Knaresborough of my mind, and how that he should desire you in my name to send for me to come home to you, and as yet I have had no answer again, the which desire my lady [Darcy] has gotten knowledge. Wherefore she is to me more better lady than ever she was before, in so much that she hath promised me her good ladyship as long as ever she shall live; and if she or you can find anything better for me in this part, or any other, she will help to promote me to the uttermost of her power.

Wherefore I humbly beseech you to be so good and kind father unto me as to let me know of your pleasure, how that you will have me ordered, as shortly as it shall like you; and write to my lady, thanking her good ladyship of her so loving and tender kindness showed unto me, beseeching her ladyship of good continuance thereof. And therefore I beseech you to send a servant of yours to my lady and to me, and show now, by your fatherly kindness, that I am your child, for I have sent you divers messages and writings, and I had never answer again. Wherefore it is thought in this part, by those persons who list better to say ill than good, that you have little favour to me, the which error you may now quench, if it will like you to be so good and kind father unto me. Also, I beseech you to send me a fine hat and some good cloth to make me some kerchiefs. And thus I beseech Jesu to have you in his blessed keeping, to his pleasure and your heart's desire and comfort. Written at the Hirst, the 18th day of May, by your loving daughter Dorothy Plumpton.

41

To the worshipful and my most entirely beloved good, kind father Sir Robert Plumpton knight lying at Plumpton in Yorkshire be these delivered in haste.

(Plumpton Letters, no. 201)

WOMEN AND THEIR MOTHERS

Many of our perceptions of medieval family relationships are derived from the Pastons, and some of the Paston women seem barely to have tolerated the presence of their daughters in the house. It would be wrong, however, to generalise about medieval attitudes to unmarried daughters from their example, as the loving possessiveness of a mother such as Eleanor of Provence demonstrates and other letters here illustrate. Elizabeth Paston was the daughter of Justice William Paston and the heiress Agnes Berry, and her parents seem from all the evidence to have been unappealing people, hard-hearted, ambitious and cold. Her father died in 1444 when she was fifteen and her mother assumed the responsibility for finding a husband for her daughter. Elizabeth was already about twenty when the first candidate appeared. He was Sir John Fastolf's stepson, Stephen Scrope, an unprepossessing widower of fifty who had suffered a long, debilitating and disfiguring illness. Agnes's treatment of her daughter during the negotiations is described elsewhere (see chapter 5), but we do not know whether Elizabeth was resisting the match or saw it as a means of escaping from her mother's control. It eventually came to nothing and the search by her family and friends for a suitable husband continued for nearly ten years with several other proposed matches failing to materialise. In 1454 Elizabeth's sister-in-law, Margaret Paston, wrote to her husband John in London 'My mother [Agnes] prays you to remember my sister, and to do your part faithfully ere you come home to help to get her a good marriage. It seems by my mother's language that she was never so fain to have been delivered of her as she is now'.

Elizabeth's position as an unmarried woman in her twenties living at home seems to have been well-nigh intolerable, which raises the question of why she was not found a place in another household earlier than 1457/8, when she joined that of Lady Pole in London. Whether this move was responsible for providing a husband is impossible to tell, but she may not have been happy even there, because her mother made a note to herself to tell Elizabeth that she 'must use herself to work readily, as other gentlewomen do, and somewhat to help herself therewith'. Elizabeth's sufferings as an unmarried woman finally ended in 1459 when she married Robert Poynings. The letter she wrote to her mother soon after her marriage is an interesting one. She addressed Agnes with respect and humility, but hardly with love, and it is difficult not to detect a note of satisfaction when she described Robert's kindness to her. Her main purpose in writing to her mother was to ensure that her husband received money owed him for her agreed marriage portion and her bequest under her father's will, which became due on her marriage. It also appears that Lady Pole had been initially responsible for much of the pre-marital expenditure that might have been expected to come from the Pastons. The final request for her mother to give credence to William Worcester is a comment on the method by which letters were transported round the country. The richest families had their own messengers, but lesser folk had to rely on the journeyings of their acquaintances. Worcester was secretary to the Paston patron, Sir John Fastolf, and would certainly have been known to Agnes. Such messengers would also be able to expand on the current affairs and well-being of the correspondent. Robert Poynings was killed at the second battle of St Albans only two years after his marriage to Elizabeth, and she later married Sir George Browne of Betchworth in Surrey and had children by him (see chapter 5).

Elizabeth Poynings to Agnes Paston, 3 January 1459

Right worshipful and my most entirely beloved mother, in the most lowly manner I recommend me to your good motherhood, beseeching you daily and nightly of your motherly blessing, evermore desiring to hear of your welfare and prosperity, the which I pray God to continue and increase to your heart's desire. And if it liked your good motherhood to hear of me and how I do, at the making of this letter I was in good health of body, thanked be Jesu. And as for my master, my best-beloved that you call, and I must needs call him so now, for I find none other cause, and as I trust to Jesu none shall; for he is full kind unto me, and is as busy as he can to make me sure of my jointure, whereto he is bound in a bond of £1000 to you mother and to my brother John, and to my brother William, and to Edmund Clere, the which needed no such bond. Wherefore I beseech you, good mother, as our most singular trust is in your good motherhood, that my master, my best-beloved, fail not of the hundred marks at the beginning of this term, the which you promised him to his marriage, with the remnant of the money of father's will; for I have promised faithfully to a gentleman called Bain, that was one of my best-beloved's sureties, and was bound for him in £200, of which he rehearsed for to receive at the beginning of this term £120, and if he fail thereof at this time, he will claim the whole of us, the which were to us too great a hurt; and he cannot make an end with none of his other sureties without this said silver, and that can my brother John tell you well enough, and it lusteth him to do so, and in all other things. As to my Lady Pole, with whom I sojourned, that you will be my tender and good mother that she may be paid for all the costs done to me before my marriage, and to Christopher Houson, as you wrote to my brother John that I should have been so; and that it please your good motherhood to give credence to William Worcester. And Jesu for his great mercy save you.

Written at London, the Wednesday the 3rd day of January. By your humble daughter, Elizabeth Poynings.

(Paston Letters, no. 374)

Like the Pastons, the Oxfordshire Stonors were a gentry family, but rather than being lawyers on the make, they were much longer established, richer and of a higher social standing; this was true of the Thames Valley as a whole, which was more settled than East Anglia and less full of competitive, litigious social climbers. Jane Stonor, the author of the following letter and wife of Thomas Stonor, was almost certainly the illegitimate daughter of William de la Pole, Duke of Suffolk. Her husband, orphaned young, had been left to the guardianship of Thomas Chaucer, whose daughter Alice later married Duke William. Although the daughter to whom Jane was writing is not identified, she had two, Mary (see chapter 2) and Elizabeth, who were definitely in the household of her half-sister-in-law, the Duchess of Suffolk, and a third, Joan, may have been there as well. The Duchess Elizabeth was married to Alice Chaucer's son John and was herself the elder sister of King Edward IV. It is clear from the letter that not only had she sought her husband's Stonor relations for places in her household, but also that the queen, Elizabeth Woodville, had been involved in the negotiations. One or other of the girls wanted to come home and, although the Stonors would have happily had her back, they clearly felt that they must have the queen's permission first. Unfortunately, the reason for the royal displeasure with the Stonors is unknown. Jane's letter is affectionate but firm: the girl must stay where she is and make the best of it, but that if her mistress wishes to be rid of her, then of course she may come home. The tone is very different to that of the Pastons, and should be used as a counterbalance to views of the parent–child relationship derived solely from that family. The reference to the queen's writing in her own hand should not be taken literally, but simply means a letter directly from the queen.

Jane Stonor to ?Mary Stonor, c. 1472

Wellbeloved daughter, I greet you well; and I understand you would have knowledge how you should be demeaned. Daughter, you know well you are there as it pleased the Queen to put you, and what time that you came first from mine; albeit my husband and I would have had . . . wherewith the Queen was right greatly displeased with us both; albeit we know right well it came not of herself. Also methink they should not be so weary of you, that did so great labour and diligence to have you; and that whereas you think I should be unkind to you, verily, that I am not, for an you be as I left you, as I trust verily that you be, I am and will be to you as a mother should be, and if so be they weary of you, you shall come to me and you will yourself; so that my husband or I may have writing from the Queen in her own hand, and else he nor I neither dare nor will take upon us to receive you, seeing the Queen's displeasure before; for my husband sayeth he has not willingly disobeyed her command heretofore, nor he will not begin now. Also I understand . . .

[No conclusion or endorsement.]

(Stonor Letters, no. 120)

The next letter comes from the third of the great fifteenth-century collections of gentry letters, that of the Plumptons of Plumpton, near Knaresborough in Yorkshire. The writer is Edith, widow of Ralph, Lord Neville, whose daughter Isabel had become the second wife of Sir Robert Plumpton in 1505 (see above). Despite the fact that she had remarried, becoming the wife of Thomas, Lord Darcy of Templehurst, Edith used her former title when writing to her daughter. Whether she did so only to her children of her marriage to Neville or more generally, we do not know, but widows whose second marriage was a disparagement frequently retained their former titles; Ralph Neville's distant cousin, Katherine Neville, Duchess of Norfolk, for instance, retained the Norfolk title through three subsequent marriages. Edith's husbands were both barons, but her first husband came from a much older and more distinguished line, while her second husband's title was a new creation. Isabel Plumpton had been plunged, upon her marriage, into Sir Robert's legal and financial disasters. Her mother's letter is brisk and businesslike, but not unsympathetic, and Lord Darcy was generous enough to forego most of a debt owed him by Sir Robert. The request to give credence to the bearer, probably a retainer of the Nevilles and certainly someone whom Isabel knew well, means that news and gossip were reported verbally rather than via the letter.

Edith, Lady Neville, to Dame Isabel Plumpton, 28 April (?1506)

My own good Lady Plumpton, I recommend me to you and to your good husband, and right sorry I am of his and your troubles. If I could remedy it. But God is where he was and His grace can and will purvey everything for the best, and help his servants at their most need. And so I trust his Highness will do you. My lord, my husband, recommends him unto you both and sends you your obligation, and has received but £4 and a mark of the £20 and £2. The remnant my lord gives to your good husband and you. And I pray Almighty Jesu send you both well to do, as your own hearts can desire. Written in haste with the hand of your mother, the 28th day of April. Give credence to this good bearer, for surely he loves you full well. Edith Neville.

To my Lady Plumpton

(Plumpton Letters, no. 200)

The last letter in this section is brisk, businesslike but affectionate. Nothing is known of the family of Jane Empson, but she was the wife of one of Henry VII's most notorious ministers. Sir Richard Empson was a talented lawyer, rising in the service of the Duchy of Lancaster under the Yorkists and then an MP, who was Speaker in the 1491 Parliament. In 1504 he was knighted and made Chancellor of the Duchy of Lancaster. His zeal and success in raising cash for the Crown made him plenty of enemies, and on the death of Henry VII he lost his protector. Courting popularity, the young Henry VIII had Empson and his colleague, Edmund Dudley, tried on a trumped-up charge of treason. Jane shared her husband's imprisonment in the Tower, but was released when Empson was executed in 1510. The Empsons came from Towcester, Northamptonshire, and the husband they found for their daughter Elizabeth was from a local family based at Ashby St Leger. George Catesby was the son of another successful lawyer, William Catesby, and his wife, Margaret, daughter of William, Lord Zouche. William had prospered under Richard III, becoming one of his leading ministers, but was executed by the new regime after Bosworth. Henry VII reversed the attainder on his family in George's favour in 1496 and his marriage to Elizabeth followed shortly afterwards. After George's death, Elizabeth married Sir Thomas Lucy in 1509. Despite the dramas and tragedies in their families, here the women are discussing nothing more momentous than business dealings with butchers. Jane could not agree to an arrangement Elizabeth had made because she had just come to another arrangement herself.

Jane Empson to Elizabeth Catesby, 2 December 1506

Daughter Catesby, I greet you well and send you God's blessing and mine. I have received your writing that you sent by the carter of Towcester and perceive thereby the bargain that Richard of Challake [?Challock Lees, near Canterbury] made and Henry Barker and good game made with the butcher of Baldock [Hertfordshire], which butcher was with me upon Tuesday in the morning afore your writing. And I was content with the same bargain and so he and I went through that he upon New Year's Day should come for them, wherefore I can none otherwise do but rest upon the same point, but I pray you say to Richard of Challake that he make as good shift as he can with some butchers about him and he see it will no better be. No more at this time but I trust to be with you at Eston the Friday or Saturday next after Lady Day [25 March] by God's grace who keep you. From London this Wednesday after St Andrew's Day. By your loving mother, Dame Jane Empson.

To my right wellbeloved daughter Elizabeth Catesby at Eston by Towcester [Easton Neston?] be this delivered.

(PRO SC 1/51/159)

TWO

'Very dear lord and brother':
Women and their brothers

This chapter was originally intended to relate to all siblings, but it soon became apparent that while a handful of letters survive from women to their brothers, there are no obvious examples of any written to their sisters. This should certainly not be taken to mean that no such letters were written, indeed there is evidence of them from other sources. It is clear from a variety of records, household accounts and wills as well as letters, that the interests of women were generally concentrated on the nuclear, rather than the extended family. The principal reason for this was that once married, women were required to identify with their husband's family rather than their own, something that became easier once children were born. There is evidence, particularly in the case of heiresses, that this did not necessarily prevent women retaining a strong sense of their own family identity, but it served to loosen ties with the birth family. In the families of the gentry and nobility where, perforce, our examples are taken, other factors reinforced this tendency. Most children of gentle birth spent periods in other households once they reached adolescence, thus reducing the amount of time they spent with their siblings and loosening any close attachment there might have been in childhood. In many cases girls may have known young men serving in the same household as themselves rather better than their own brothers. Nonetheless, siblings formed an important part of women's networks and the relationships of medieval women with their siblings were probably as varied as those today, tempered by affection, indifference, mistrust, loyalty and jealousy. Brothers were brought up to be protective and of help to their sisters. Sometimes pleas for help came from the sisters themselves, sometimes brothers were called upon by their parents to be of service; for example, Margaret Paston urged her eldest son to arrange for his sister Margery to be placed with the Countess of Oxford, or some other noblewoman.

The letters from women to their brothers that have survived fall here into two categories. The earliest are from English princesses to the kings who were their brothers. The fact that their letters are of diplomatic importance explains their survival, and gives them an added level of political interest. One of the classic roles expected of a princess was to be an intermediary between her husband's domain and her own, and since many royal marriages were arranged to conclude a peace, or at least a truce, or bring a recalcitrant vassal back within the orbit of his overlord, it was by no means a nominal one. Its fulfilment, nevertheless, tends to be overlooked in diplomatic history because evidence rarely survives, and it is sometimes only by accident that we learn that married princesses did return to their native lands to visit their parents or brothers, sometimes accompanied by their husbands, and indeed more than one princess died while in London on a visit to her family. It would be surprising if on such occasions political affairs were not informally discussed, agreements reached and other marriages arranged. Such family networking would have been replicated lower down the social scale. It is of particular interest that two of the royal women whose letters are included here were bastards, but recognised as members of the royal family and married accordingly. In the case of Henry III, both his full and his half-sister are confusingly called Joan. Henry and his full sisters grew up in one of the most seriously dysfunctional of all the medieval royal families. The stormy marriage of King John and their mother, Isabella of Angoulême, ended with the early death of the king and Henry's accession when he was nine, and his siblings all younger. Isabella then abandonned her children to return to her county of Angoulême in southern France, to which she was the heiress. Her young children, not surprisingly, seem to have clung together and remained close all their lives. Joan, three years younger than the king, was his eldest full sister. She had been betrothed to Hugh de Lusignan, Count de la Marche, as a small child and sent to southern France to be brought up in his household, since he was already adult. When her mother Isabella returned to Angoulême she promptly married Hugh herself. Joan was sent home after some difficulty – Isabella and Hugh detained her as a hostage for her dowry, which they had no intention of returning. Her first letter, written when she was with her mother and had not yet returned to England, is the only letter among our examples to be written by a child, for Joan was probably about nine or ten when it was composed, presumably under the strict guidance of Queen Isabella, but still informal and full of affection for her brother.

Joan of England to Henry III, c. 1220

To the most excellent lord and her most beloved brother, Henry by the grace of God King of England and Lord of Ireland, Duke of Normandy and Acquitaine and Count of Anjou, Joan his sister sends greetings, if this is sweet enough.

My messenger will know that I am safe and unharmed and I would like to know and hear of you and my brother Richard. Moreover I strongly beseech you not to credit what unfaithful persons say to you against our lord Hugh de Lusignan, but believe without hesitation the words of our lord William de Batill and R. de Barnville [the bearers of the letter], and as soon as you are able, let me know your circumstances and your wishes.

(PRO SC 1/3/187; Everett-Green, vol. 1, p. 382; Latin)

A letter from the Count de la Marche to his step-son, Henry III, dated November 1220, says that he has delivered up Henry's sister. On Joan's return to England, a new match was arranged for her and she was subsequently married, at the age of eleven in 1221, to Alexander II, King of Scots. The couple paid fairly frequent visits to

England, often when the court was at York. The marriage brought peace on the borders and a degree of prosperity and increased trade to Scotland. Royal revenues increased to the extent that Alexander was able to lend both his brothers-in-law money. Joan's second surviving letter, written only a few years after her marriage, is a political one and appears to reassure her brother of her husband's support, the implication being that Henry was worried that Alexander was helping to foment rebellion against him in Ireland; the letter is damaged, hence the gaps in the text. A letter also survives from Henry to his sister, telling her of their sister Isabella's forthcoming marriage in 1235 to the Emperor Frederick II, in which his affection is clear, and he alludes to Joan's continuing concern for her own family. He conferred two English manors on her for life, and she became closely attached to his wife, Eleanor of Provence. She and Alexander had no children and it appears that her health was poor. She died on a visit to London, aged twenty-eight, with both her brothers, King Henry and Richard, Earl of Cornwall, in attendance.

Joan, Queen of Scotland, to Henry III, March (?1224)

To Henry, by the grace of God, illustrious King of England, Lord of Ireland, Duke of Normandy and Aquitaine, Count of Anjou, venerable lord and her dearest brother, Joan, by the same grace, Queen of Scotland, sends greetings and prayers for favourable successes.

We have received the letters which your excellency sent to us with great joy, as was fitting, on the Wednesday before the Annunciation of the Blessed Virgin Mary. May you hear, however, that we have been grieved by the letters because of the troubles you have revealed to us from Ireland . . . how with serious wrong Hugh de Lasceles has moved against you and your loyal men. But, with divine grace mediating, soon the war will be without effect, through the advice and support of your loyal men. With regard to this, you should know that my husband the King of Scotland has told us that . . . present state of affairs . . . that some armed man, horsed or on foot may want to set out from his territories into Ireland. And if it were possible . . . to know from someone from his own lands or another, and then he could be intercepted, it would be taken from him with payment owed. Indeed, more secretly in our parts . . . we heard . . . that the king of Norway will land in Ireland next summer to offer help to the said Hugh. . . . We point this out to you so that you may forestall him. Farewell.

(Royal Letters Illustrative of the Reign of Henry III, no. CXCV; Latin)

Henry III's half-sister, Joan, was a bastard daughter of King John by an unknown mother, of whom only her name, Clementia, is recorded. John had many mistresses and at least seven bastards, almost all born before his accession to the throne and his marriage to Isabella of Angoulême. He had no scruples about seducing gently born women, married or otherwise, but whoever her mother was, Joan was recognised as the king's daughter and brought up in his household. Bastard daughters could serve the same useful purposes as legitimate ones, though their husbands might be lower down the pecking order of rulers, and Joan was married in 1205 or 1206 to Llywelyn the Great, Prince of Gwynedd. She became an influential figure in diplomatic affairs between England and Wales, in one of the rare cases where a woman's role has been fully recognised. During an attack by John on North Wales in 1211, Llywelyn was so hard pressed that it was reported that 'on the advice of his leigemen, he sent his wife, who was the daughter of the king, to make peace between him and the king in any manner she might be able'. Llywelyn was granted a safe conduct and John accepted his submission for Joan's sake. She maintained a friendly relationship with her half-brother, Henry III, who was born after her marriage, meeting him formally on occasion in the Marches, and in 1229, she and her son David did homage to the king at Westminster on behalf of Llywelyn. In 1226, Pope Honorius declared her legitimate, but without prejudice to Henry III or the realm of England, meaning that she and her children had no rights of inheritance. Her surviving letter to Henry, which cannot be dated with any accuracy, shows that she continued her diplomacy, smoothing relations between her brother and her husband, and assuring Henry of the loyalty of the clerk, Instructus, who appears from the letter to have been their chief go-between. Joan died in 1237 and Llywelyn built a Franciscan house over her grave at Llanvaes in Anglesey.

Joan, Princess of Wales to Henry III, c. 1217–37

To her most excellent lord and dearest brother, Henry, by the grace of God, King of England, Lord of Ireland, Duke of Normandy and Aquitaine and Count of Anjou, Joan sends her own greetings.

Know, lord, that I am grieved beyond measure, that I can by no means express, that our enemies have succeeded in sowing discord between my husband and you. I grieve no less on account of you than on account of my husband, especially since I know what genuine fondness my husband used to have, and still has, for you, and how useless and dangerous it is for us, with due respect, to lose true friends and have enemies instead. Thus on bended knee and shedding tears, I beg your highness to alter your decision, as you may easily do, and do not fail to be reconciled to those who are joined to you by an unbreakable bond and learn both to love friends and oppress enemies. With regard to this, lord, you may know how some have wrongly suggested to you that you should not trust Instructus, your clerk and my lord's, in whom I do not believe you could have a more faithful clerk in England, may God help me. For this reason, he is no less faithful to you if he is faithfully carrying out the business of his lord, because he behaves in the same way carrying out your affairs in the presence of his master; neither you nor anyone would rely on him if he handles the business of his master in a half-hearted or careless manner. Therefore if you wish to have confidence in me for anything, put your faith in me for this. Farewell.

> *(Royal Letters Illustrative of the Reign of Henry III,*
> *no. CCCIII; Latin)*

Mary, daughter of Edward I, was the fourth of his five surviving daughters (see chapter 1). When she was seven years old she joined her cousin, Eleanor of Brittany, as a novice at Amesbury, where their grandmother, the widowed Queen Eleanor of Provence, had taken the veil. On the death of Queen Eleanor, Eleanor of Brittany moved to Amesbury's mother house of Fontevrault, where she became Abbess, but Mary had no wish to leave her comfortable and self-indulgent life in England. Although Mary had become a nun before her brother Edward was born, her frequent visits to court during her father's lifetime presumably meant that she knew her brother quite well. It was obviously convenient for the convent to have such a channel to the king, as is shown by Mary's letter to Edward about the appointment of a new prioress. Although the Abbess Eleanor of Fontrevault won the dispute, she diplomatically appointed Mary as her attorney in England. Quite what Mary was doing in the Isle of Wight is not clear, but Amesbury was in Hampshire, and it may have owned property on the island.

Mary, nun of Amesbury, to her brother, Edward II, 9 May (c. 1309)

To the very high and noble prince, her very dear lord and brother, my lord Edward, by the grace of God King of England, his sister Mary sends health and all manner of honour and reverence.

Very dear sire, as a long time has passed since God did his will upon our prioress, we, after her death, sent in all haste to our dear cousin, the Lady-Abbess of Fontevrault, both on my part and on that of the convent, asking for a lady from this our convent, to wit, for the Lady Isabella, whom we understand to be well able and sufficient for the office, that she might be granted to us for our prioress. And we thought, dear sire, that she [the Abbess] would have willingly granted us our request, for she is bound to do so since she was brought up and veiled amongst us, as so she should neither wish nor permit that the church should be so long without prelates; but as yet we have had no answer, only we understand from certain people that she intends to send us a prioress from beyond the sea there, and a prior by her counsel out there. And know, certainly, my very dear brother, that should she send any other than one belonging to our own convent, it would prove matter of discord in the convent, and of the destruction of the goods of the church, which I know well, sire, that you would not suffer willingly and wittingly; wherefore I pray you, dearest lord and brother, and require you, both for the love of me and of our convent – which after God trusts surely in you – that you would please send word to my said Lady-Abbess, that she do not undertake to burden our church with any prioress out of the convent [Fontevrault], nor with prior other than the one we have now, but that she would grant us her whom we have requested. Do this, most dearest brother, that our convent may receive your aid and sustenance in this case as they have always done in their needs. May Jesus Christ give you a long life, my dearest brother.

Written at Swainton, in the Isle of Wight, the 9th day of May.

(PRO SC 1/34/128; Wood, I, pp. 61–3; French)

The next two letters are written by two of the sisters of Henry IV, again, one by a full sister and one by an illegitimate half-sister. All were children of John of Gaunt, Duke of Lancaster, and therefore members of the royal family. Philippa and Henry were the children of Gaunt's first wife, Blanche of Lancaster, who died of the plague while they were still young. Philippa was married to John I of Portugal in 1387, long before her brother usurped his cousin Richard II and took the throne as Henry IV. She bore him many children and accepted at court an equally large number of his bastards. One of them, Beatrix, had accompanied Queen Philippa on a visit to England in 1405 after her brother had become king. At Philippa's urging, she was married to Thomas Fitzalan, Earl of Arundel. Thomas' father had been executed and attainted by Richard II in 1397, and he himself put in the wardship of the Duke of Exeter. He was very harshly treated and managed to escape to the continent where he joined his uncle, the deposed Archbishop of Canterbury, in exile. He landed in England with the future Henry IV in 1399 and was much favoured by him, despite being under age. It was presumably at this time that he sought permission from the king to choose his own wife, agreeing to pay the fine that the situation required. In 1400 his father's attainder was reversed and he became earl. Why, when Thomas was acquiescing in the queen's plan to marry him to Beatrix, Henry was still demanding the fine is unclear, but Philippa was doing her best to rescue the young earl.

Philippa, Queen of Portugal, to Henry IV, 4 November 1405

Most high and most puissant prince, my most supremely beloved brother, I recommend myself to your high nobleness as humbly and entirely as I can or know with all my entire heart, supremely desiring to hear and to know often of your estate and health; and in especial of the prosperity of your most noble person, as good, pleasant and joyous news as you yourself, most noble prince, could best devise, or in any manner desire, for your sovereign ease and comfort. And because I am certain that you would most willingly hear similar things from here, I signify to you that the King my sovereign lord, all my children, your own nephews, who wish always humbly to be recommended to you, and I their mother, your own sister, at the making of these presents are all well and hearty of body, thanks to our Creator, who ever maintain you in honour and prosperity according to your desire.

Most high and puissant prince, my best beloved brother, please it you to know that by Sir John Wiltshire, knight and ambassador of our cousin the Earl of Arundel, I am here informed how a sum of gold is yet owing to you by the said Earl, which he pledged himself to pay you for the licence which it pleased your gracious lordship to grant and give him in his nonage, that he might marry according to his wish, and in whatever place he saw fitting to his estate. And since you know well, my supremely best beloved brother, that he is now married not after his own seeking but as by your commandment, in part at my instance, I therefore supplicate you, since you are so great and noble a prince, as entirely as I know how, that it will please you to quitclaim to the said sum at this my request, in order that I, who am in part the cause of his marriage, may be the cause of the acquittal of the said sum. And if there be anything in these parts which might give you pleasure, may it please you to command and certify it to me, and I will do it to my utmost power without hypocrisy.

So I pray our sovereign Lord Jesu ever to give you prosperity, pleasuance and joy, and very long to endure.

Written at the palace of Lisbon, the 4th day of November,

Your entire and loyal sister, P de P.

(Moriarty, pp. 193–4; French)

The Beauforts were the most famous family of royal bastards in medieval England, children of John of Gaunt, Duke of Lancaster, by his mistress, Katherine Swynford, who later became his third wife and whose children were subsequently legitimated. Joan was the only daughter of their union and was first married to Sir Robert Ferrers. She was a widow at the time of her parents' marriage and a second, more ambitious, marriage was arranged for her with Ralph Neville, Earl of Westmorland. The only snag was that Ralph was a widower with nine children. He and Joan went on to have fourteen more. Under the influence of his determined and ambitious wife, Ralph stripped his heir of most of the lands that should have been his by right, in favour of his eldest son by Joan: Richard, later Earl of Salisbury. Ralph played a prominent role in the abdication of Richard II and the usurpation of his wife's half-brother, Henry. How friendly Joan herself was with Henry is difficult to judge from this letter; the favour she was seeking was not for herself, but for a young couple she felt deserved better treatment at the hands of her brother than they had received to date. If Joan had taken the unfortunate Margaret into her own household, that would have separated her from her husband, while a position in Queen Joan's household would be a better solution. It is an appealing letter (and like that of her half-sister, Philippa), written entirely on behalf of people she regarded as unfortunate and to whom, particularly the wife, she feels a sense of responsibility. It incidentally reveals the price that a couple could pay for failing to fulfil family expectations and marrying for love.

'Very dear lord and brother'

Joan, Countess of Westmorland, to Henry IV, 1406

Most high and puissant prince and most excellent sovereign lord, I recommend myself to your royal and high lordship in the most obedient manner which, with my whole entire and simple heart, I can most humbly do, as she who desires to know of you and your most noble estate and most perfect health, such prosperity as your royal and honourable heart can desire. And may it please your high nobleness to understand that I write now to your royal presence on behalf of your loyal liege and esquire, Christopher Standish, who, he has certified me, has been in your service in Wales every time you have been there against your enemies, and besides, in all your most honourable journeys since your coronation, in which he has expended the substance that he could acquire of his own and of his friends, in such wise that, whereas he and my wellbeloved, his wife Margaret (daughter to Thomas Fleming, who was chancellor and servant during his life to my most honoured and redoubted lord, your father) kept house and establishment, they have left it and the said Margaret is lodged very uncomfortably with her children, of whom she has many, having one or two every year; and all this on account of the great charge which her said husband has incurred and still incurs in your service; to whom, of your gracious goodness and gentleness you have aforetime promised guerdon of his labour, whenever he should spy out [something] from which [he could have a living] of 40 marks or £40. And, most puissant and excellent prince and my most sovereign lord, he is the youngest [and his father has dismissed him from] his ser[vice], and that merely because he and his wife married each other for downright love, without thinking this time [what they should have to live on. Wherefore I] entreat your most high and puissant lordship to consider that this same Margaret should dwell [in some suitable place or else with the Queen] your wife, whom God protect; and that she is come to me trusting that my [intercession] might avail her with you. May it please you to be gracious lord to her and her said husband, and of your guerdon [assist them] to support their persons in poor gentility, that their affiance may turn to good effect for them, and to my

59

honour if it please you, by their finding succour from your royal and most excellent nobility, on account of this my most effectual supplication.

Most high and puissant prince and most excellent sovereign lord, I pray God to grant you a most honourable and long life, and preserve you in his most excellent keeping, and give you entire joy and gladness as much as your gentle and most noble heart would choose or desire. Written at the castle of Raby.

Your most humble and obedient subject, if it please you, J de W

(BL Cotton MS Vespasian F, xii, art. 27, fol. 32;

Wood, I, pp. 83–5; French)

Note: the original letter is damaged and Wood has supplied conjectural lost words in [ ].

The next two letters take us away from the royal family, because they are from married gentlewomen, each seeking help of one sort or another from her brother. In both cases there is clear evidence of affection coupled with the belief that the help being sought would be forthcoming; they are part of the ample evidence that many women retained close links with their own families after their marriage. The first letter is from Katherine, daughter of Sir William Plumpton (executed for treason in 1405 for his complicity in the rebellion of his uncle, Richard Scrope, Archbishop of York), who was married to a Chadderton of Chadderton Hall, Lancashire. The family were comfortably off, as illustrated by the fact that they had just added a new chapel to their home; this was a distinctly expensive status symbol. Katherine's brother George, the recipient of the letter, was a priest, hence the request by Katherine's husband for some gift for the altar, a suggestion which had been taken very much amiss. Their elder sister, Isabel, had married a Lincolnshire knight, Sir Stephen Thorpe, in 1425. Both girls had had their marriage portions provided by their widowed mother, Alice, who also left them devotional and household items in her will when she died in 1423. The Thorpes had clearly fallen on hard times if they could not afford for Dame Isabel to have a single female servant or companion, and Katherine was deeply upset and worried by her sister's situation, and held a low opinion of her brother-in-law. Since Isabella married after her mother's death, her elder brother, Sir Robert Plumpton, should be seen as bearing the responsibility if the husband chosen for her could not keep her in a manner appropriate to her status. After expressing her worries about her sister's companionless state, it was rather tactless of Katherine to ask George to keep a look out for a young woman for her own household, but it is a good illustration of the widespread custom of young girls (and boys) being sent to serve in other households. Although in general the practice was aimed at widening networks, so the households of non-kin were preferred, it was not unusual to serve kinfolk who were of superior social status. It is just such a link which caused Katherine's indignation in the last paragraph of the letter. Lord Scrope of Masham was a second cousin, since her grandfather had married Isabella, daughter of the first Lord Scrope, and as a kinswoman she should have received greater courtesy than she felt she got from Elizabeth, Lady Scrope, who for some reason refused to see her. Mistress Darcy was the Scropes' daughter, making her mother's excuses. She had been widowed in 1452 and may have been living with her parents. The fact that Katherine had a retinue of five attendants was clearly a matter of some pride, and a dig at the Scropes, who were one of the poorest of the baronial families. All in all, Katherine's letter gives some fascinating insights into the social customs of the upper gentry in the fifteenth century. It is fluently written, probably not too dissimilar to the manner in which she spoke, and full of naturalness, even to her husband's semi-joking comment about the chapel.

Katherine Chadderton to George Plumpton, c. 1450–5

My best brother, I am sorry, by my troth, that I shall not see you and have come thus far to York. God knows my intent was not for no great goods that I thought to desire, but I know well now you trusted [believed] the contrary. But, brother, it is not unknown to you that I am right sickly and my heart would have been greatly comforted to have spoken with you, but I trow, and so does my

61

daughter, that you be displeased, denying that my writing before, because she desired a book of you, and as ever I be saved, she prayed me write for either psalter or primer, and my husband said, half at play, 'pray my brother to get somewhat to my new chapel'. God knows, he meant neither gold nor silver, but some other thing for the said altar. But had I known you would have been displeased, I would not have written, for as much as I have displeased my best brother. My sister, Dame Isabel, lives as heavy a life as any gentlewoman born, for the which cause I fared never well since I saw her last month. How such, she hath neither woman nor maid with her, but herself alone. And her husband comes all day to my husband and says the fairest language that ever you heard. But all is wrong, he is ever in trouble, and all the joy on earth has she when my husband comes to her. She swears there is no creature she loves better. Also, brother, I beseech you entirely, if there be any goodly young woman that is a good woman of her body, and pay four and twenty [pounds] or more, and I would have one of my own kin, an there were any, for myself. And dear brother, an you or any for you can espy, I beseech you to get her for me as hastily as you may, soon upon Easter, an it may be. I can no more, for great haste of my journey, but I beseech the Blesed Trinity, with all the saints in heaven, give me grace to see you ere I die, to God's pleasure and your bodily health.

And brother, I goed to the lord Scrope to have seen my lady, and by my troth, I stood there a large hour, and yet I might see neither lord nor lady; and the strangest cheer that ever I had of my Mistress Darsie, and yet I had 5 men in a suite. There are no such 5 men in his house, I dare say.

To Master George Plumpton at Bolton Abbey.

(Plumpton Letters, no. 2; see also Ward.)

Mary Barantyne was desperately worried on her own behalf when she wrote to her brother, William Stonor. Unlike the northern Plumptons, the Stonors came from the Thames Valley and had risen in importance by successful careers in the law and royal service. Like Katherine Plumpton, Mary Stonor was unwed at the time of her father's death in 1474. She was probably married to John Barantyne in about 1476, with a dowry of land worth £10 per annum. She and her younger, unwed sister Elizabeth, were in the household of Elizabeth, Duchess of Suffolk, sister of Edward IV. William Stonor's new wife, a wealthy London widow called Elizabeth Riche, noted that the duchess was half-minded to dismiss the two girls unless their family could provide them with better apparel, and it was probably Elizabeth's money which supplied the new clothes. At the time of her letter to her brother, both Mary and her husband seem to have been still under age and in the care of John's mother, who under the will of her husband, held all his lands for life, save for a small amount set aside for his heir, John. This in itself was unusual, and implies not only a belief in the competence of his widow, but perhaps hints at less than full confidence in his son, who was fourteen at his father's death. In the will, made two days before his death in 1474, John Barantyne Senior directed that his children should be 'ruled and guided by Elizabeth, my wife'. The disadvantages of this arrangement became apparent two years later when the widow married Sir John Boteler, carrying with her most of the Barantyne lands. John Barantyne was clearly under his mother's thumb, and the two were involved in a good deal of litigation at this period. It seems that despite any intervention by Sir William Stonor, the lands in Henton were sold in 1482. Mary's son, William, was born a little over a month after her letter was written. In a charming glimpse into late medieval life, John Parson recalled much later that for the baptism there was a fire in the belfry and the midwife stripped the child, and that Sir William Stonor, his uncle and godfather, said that the child loved it. This is hardly surprising, given the common custom of binding babies in swaddling clothes to ensure their limbs grew straight.

Mary Barantyne to Sir William Stonor, 13 November 1481

Right reverend and worshipful brother, I recommend me to you as heartily as I can; thanking you of your good brotherhood to me before this time showed, which I pray you of continuance: letting you wit, as I am informed, that my husband by the moving, procuring and striving of my lady his mother, that they will sell certain of my husband's livelihood: what it is I cannot inform you, but as a credible man that should know my reason it should be Henton. Wherefore I beseech and require you, as you are a true God's knight and the King's, that you advise and counsel my husband the contrary, so being disposed, as my very trust is in you. For I thank God we have fair issue and by possibility be like to have. And I beseech you that this said counsel and advice come by yourself and not of me in no wise. And I shall pray to God for your honour and welfare, which preserve you bodily and ghostly. Written at Little Haseley the Tuesday before the feast of St Hugh the Bishop. By your own sister, Mary Barantyne.

To my right reverend and worshipful brother, Sir William Stonor, knight, be this bill delivered.

(Stonor Letters, no. 294)

THREE

'Right entirely and best beloved husband':
Women and their lovers and husbands

The stereotypical picture of medieval marriage is of young people married off at their parents' behest to suit family politics, or to add to its wealth and status, with little or no consideration for their feelings. This is very far from being an accurate or complete picture. Marriage in the circles of the nobility and landed gentry was a means of social advancement for the family as well as the individual, and its aim was the preservation of landed property and acquisition of further estates, but that was by no means all that was involved. Romantic love was a well-known concept in the Middle Ages, it featured in songs and stories, but it was not something that most people expected to base anything as important as the business of marriage upon. Love, they believed, if it came, was a result of marriage, not a prerequisite for it; marriage was initially based on politeness and respect. And yet there are plenty of well-documented examples of marriages made purely on the basis of the desires of the two people involved, sometimes with the blessing of their parents, sometimes without. In this they could count the Church as an ally. While it did not encourage young people to flout the wishes of their parents, the Church recognised as a valid union one where there were no canonical impediments and where solemn vows had been exchanged between the two, even if they had not been said before a priest. This constituted a pre-contract, a legally binding agreement to marry, and if the vows were followed by consummation, then it became a legal marriage. Love is often expressed in letters, sometimes between prospective partners, based on a few short meetings and quite probably no private converse. It was therefore likely to be no more than convention, based on favourable first impressions, shared interests and hope. Yet this initial liking in many cases deepened into the solid marital love illustrated in some of the letters, for others the best that could be hoped for was affection and respect based on mutual interests. Conversely, if a young couple took an instant dislike to each other on meeting, then most parents would be willing to end negotiations.

Unless a son was called, or chosen, for the Church, or a daughter wished to enter a convent, a single life was not an option, so every child from a gentle family expected to marry. Barring unforeseen circumstances, they expected their future partner to be selected by their parents and for the match to serve their family economically or politically. Arranged marriages should not be rejected out of hand as incompatible to happiness, since even in the modern era, people tend to choose their partners from those with a similar background and outlook. Medieval parents generally looked for their children's future spouses among the sons and daughters of their neighbours and acquaintances, fellow office holders or members of their lord's affinity, business or legal contacts or more distant members of their kinship network. The difference to modern eyes lies in the business element of the match. A daughter went to her marriage with a dowry, either a sum of money or parcel of land, or if her family was of high enough rank, a manor or more. A son, if he were to be regarded as a suitable match, had to be endowed with an estate, or settled in a lucrative career in the law or royal service, so that he could support a wife. The heiress of an estate might expect to look slightly higher than her own status for a husband, an heir likewise. Heirs and heiresses sometimes made a child marriage, when a girl was under the age of twelve and a boy less than fourteen. If this was the case, then the children concerned were often either already living in the household of their new spouse's family, or had moved into it, so that they might be brought up in their company. If a child marriage rather than a betrothal actually took place, then as far as the Church was concerned, it had to be validated at the time the children reached maturity and were old enough to give their formal consent. Technically at least, either party could repudiate a match made when they were too young to consent. It took a brave young person to do so, but it did occasionally happen.

Marriage in the Middle Ages often took the form of serial monogamy, but unlike the modern era of divorce, it was concluded by death. With a much shorter life expectancy, many people could expect to marry twice, possibly even three or four times. A widow, still young enough to bear children and with a good dower from her deceased husband, was a very marriagable prospect. With so much remarriage, step-parents and children were the norm, and marriages were often subsequently arranged within the newly extended family. While first marriages were usually made between young people of a similar age, there are examples of matches with a great discrepancy in age. Usually this was the marriage of a young girl, perhaps with nothing much in the way of a dowry, to a much older man, often with children of her own age. There are, however, occasional examples of the age gap in reverse: Katherine Neville, the wealthy dowager Duchess of Norfolk, was married off to Queen Elizabeth Woodville's youngest brother, John, who was almost young enough to be Katherine's grandson, but the cynicism of the match shocked contemporary opinion, and this is probably an indication that it was very rare.

Once married, a medieval couple from the gentry or nobility formed a working partnership. Naturally the woman was expected to run her household, ensuring that its members were clothed, fed, doctored and lived in a seemly manner. Since a household might number anything from a dozen or so in the lower ranks of the gentry to hundreds in those of the great nobles, such a task was never a sinecure. In addition to running a sizeable household, a man expected his wife to be able to deal with his estate officials in his absence on a day to day basis and refer only important matters to him. Since gentlemen of the shire were quite often away from home, serving in Parliament or on the bench, or as part of a fighting force, as well as dealing with their own business in outlying parts of their estates or with legal business in the king's courts, a wife might well be left in charge at home for weeks at a time. It is, of course, to these absences that we owe the surviving letters. No early medieval letters survive from women to their lovers or husbands; and from the later period they come from three great fifteenth-century collections, which enable us to make a more detailed study of the three families concerned, the marriages within them and their attitudes toward it.

We know nothing about the matchmaking on behalf of Thomas Stonor and and his wife, Jane, who was probably the natural daughter of William de la Pole, Duke of Suffolk, but the Stonor family was closely linked to Thomas Chaucer, one of the most powerful men in their Oxfordshire locality, and whose daughter, Alice, had married the duke. Jane was born and brought up in France, and received letters of denization (naturalisation) when she married in about 1453. By the time this letter was written, Thomas and Jane were a couple with a growing family; they eventually had three sons and three daughters who grew to adulthood. The letter is not one about personal or family affairs, but was dashed off quickly to let her absent husband know of a summons by the new Yorkist king, Edward IV, to join him at Northampton for a campaign against Lancastrian dissidents. The castle concerned was Alnwick, in Northumberland, which had been held by Lancastrians, then successfully beseiged by a Yorkist army, only to be lost again through treachery. The Scots, always keen to get involved in warfare on the borders, had not unnaturally given aid to Queen Margaret of Anjou when she, King Henry and their son escaped to Scotland after the seizure of the throne by Edward IV and their defeat at Towton. Twice a Scottish army had crossed the border to support the Lancastrians' rearguard action in Northumberland. As it turned out, while Edward was still at Northampton, Yorkist forces under the Earl of Warwick sent the Scots fleeing back over the border, and on this occasion Edward did not lead north an army containing a Stonor contingent. Alnwick remained in rebel hands for almost another year until the Yorkists' final victory in the north at Hexham in May 1484. 'Langforth', who forwarded the privy seal letter to the Stonors, was probably Edward Langford, a Berkshire neighbour and kinsman.

Jane Stonor to Thomas Stonor 2 August (1463)

Sir, I recommend me to you. Pleaseth you to know that upon Wednesday last passed my cousin Langforth's son brought you a privy seal [letter] and to all the gentlemen of the shire. So I received sore against my will. I desired of him to have kept it still, for you were not at home: but he would not do so, but counselled me to send you in all haste. And he promised me that he would inform the King that you were not at home, and he told me that upon the Thursday following the King removes northwards and purposes into Scotland, if then he come again. For that other party has besieged the castle that was late rescued, and there is of them more than 5,000, as the King has word. Other tidings I can none send, but I beseech the Holy Ghost be your guide. Written at Stonor the Tuesday after St Anne's day.

Your own J S.

(Stonor Letters, no. 70)

As far as may be judged, the marriage of Thomas and Jane seems to have been a successful one. While we know nothing of their feelings at the time they were married, writing in October 1468 with the news of the death of his mother and stepfather, Thomas addresses her as 'Mine own good Jane' and then says 'good, sweet leman (lover), be you merry and of good comfort for to comfort me when I come. I cannot come to you as soon as I would'. Jane's letters to her husband were rather more formal, and there is a distinct note of exasperation in this one in response to a note from her husband announcing that William Lovel, Lord Morley (see below), wanted to stay at Stonor. But Thomas had failed to tell her what answer he had given to Morley, causing Jane to assume his mind was elsewhere at the time. She was less than anxious to have an important guest at a time when the household was at sixes and sevens after Thomas's hasty departure for their Devonshire estates. Her comment that servants were not as diligent as they used to be is a complaint that has echoed down the centuries. So too does the reminder of the shopping he had promised to do for her; some of the things that she wanted are now hard to identify. The use of the word 'brother' in relation to her husband is by no means unusual at this period, when words like brother and cousin which for us imply a specific relationship were used much more loosely. Thomas addresses his letter to Jane as 'To my Cousin Jane Stonor', and see the letter of their daughter-in-law, Elizabeth, that follows.

Jane Stonor to Thomas Stonor (c. 1470)

Sir, I recommend me to you as lowly as I can; pleaseth you to wit I have received a bill from you whereby I understand my lord Morley desires to sojourn with you. What answer that you have given him I cannot understand by your bill; I suppose your mind was upon some other matters when that you wrote it, but an you have not granted, I beseech you to eschew it and to contend your little abiding at home, and also the joberde [*sic*] of your children and of all your house at your hasty going into Devonshire; for an your abiding at home be no otherwise than it is, that will be none profit unto you and heartsease unto me; rather break up household than take sojourners, for servants be not so diligent as they were wont to be. Now farewell, good sir, and God give you good night and bring you well home and in short time. Written at Stonor upon St Simon and St Jude's Day at eve by your own Jane Stonor

Please it you remember upon gentian, rhubarb, bays, caps, pouttys [*sic*], cheverellaseys [*sic*], an ounce of flat silk, laces, tryacyl [*sic*]

To my brother [*sic*] Stonor in haste, at the Sword in Fleet Street

(Stonor Letters, no. 10)

William, the eldest son of Thomas and Jane, was unmarried at the time of his father's death in 1474, although a match had been mooted with Margery, widow of William Blount, son of Lord Mountjoy, which seems to have foundered on financial considerations. It seems likely that when Thomas died, negotiations were in hand for a less socially advantageous bride, but one who had much greater financial attractions. Elizabeth Riche was the daughter of a London alderman and the wealthy widow of a city mercer; she was probably older than William, who married her in 1475. She also had three daughters and a son by her first marriage, the eldest, a girl called Katherine, was probably about twelve at the time of her mother's remarriage. When she wrote the following letter, Elizabeth was in London, probably attending to business affairs, but was clearly distressed at news of her daughter's illness; the word 'crazed' may mean she was running a fever. She therefore made arrangements to have her carried from Stonor to London, where she could get better medical attention and sent down three trusted servants, including a clerk or chaplain, Sir William, to help with the move. The reference to her brother Stocker was to Sir William Stocker, husband of her sister Margaret, while that to her brother Crooke was probably to her own brother, John.

Travelling and the transport of valuables was never entirely safe, so Elizabeth took advantage of her husband's probable journey to town as an escort for her daughter, by asking him to bring some of her family silver with him for the service marking the anniversary of her first husband's death. The use of the term 'cousin' to her new husband and the reference to her first husband as 'husband' would not have seemed as strange to William Stonor as it does to a modern reader. Unlike most of the other letters in this collection, and of Elizabeth's own, this one was written entirely in her own hand. Her use of French in dating the letter was probably a little affectation indicating her newly acquired gentility.

Elizabeth Stonor to William Stonor, 18 August 1476

Right well beloved cousin, I recommend me unto you with all my heart, and I thank you heartily, gentle cousin, of your expedition that you have made in pleasing my brother Stocker of his buck; he is beholden unto you and at your coming to London he will thank you I doubt not as reason is; and I for my part thank you for my venison, the which I have received by my brother Crooke. Also, gentle cousin, I understand that my daughter Katherine is crazed and has a disease on her neck: I marvel what it should be: if it would like you, I pray you heartily to suffer her to come to London to me to the intent she may be helped thereof. I send Sir William, Agnes Dibdale and Howlake for her, and on Tuesday next I trust to see you here at London, and when you come you shall be welcome with more. Jesu speed you ever, amen. At London le 18 jour d'aoust. Elizabeth Stonor

PS Gentle cousin, I pray you bring with you the 2 basins and ewers of silver, the silver candlesticks and the monstrance, and the little silver basin to set it in. I would have it here against my husband's terement, and it can not come better at no time than with you now because of strength.

To my most worshipful cousin William Stonor Esquire, this be delivered. At Stonor.

(Stonor Letters, no. 168)

Elizabeth's next letter, written only a month after the last, shows that all was not well at Stonor in her absence. William had been ill and then her brother, John Crooke, staying with him, had contacted the pox. This was a generic term meaning a disease with spots or 'pocks' and could be chickenpox, smallpox or measles or even the plague; it was also used colloquially for venereal disease, but that is not the meaning here. Elizabeth was anxious for William to leave the contagious air of Stonor and come to London as soon as he was well enough to travel (an interesting reversal of the usual health-giving properties of town and country), and she also offered to come home to nurse him if he was still incapacitated. While she displayed great anxiety about her new husband's well-being, she seems less concerned with her unfortunate brother. She was also grateful to her husband for being willing to look after all her children at Stonor, but again, preferred to have them safe under her eye in London. She was very busy with business matters, presumably concerned with her late husband's affairs, over which she wanted her husband's advice. The reference to her son Betson, is to Thomas Betson, who was a partner of William Stonor's in the wool trade and Elizabeth's man of business. At about the time of William and Elizabeth's marriage, he had become betrothed to Katherine Riche, Elizabeth's eldest daughter, who, at the time of these letters, was still too young for marriage. This letter affords an interesting example at the speed of travel. Elizabeth was writing on the Thursday in London and expected to receive a reply from Stonor on the Saturday, implying that when the matter was urgent, Stonor could be reached in one long day's ride of about 40 miles.

Elizabeth Stonor to William Stonor, 12 September 1476

Right reverend and worshipful and entirely best beloved cousin, I recommend me to you in the most lowliest wise that I best can or may. And, sir, as this day by your servant Thomas Matthew, I received a letter from you, by the which letter I understand that you be somewhat amended and shall every day better and better than other by the grace of God. Also, gentle cousin, I understand that my brother and yours is sore sick of the poxes: wherefore I am right heavy and sorry of your being there, for the air of pox is full contagious and namely to them that be not nigh of blood. Wherefore I would pray you, gentle cousin, that thee would come hither, and if it would please you so to do. And if that it like you not so to do, gentle cousin, let me have hither some horses I pray you and that I may come to you, for in good faith I can find it in my heart to put myself in jeopardy there as you be, and shall do whilst my life endures to the pleasure of God and yours. For in good faith I never thought so long since I saw you, for in troth I had well hoped that your horses should have been here as this night; and that I thought verily, and so pointed myself to be with you as the morrow at night with God's mercy, which should have been unto me right a great comfort; for in good faith I have not been merry at my heart this sevennight day for divers matters the which have been broken to me. Wherefore I wist full heartily divers times that you had been here; for I wot well that you could an [have] answered in certain matters better than I; for truly I had not so busy a week since I came hither, except one day, which Sir William, and John Matthew both can inform you part thereof. And, sir, touching my children I heartily thank you that it like you so for to tend them: but that, gentle cousin, if it please you to send them up with such horses as it like you to send for me, I would heartily pray you, for the pox been passed out of this country and city as far as I understand, blessed be God. Gentle cousin, I pray you heartily that I may have a ready

73

word from you on Saturday at night at the farthest; for in truth I can not be merry unto the time that I know verily how that you will I be demeaned herein. No more to you at this time, but almighty Jesu preserve you, and keep you long in good health of body and long to live in virtue to God's pleasure, and so to your most heart's desire, amen. At London, the 12th day of September.

And my son Betson recommend him unto you as heartily as he can or may, and besought to vouchsafe to pray for him etc; and you shall rec[eive] 2 letters of him by John Matthew. And as this day at 8 of the clock in the morning he took his barge. I pray God send him good speed. By your own Elizabeth Stonor

To my right worshipful cousin, William Stonor, squire, this be delivered.

(Stonor Letters, no. 169)

Another month had elapsed by the time the third letter from Elizabth in London reached Stonor. This time she changes her mode of address from 'cousin' to the more familiar 'husband'. Business rather than ill health had finally kept William in Oxfordshire, from where he had kept the London household supplied with venison and fresh fish and rabbits (or conies). Since there can be no doubt that Elizabeth bettered herself socially by marrying into the gentry from her rich City merchant background, it is possible to detect a great deal of satisfaction in the report she makes of her dealings with the Yorkist royal family. Edward IV was well known for his lack of snobbery, dealing as comfortably with men of the City as with his nobles, and it would seem his sister Elizabeth, Duchess of Suffolk, was the same. When she was in London she was happy to include women like Elizabeth in her train, but Elizabeth owed the Suffolk connection to her husband's close relationship to the ducal family. His sisters, Mary and Elizabeth, were in the duchess's household, and his wife reports the duchess's displeasure at their lack of suitable clothing, but that she recognised the Stonors were only responsible for Elizabeth and any new clothes for Mary would come from her new family. The elder of William's two sisters, Mary (see chapter 2), was married to

John Barantyne, who was still under age. His widowed mother had recently married Sir John Boteler, who was proposing that the young couple live with them, a suggestion that Mary regarded as part of a plan to control her young husband's livelihood. Elizabeth Stonor's reference to money in connection with the duchess is not explained, but it reads as though the duchess either owed them money or was about to pay them some for another reason. The king's mother, of course, was Cecily, Duchess of York (see chapters 4 and 6). The reference to 'cousin Rokes' is to Thomas Rokes, who was a cousin of William's through the marriages of two of his Stonor aunts. His business on behalf of the Stonor servant, John Matthew, is obscure, but he seems to have been particularly displeased by Matthew's attitude. 'Cousin Fowler' was probably Richard Fowler, from a local family, a successful royal servant who became Chancellor of the Duchy of Lancaster; Stonor was hoping to benefit from Fowler's influence in high places. Although her husband did not join her in London, her children had done so, and were some consolation to Elizabeth in his absence. That William, too, was missing his wife, may be inferred from the gift of a ring he sent her, not, unfortunately, a very well-made one.

Elizabeth Stonor to William Stonor, 22 October 1476

Right entirely and best beloved husband, I recommend me unto you in my most hearty wise, evermore thanking you right heartily of all kindness to me showed at all times, and now for your good venison and conies, the which you sent me by Harry Blackhall, the which is great dainties to have here in London: wherefore I sent the half haunch to my father and a couple of conies: and they recommend them unto you and thank you right heartily. And, sir, you shall understand that I have been with my lady of Suffolk as on Thursday last was, and waited upon her to my lady the King's Mother, and hers, by her commandment. And also on Saturday last was I waited upon her hither again, and also from thence she waited upon my lady her mother, and brought her to Greenwich to the King's good grace and the Queen's: and there I saw the meeting between the King and my lady his Mother. And truly methought it was a very good sight. And, sir, I was with my lady of Suffolk at this day, hoping that I might have had her at some leisure that I might have spoken to her for the money, but truly she was very busy to make her ready, for she is riding to Canterbury as this same day, and she will be here again as on Saturday next coming, for she told me so herself. Also, sir, I spoke with my cousin Fowler at my lady the King's Mother's: and I thanked him as heartily as I could for his great kindness that he showed to you and to me at all times, praying him of his good continuance: and he asked me when you would come hither. And I told him that I supposed that you would be here as this week. And also I spake with my cousin Rokes and he asked me in like wise, and he sayeth it is not his fortune to meet with you here in London: and I spake to him for John Matthew's matter, and prayed him to be a good master unto him, and he answered me again, and said that he had little cause, for he sayeth that he has been the most importunate man that might be to himwards. And I answered and said to him, that I could never understand it but that he owed him his service to his power. And, sir, my lady of Suffolk is half displeased because that my sister Barantyne is no better arrayed, and likewise my sister Elizabeth. And she says without they be otherwise arrayed, she says, she may not keep them: and she says that my mother and yours should say that you have enough to find my sister Elizabeth with all. Also I understand that Sir John Boteler hath spoken to my lady to have my sister Barantyne with him: what he means therein we wot not, without that he would have the rule of her husband's livelihood by that means. Wherefore my sister would speak with you for that matter to have your counsel in what is best to do. And, sir, as for my son Betson I heard no word from him since you departed: for there comes no passage these 8 days. And, sir, I would pray you when Davy Wrexham comes to you out of the Cotswolds, that you will send him hither that he might write to my son how he has done in the country. And good sir, I pray you that my blue gown of damask may be sent to me against Allhallows day, and my coffers and my daughter Katherine's, that I spake to you afore. And sir, such kerchiefs and smocks and small japys that be in the chest that Catherine my woman had rule of, which chest stands in my son Betson's chamber. And sir, I would pray you that you would send this gear to me that I might take reckoning of her: for she 'skeevisith' her and says that such gear as I ask her is there. Sir, I pray you send me no more rings with stones: for the ring that you sent me by Harry Blackhall, the stone is fallen out by the way and lost: wherefore I am sorry. Good sir, let it not be long ere I may see you: for truly me think right long since I see you. Your children and mine fare well, blessed be God, and they be a great comfort to me in your absence. No more to you at this time, but Almighty Jesu preserve and keep you in long health and virtue to His pleasure. At London the 22nd day of October.

My own cousin, I send you a bladder with powder to drink when you go to bed, for it is wholesome for you. By your own to my power Elizabeth Stonor.

To my right well-beloved cousin William Stonor, esquire, at Stonor, this be delivered.

(Stonor Letters, no. 173)

Three years later, it was Elizabeth who was at home at Stonor, and Sir William (knighted in 1478 at the marriage of the king's younger son, Richard, Duke of York) who was briefly away. His wife's letter, written urgently and late at night, was chiefly concerned with the possibility of them gaining the wardship of 'Lovell's daughters'. Lovel was William Lovel, Lord Morley, in the right of his wife Eleanor, whose grandmother was a de la Pole. It was almost certainly this connection with the Duke of Suffolk which enabled the Stonors to learn that the wardship was available. Both William and Eleanor Lovel died in the summer of 1476, when their son, William, Lord Morley, was only ten and his sister Alice two or three years older. William's wardship was granted to the Bishop of Salisbury, and he later married Elizabeth, daughter of the Duke of Suffolk, but it is unclear who initially was granted Alice's wardship, as it had become vacant a couple of years later. Alice did indeed become a ward of the Stonors, and following the death of her brother in battle in Flanders without heirs, she became Baroness Morley in her own right in 1489. Baronies were the only peerages that women inherited automatically; more senior titles were in the gift of the king who decided whether or not to grant them to the husband of the heiress. The stewardship of Henley, just five miles from Stonor, to which Elizabeth Stonor refers in her letter, seems to have gone elsewhere. The interest in the death of the vicar of Fawley, Buckinghamshire, was because the Stonors owned property in the parish. This letter of Elizabeth's is a good example of the way that important family business and personal concerns are reflected in a single letter.

Dame Elizabeth Stonor to Sir William Stonor, 26 March (1479)

My best beloved husband, I recommend me unto you in my most hearty wise, desiring to hear of your welfare and trusted verily to have had you at home on Our Lady day (25 March) by night; if you had been I would have trusted you should have had the ward and possession of Lovell's daughters ere this, for whom Stedolfe, the Queen's attorney, rode on Tuesday last all night towards the King's grace. And if you would speed you home to speak with him at his coming I doubt not that you shall have the one at the least, for I understand they be not wards neither to the King or Queen: praying you therefore to speed you home, for understand he be with Bryan tonight or tomorrow without fail. Also for all such stewardships you wrote unto me for, they were granted away in his lifetime ere he deceased. As for the stewardship of Henley, I cannot tell whether it be gone or no: wherefore Vyne shall ride according to your commandment. Sir, I thank you heartily for the venison that you wrote to me to receive: how be it, as yet I have not received. Over this, the parson of Fawley deceased yesterday in the morning and the parson of Hamelden and Sir William, priest there, be executors. No more unto you at this time, but the Holy Trinity preserve you. Written at Stonor, when I would fain have slept, the morrow after our Lady day in the morning. Sir, I send you your boots and your cloak, for there hath been a wet weather here since you departed. By your own wife, Elizabeth Stonor.

To my best beloved husband, Sir William Stonor, Knight

(*Stonor Letters, no. 237*)

Sadly, the lively and fashionable Elizabeth died late in 1479, and very soon afterwards Sir William began to look for another wife. The lady he decided upon also owed her wealth initially to trade, this time in Exeter, but Annys, or Agnes, Wydeslade's family had invested in land and she was her grandfather's heiress to considerable estates in both Devon and Cornwall. Sir William's second marriage, therefore, was a step up socially from his first. At the time he met Annys, she was the childless widow of a Devon gentleman and, as her letter indicates, in poor health. Her first husband had predeceased his father, hence the agreement over dower that Annys was making with her late father-in-law, Richard Wydeslade, who had been her own guardian when she inherited under age. Sir William married her sometime in the spring of 1480, but Annys's health failed to improve and within a year, she too was dead.

Annys Wydeslade to Sir William Stonor (early 1480)

Right worshipful master, I heartily commend me unto you with all such service as I can or may: thanking you of your kindness showed unto me, so poor a woman as I am, and unto your mastership undeserved: desiring to hear of your welfare, the which I pray almighty God to preserve you to your most pleasure and heart's desire. Please you to have knowledge of my poor welfare: at the making of this my letter I was in good health and I trust in God within short space to be better: for I am now at my liberty, whereof I thank you, in my own house at Exeter. The physician will do his cunning upon me, but undertake me he will not, nor never did none in his life. Comfort in him I find, and in my mind I think he will do me good. Furthermore, the dealing of my father-in-law, you shall have knowledge by a bill which Thomas Matthew shall deliver you.

A very end between him and me will not be had into the time of your coming, which I trust will not be long. Methinketh a thousand years gone that I heard any tidings from you. And in good faith you may say unto me that I am unkind that I wrote nor sent unto you since your last being at Wideslade. The cause is, for my excuse is that I have been in hell, where I had little comfort, but as soon as I came to Exeter, then was I in heaven: and because that I am now in joy I do send you this letter. Master, it is so that the physician is in hand with me, and he desireth to have me in cure 3 months, for which cause I pray you remember your worship and my poor quest. And as I amend, I shall put you in knowledge by the grace of Jesu, who keep you. From your true lover, Annys Wydeslade

To his right worshipful master, Sir William Stonor, Knight, be this delivered

(Stonor Letters, no. 262)

Some of Annys's lands in Devon were held of the Marquess of Dorset, in the right of his wife, and it may be this connection which brought Sir William into the orbit of the queen's family, the Woodvilles; Thomas Grey, Marquess of Dorset was her son by her first marriage. Equally, it may have been through Jane Stonor, his mother, who had some influence with the queen. Whatever the channel, Sir William's third marriage was a piece of major social advancement. Anne Neville, daughter of John, Marquess Montagu, brother of Warwick the Kingmaker, was a second cousin of Edward IV. However, since the death of both her father and uncle at the Battle of Barnet fighting Edward, the Nevilles were in disgrace, which is why the family were willing to countenance a match with a wealthy widower from the gentry class. Dame Annys Stonor died in May 1481 and Anne Neville bore a son in August 1482, so for the second time Sir William remarried very quickly. In the early stages of pregnancy, Anne was away from home, attending Dorset and his wife in Taunton and longing to see her husband, who was due to join her at the time of the local assize court. In the following summer, the death of her only brother, George, left Anne and her sister Elizabeth as co-heiresses; a bonus Sir William could hardly have looked for. Yet again he was unfortunate, for Anne died in 1486. The brief period of her marriage had seen Stonor attainted for his involvement in Buckingham's rebellion in 1484, his exile in the company of Dorset and his triumphant return in the train of Henry VII. Sir William did not remarry; he died in 1494, aged about forty-five. All three of his marriages had been clearly made for money or position, but that did not preclude subsequent marital happiness, and it would be fascinating to know which of his three wives was his personal favourite.

Dame Anne Stonor to Sir William Stonor, 27 February 1482

Sir, I recommend me to you in my most hearty wise, right joyful to hear of your health: liketh you to know, at the writing of this bill I was in good health, thinking long since I saw you, and if I had known that I should have been this long time from you I would have been much lother than I was to have come into this far country. But I trust it shall not be long or I shall see you here, and else I would be sorry on good faith. Sir, I am much beholden to my lady [Dorset], for she maketh right much of me, and to all the company, officers and others. I have early trust upon your coming unto the time of the assize, and else I would have sent Harry Tye to you long or this time. I have delivered a bill to Harry Tye of such gowns as I would have for this Easter. And I beseech our blessed Lord preserve you. From the Castle of Taunton the 27th day of February. Your new wife Anne Stonor.

[No endorsement.]

(Stonor Letters, no. 306)

Leaving the Stonors of Stonor Park in Oxfordshire, we move to East Anglia and the best-known family of fifteenth-century England, the Pastons. The marriage of William Paston and Agnes Berry was one of the two or three matches which set the Pastons on their road to worldly success. William was too intent on advancing his career in the law to marry young and was forty-two in 1420 when he decided

81

the time had come to find a wife. He did moderately well. Agnes was only eighteen and she and her sister were the co-heiresses of Sir Edmund Berry, so on his death in 1433 she brought William three manors, including Stanstead in Suffolk and Orwellbury in Hertfordshire; he in turn purchased Oxnead in Norfolk and settled it on her by way of jointure and it became a favourite family residence. It was hardly a love match and both William and Agnes appear cool and businesslike in all their dealings with each other and their family. Agnes outlived her husband by many years: William died in 1444 and for the next thiry-five years Agnes held on to Paston property worth £100 a year, which was made up of her inheritance, her jointure and her dower. On her death she chose to be buried beside her parents in the chapel of the White Friars in Norwich rather than with her husband in the cathedral. Their son John (known as John Paston I to distinguish him from his son and grandson who are known as John Paston II and John Paston III) was born in 1421 and because of his own late marriage, Judge William appears to have been anxious to have his son's match settled early and producing grandsons before he died. John was married at nineteen, while he was still at Cambridge, and in the following letter Agnes describes to her husband their son's first meeting with the girl they had chosen for him. Margaret Mautby, who was eighteen, was already an heiress, for her father, John Mautby, had died when she was eleven. She was a greater catch than Agnes Berry had been, for she brought with her eight manors, including Sparham and Mautby, situated for the most part in those areas of Norfolk where the Pastons already held land. According to Agnes the meeting between the young couple went off well. It is worth noting that although the Paston women could both read and write, they invariably employed the services of a secretary, despite the final comment which implies that Agnes wrote the letter herself. The comments at the end of the letter are instructive. William was to buy a gown for their prospective daughter-in-law and Agnes tells him firmly to get a red or blue one. The reference to two pipes of gold is slightly puzzling, since it clearly did not refer to gold coin; it may perhaps be to gold thread for embroidery. This is the only one of Agnes's letters to William to survive.

Agnes Paston to William Paston, 20 April (1440)

D ear husband, I recommend me to you etc. Blessed be God I send you good tidings of the coming, and the bringing home, of the gentlewoman that you know of from Reedham, this same night, according to appointment that you made there for yourself.

And as for the first acquaintance between John Paston and the said gentlewoman, she made him gentle cheer in gentle wise, and said, he was verily your son. And so I hope there shall need no great treaty between them.

The parson of Stockton (Norfolk) told me, if you would buy her a gown, her mother would give thereto a goodly fur. The gown needed for to be had; and of colour it would be a goodly blue or else a bright sanguin.

I pray you do buy for me 2 pipes of gold. Your stews [fishponds] do well.

The Holy Trinity have you in governance.

Written at Paston, in haste, the Wednesday next after Deus qui errantibus, for default of a good secretary. Yours, Agnes Paston.

(Paston Letters, no. 34)

The newly-wed Margaret Paston was to become one of the most prolific correspondents in the collection (sending a total of 104 letters which have survived and which are written in a great variety of hands), largely because her husband, John, was so frequently away from home on business defending his inheritance. For a lawyer, Judge William left his affairs in an inexcusable mess when he died in 1444. His will was out of date, and he had only tinkered with it at the end of his life, assigning manors to his younger sons and setting aside money for his daughter. On his death, his heir, John, found himself virtually landless, because much of the Paston estate was still being enjoyed by his mother. He frustrated the intentions of his father's will, holding on to manors which should have gone to his brothers and alienating the rest of the family. John Paston's chief patron was the veteran soldier, Sir John Fastolf, whose chief seat, the fine castle of Caister, was very close to

Margaret's manor of Mautby, and it was through his wife that he met Fastolf; Margaret was distantly related to him through her mother. A decade or so later Fastolf, dying childless, left a nuncupative, or verbal, will bequeathing the whole of his estate to Paston, provided he establish a college and almshouse at Caister. The trouble was that John was the only witness to the will and not unnaturally many regarded him as lying and the will invalid. It was bitterly contested by some of Fastolf's other trustees, including Justice William Yelverton, William Worcestre, Fastolf's secretary and Thomas Howes, his chaplain. The result was nearly twenty years of wrangling and litigation which drove John to an early grave half way through and which his son, John II, managed to resolve largely through his connections at court. The Pastons lost most of the inheritance, but eventually got Caister itself. A great many of Margaret's letters relate to these legal struggles over the estates, which it would take a great deal of tedious detail to explain, and therefore the emphasis here is on letters which deal more with personal affairs. The first was written only three years after her marriage and while Judge William was still alive. It indicates how strong the bond between Margaret and John had become and is a perfect example of the medieval concept of marital love developing after an arranged marriage had taken place. Their eldest child, John II, had been born the previous year. The reference to Margaret's father Garneys is to Ralph Garneys of Gelderston, the second husband of her mother, Margery Berney.

Margaret Paston to John Paston, 28 September 1443

Right worshipful husband, I recommend me to you, desiring heartily to hear of your welfare, thanking God of your amending of the great disease that you have had. And I thank you for the letter that you sent me, for by my troth my mother [her mother-in-law, Agnes] and I were nought in heart's ease from the time we knew of your sickness til we knew truly of your amending. My mother promised another image of wax of the weight of you to Our Lady of Walsingham, and she sent four nobles [26s 8d] to the four Orders of Friars at Norwich to pray for you, and I have promised to go on a pilgrimage to Walsingham and to St Leonards [Priory, Norwich] for you. By my troth, I had never so heavy a season as I had from the time that I knew of your sickness til I knew of your amending, and yet my heart is in no great ease, nor shall be, til I know that you be very hale. Your father and mine [Justice William] was this day seventh [a week ago] at Beccles (Suffolk) for a matter of the Prior of Bromholm, and he lay at Gelderston that night and was there til it was 9 of the clock and the other day. And I sent thither for a gown and my mother said I should have then, til I had been there anon, and so they could none get.

My father Garneys sent me word that he should have been here the next week, and my uncle also and play them here with their hawks, and they should take me home with them; and so God help me, I shall excuse me of my going thither if I may, for I suppose that I shall readier have tidings from you here than I should have there. I shall send my mother a token that she took me, for I suppose the time is come if I keep the behest that I have made; I suppose I have told you what it was. I pray you heartily that you will vouchsafe to send me a letter as hastily as you may, if writing be no dis-ease to you, and that you will vouchsafe to send me word how your sore doeth. If I might have had my will, I should have seen you ere this time. I would you were at home, if it were to your ease, and your sore might be as well looked to here as it is there where you are, now liefer than a gown though it were of scarlet. I pray you, if your sore be whole, and so that you may endure to ride, when my father comes to London, that you will ask leave and come home when the horses be sent home again, for I hope you should be kept as tenderly here as you have been at London. I may none leisure have to write half a quarter so much as I should say to you if I might speak with you. I shall send you another letter as hastily as I may. I thank you that you would vouchsafe to remember my girdle and that you would write to me at the time, for I suppose that writing is none easy for you. Almighty God have you in his keeping, and send you health.

Written at Oxnede, in right great haste on St Michaelmas Eve. Yours, M Paston

My mother greets you well and sends you God's blessing and hers; and she prayeth you, and I pray you also, that you be well dieted of meat and drink, for that is the greatest help that you may have now to your health ward. Your son fares well, blessed be God.

(Paston Letters, no. 47)

Margaret's next letter is a result of a scolding she had received from her husband, though we do not know the cause. Her plea for forgiveness is touching, but she does not seem to doubt that she will receive it and moves easily on to domestic matters. Ingham was presumably one of their tenants, hence the dispute about who was responsible for the windows in the property.

Margaret Paston to John Paston, 22 March (?1451)

Right worshipful husband, I recommend me to you, beseeching you that you be not displeased with me, though my simpleness caused you to be displeased with me. By my troth, it is not my will neither to do nor say that should cause you for to be displeased; and if I have done, I am sorry thereof and will amend it. Wherefore I beseech you to forgive me, and that you bear none heaviness in your heart against me, for your displeasure should be heavy to me to endure with.

I send you the roll that you sent for, in sealed, by the bringer hereof; it was found in your trussing coffer. As for herring, I have bought a horseload for 4s.6d. I can get none eels yet; as for bever [beverages?], there is promised me some, but I might not get it yet. I sent to Joan Petche to have an answer for the windows, for she might not come to me. And she sent me word that she had spoken thereof to Thomas Ingham, and he said that he should speak to you himself, and he should accord with you well enough, and said to her that it was not her part to desire of him to stop the lights; and he also said it was not his part to do it, because the place is his but for years.

And as for all the other errands that you have commanded for to be done, they shall be done all as soon as they may be done. The blessed Trinity have you in his keeping. Written at Norwich, on the Monday next after St Edward, Yours, MP.

(Paston Letters, no. 183)

A visit of Queen Margaret of Anjou to Norwich was a major event, even for those, like the Pastons and the Cleres, whose sympathies inclined towards the Duke of York. Elizabeth Clere, to whom Margaret refers, was a niece of Fastolf's and the widow of Robert Clere of Ormesby, her second husband. Both William and John Paston were on close terms with Elizabeth and her sons, and the families addressed each other as 'cousin' although the relationship, via Margaret Paston, was a distant one. Margaret and Elizabeth were close friends, despite the fact that Elizabeth was somewhat the elder. The queen's attempt to find a new husband for the widowed Elizabeth came to nothing, largely because the latter had no wish to change her state. She was very well provided for, and was able to lend her friend suitable jewellery for the occasion. Margaret's plea to John that he buy her some for herself so that she is not shamed on future occasions is a touching one. The king's brother, who wanted to see John Paston, was one of Henry VI's half-brothers, either Jasper Tudor, Earl of Pembroke, or Edmund, Earl of Richmond.

Margaret Paston to John Paston, 20 April 1453

Right worshipful husband, I recommend me to you, praying you to know that the man of Knapton [Norfolk, where the Pastons owned some land] that owes you money sent me this week 39s. 8d; and as for the remnant of the money he has promised to bring it at Whitsuntide. And as for the priest, Howard's son, he went to Cambridge last week and he shall no more come home and therefore I might not do your errand.

As for tidings, the Queen come into this town on Tuesday last past after noon, and abode here til it was Thursday, 3 after noon; and she sent after my cousin Elizabeth Clere by Sharynborn, to come to her; and she durst not disobey her commandment and come to her. And when she came in the Queen's presence, the Queen made right much of her and desired her to have a husband, the which you

87

shall know of hereafter. But as for that he is never nearer than he was before. The Queen was right well pleased with her answer and reporteth of her in the best wise, and sayeth by her troth, she saw no gentlewoman since she came to Norfolk that she likes better than she doth her.

Blake, the bailiff of Swaffham [Norfolk], was here with the King's brother, and he came to me thinking that you had been at home and said that the King's brother desired him that he should pray you in his name to come to him, for he would right fain that you had come to him if you had been at home; and he told me that he knew well that he should send for you when he came to London, both for Cossey and other things.

I pray you that you will do your cost on me against Whitsuntide, that I may have something for my neck. When the Queen was here, I borrowed my cousin Elizabeth Clere's device, for I durst not for shame go with my beads amongst so many fresh gentlewomen as were here at that time. The blessed Trinity have you in his keeping. Written at Norwich on the Friday next before St George. By yours, M Paston.

(Paston Letters, no. 226)

Margaret's next letter comes back to the vexed question of a husband for her sister-in-law, Elizabeth Paston (see chapters 1, 4 and 5). Because of the uncertain dating of the letter, it is impossible to tell which of the men suggested over the years as suitable matches is being referred to here, but Elizabeth, desperate to be married and away from home, is clearly encouraging her brother John to be more active in her cause. Agnes was being her usual unpleasant self and scoffing at her daughter's chances. John Brackley, to whom Margaret refers, was a well-known preacher from the Grey Friars in Norwich, and her 'cousin Crane' was probably Alice, daughter of John Crane (see chapter 5); although the Cranes were only distant relations of Agnes Paston, the two families had close dealings. The subject of Alice's matter is not revealed: a potential husband? a lawsuit? The possible dating of this letter to 1454 comes from Margaret's reminder to her husband that she is still waiting for the necklace she had asked for.

Margaret Paston to John Paston 29 January (?1453/4)

Right worshipful husband, I recommend me to you, praying you to know that I spake yesterday with my sister [Elizabeth Paston] and she told me that she was sorry she might not speak with you before you went; and she desires, if it pleases you, that you should give the gentleman, that you know of, such language as he might feel by you that you will be well willing to the matter that you know of; for she told me that he hath said before this time that he conceived that you have set but little thereby, wherefore she prayeth you that you will be her good brother, and that you might have a full answer at this time whether it shall be yea or nay. For her mother hath said to her since you rode hence, that she hath no fantasy therein, but that it shall come to a jape; and sayeth to her that there is good craft in daubing; and hath such language to her that she thinketh it right strange, and so that she is right weary thereof, wherefore she desireth the rather to have a full conclusion therein. She sayeth her full trust is in you, and as you do therein, she will agree her thereto.

Master Brackly be here yesterday to have spoke with you; I spake with him, but he would not tell me what his errand was.

It is said here that the sessions [of the peace] shall be at Thetford on Saturday next coming and there shall be my lord of Norfolk and others with great [numbers of] people, as it is said.

Other tidings have we none yet. The blissful Trinity have you in his keeping. Written at Norwich on the Tuesday next before Candlemass.

I pray you that you will vouchsafe to remember to purvey a thing for my neck, and to do make my girdle. Yours, MP

My cousin Crane recommends her to you, and prayeth you to remember her matter etc, for she may not sleep at night for him.

(Paston Letters, no. 236)

Turning from Margaret we come to the tangled matrimonial affairs of her two eldest sons. The eldest, John II, usually referred to as Sir John, is described by Gairdner as 'a careless soldier, who loves adventure, has some influence at court, mortgages his lands, wastes his property and is always in difficulties', and yet he emerges from the letters as one of the most human and appealing of the Paston family. Born in 1442 and knighted in 1463 when he came of age, he became a friend of Queen Elizabeth Woodville's brother, Lord Scales, and for some time in the late 1460s was betrothed to their cousin, Anne Haute. It is not perhaps surprising that during his early twenties Sir John should have had mistresses, what is surprising is the survival of letters from two of them. It indicates that possibly they were kept for sentimental reasons; none of Anne Haute's letters have been preserved. The first, from Cecily Daune, is identified by Gairdner as being from a former lover and the tone of the letter suggests that she was possibly a servant girl whom he had seduced and discarded, but had not entirely abandoned. It is conceivable that she was only a former servant and not a lover, but the lack of any other reference to her in the family letters makes this less likely. Cecily, whoever she was, followed the fortunes of Sir John from afar, and the news of a possible marriage gave her an excuse to write, and append a plea for financial help. Nothing beyond the letter is known of her and for that she would have employed the services of a literate acquaintance or professional letter writer. The reference to a daughter of the Duchess of Somerset is obscure. There is no other suggestion in the letters that such a match was considered, but Cecily's confusion probably stemmed from the fact that Sir John's uncle, William Paston, married Lady Anne Beaufort, daughter of Edmund, Duke of Somerset, at about the time this letter was written.

Cecily Daune to Sir John Paston, 3 November (c. 1463–7)

R ight worshipful Sir, and with my faithful heart and service full entirely beloved good master, in my most humble wise, I recommend me unto your good mastership. Please it the same to wit that I think right long to I have very knowledge of your welfare, the which understanding will be to me right great comfort. And that causes me to write unto you as now. And also to let you wit that I heard report that you should be wedded unto a daughter of the Duchess of Somerset, which matter, an I spoke to you, I could inform your mastership that were long to write as now. But I shall and do pray God daily to send such one unto your world's make that will dread and faithfully unfained love you above all other earthly creatures. For that is most excellent riches in this world, as I suppose. For earthly goods being transitory and wedding continues for term of life, which with some folk is a full long term. And therefore, Sir, saving your displeasure, meseemeth wedding would have good advising.

Moreover, Sir, like it your mastership to understand that winter and cold weather draweth nigh and I have but few clothes but of your gift, God thank you. Wherefore, Sir, and it like you, I beseech your good mastership that you will vouchsafe to remember me your servant with some livery, such as pleaseth you, against this winter, to make me a gown to keep me from cold weathers. And that I might have it and such answer as you please in the promises sent unto me by the bringer hereof. And I shall continue your oratrix and poor servant and heartily pray to God for your prosperity. Whom I beseech have you, Right worshipful Sir, and with my faithful heart and service full entirely beloved good master, in His blessed governance.

Written at Hellow the 3rd day of November. Cecily Daune
(Paston Letters, no. 679)

When his engagement to Mistress Haute came to an end, there were various other marriage projects, but in 1478 at the age of thirty-six Sir John was still a bachelor. Little is known about his next correspondent, Constance Reynforth; we do not know her age or her parentage, though it is possible that her family was either from the lower gentry or the London merchant class and that she herself was an orphan. At the time of writing she was staying with a cousin in Cobham, Surrey, and in order to obtain her freedom and come to her lover, who was almost certainly in London, she needed to pretend that her uncle had sent for her. It is possible that she had been sent to Cobham to remove her from the vicinity of Sir John. His relationship with Constance lasted some time and she bore him a daughter, also called Constance, who was left ten marks in the will of her grandmother, Margaret Paston, in 1484. It probably continued until Sir John's death from sickness in November 1479.

Constance Reynforth to Sir John Paston, 21 March 1478

Right reverend and worshipful sir, I recommend me unto your mastership, effectually desiring to hear of your welfare and continual prosperity; and if it please you to hear of my poor estate, I was in good health at the making of this simple bill. Touching the cause of my writing to your mastership is, for as much as I appointed with you to be with you by the day that you assigned me of, the which, without your good support, I cannot well have mine intent, without it please you to send one of your men to me, and I shall provide a letter in my uncle's name, the which he shall deliver to my cousin as he were my uncle's messenger, and by this means I will come at your request; for my cousin would I should not depart from him without it were to my uncle's service; his and all others I refuse for yours, if my simple service may be to your pleasure. And of an answer hereof I beseech you by the bringer of my bill, and I will conform me to your intent, by the grace of God, the which may preserve you at all hours.

Written at Cobham, the 21st day of March. By your woman and servant, Constance Reynforth.

(Paston Letters, no. 928)

We come now to the most delightful correspondent among the Pastons, Margery Brews, who was to become the wife of the youngest John Paston, known as John III. John, who was the second of Margaret and John I's five sons, was born in 1444, and while his elder brother, Sir John, made his way at court, John III ran the Norfolk end of the Paston family business after their father's death. Since most of the Paston estates were in the hands of the two widows, Agnes and Margaret, much of his time and energy was taken up with the battle over the Fastolf inheritance. That did not prevent him from pursuing various matrimonial ventures with the aid of his elder brother, though none got very far, and like Sir John, he was still unmarried when he entered his thirties. Part of the problem was the lack of cash and land immediately available to the brothers, despite their good future prospects. Finally, in 1476, John heard of a young lady who was very favourably recommended by a number of his friends and once he started to investigate, his fate was sealed. Sir Thomas Brews of Topcroft, Norfolk, was not overly keen on the match, since John III was a younger son without much in the way of prospects, but his romantically inclined wife was more sympathetic (see chapter 4), while Margery herself made it quite clear that John was the husband she wanted. She and her mother worked on Sir Thomas, though they were unable to move him as far as John would have liked on the matter of her dowry. John's family were not initially very enthusiastic about the proposed marriage either, and he got no help from John II in offering an acceptable settlement. Sir John said rather grumpily that he had not been consulted and could not afford anything. Luckily, the lover convinced his mother of his seriousness sufficiently for her to invite the Brews to meet them in Norwich to discuss the financial aspects and to offer to make over to her son the manor of Sparham, provided that his elder brother agreed to forego any right he had in it. In fact two years later, the death of John II and their grandmother, Agnes, within a few months of each other transformed John III's prospects. Margery's two letters here, probably the best known of any by a medieval Englishwoman, need no further introduction. Needless to say, the lovers were successful and married at some point in the summer of 1477.

Margery Brews to John Paston, February 1477

Right reverend and worshipful, and my right well-beloved Valentine, I recommend me unto you, full heartily desiring to hear of your welfare, which I beseech Almighty God long for to preserve you unto His pleasure, and your heart's desire. And if it please you to hear of my welfare, I am not in good health of body, nor of heart, nor shall be til I hear from you;

> For there wots no creature what pain that I endure
> And for to be dead, I dare it not discure [discover]

And my lady my mother hath laboured the matter to my father full diligently, but she can no more get than you know of, for the which God knoweth I am full sorry. But if that you love me, as I trust verily that you do, you will not leave me therefore; for if that you had not half the livelihood that you have, for to do the greatest labour that any woman alive might, I would not forsake you.

> And if you command me to keep me true wherever I go
> I wise I will do all my might you to love and never no more
> And if my friends say, that I do amiss
> They shall not let me so for to do
> My heart me bids ever more to love you
> Truly over all earthly thing
> And if they be never so wrath
> I trust it shall be better in time coming.

No more to you at this time, but the Holy Trinity have you in keeping. And I beseech you that this bill be not seen of none earthly creature save only yourself, etc.

And this letter was indight at Topcroft, with full heavy heart, etc. By your own Margery Brews

To my right well-beloved Valentine, John Paston, esquire, be this bill delivered

(Paston Letters, no. 897)

Margery Brews to John Paston, February 1477

Right worshipful and well-beloved Valentine, in my most humble wise, I recommend me unto you etc. And heartily I thank you for the letter which that you sent me by John Beckerton, whereby I understand and know, that you be purposed to come to Topcroft in short time, and without any errand or matter but only to have a conclusion of the matter betwixt my father and you; I would be most glad of any creature alive, so that the matter might grow to effect. And there as you say, and you come and find the matter no more towards you than you did aforetime, you would no more put my mother and father to no cost nor business, for that cause, a good while after, which causes my heart to be full heavy; and if that you come, and the matter take to none effect, then I should be much more sorry and full of heaviness.

And as for myself, I have done and understood in the matter that I can, or may, as God knoweth; and I let you plainly understand, that my father will no more money part withall in that behalf, but an £100 and 1 mark [13*s* 4*d*], which is right far from the accomplishment of your desire.

Wherefore, if that you could be content with that good, and my poor person, I would be the merriest maiden on ground; and if you think not yourself so satisfied, or that you might have much more good, as I have understood by you before; good, true and loving Valentine, that you take no such labour upon you, as to come more for that matter, but let it pass, and never more to be spoken of, as I may be your true lover and bedewoman during my life.

To my right wellbeloved cousin, John Paston, esquire, be this letter delivered

(Paston Letters, no. 898)

Happily married and soon pregnant, Margery wrote the following letter to her husband who was on a trip to London. The need for a new gown and a bigger girdle for her burgeoning waistline make sympathetic reading, likewise her report of the midwife with sciatica, but since her son Christopher was not born until mid-August 1478, she was probably exaggerating her size in order to encourage her husband in his purchases. It is the loving postscript which is most appealing. Christopher died as a young boy and it was their second son, William, who continued the family line, becoming the ancestor of the earls of Yarmouth.

Margery Paston to John Paston, 18 December 1477

Right reverend and worshipful husband, I recommend me to you, desiring heartily to hear of your welfare, thanking you for the token that you sent me by Edmund Perry, praying you to know that my mother sent to my father to London for a gown cloth of 'mustard devillers' to make of a gown for me; and he told my mother and me when he was come home, that he charged you to buy it after he were come out of London.

I pray you, if it be not bought, that you will vouchsafe to buy it and send it home as soon as you may, for I have no gown to wear this winter but my black and my green 'a lyer' and that is so cumbersome that I am weary to wear it. As for the girdle my father behested me, I spake to him thereof a little before he went to London last, and he said to me that the fault was in you, that you would not think thereupon to get it made; but I suppose that is not so; he said it but for an excuse. I pray you if you do take it upon you, that you will vouchsafe to have it made against you come home, for I had never more need thereof than I have now, for I am waxed so fat that I may not be girt in no bar of no girdle that I have but of one. Elizabeth Peverel hath lain sick 15 or 16 weeks of the sciatica, but she sent my mother word by Kate that she should come hither when God sent time, though she should be carried in a barrow.

John of Damm was here and my mother discovered me to him, and he said, by his troth he was not gladder of nothing that he heard this twelvemonth than he was thereof.

I may no longer live by my craft, I am discovered by all men that see me.

Of all other things that you desired that I should send you word of, I have sent you word of in a letter that I did write on Our Lady's Day last was. The Holy Trinity have you in His keeping.

Written at Oxnead, in right great haste, on the Thursday next before St Thomas' Day.

I pray you that you will wear the ring with the image of St Margaret that I sent you for a remembrance, till you come home;

you have left me such a remembrance, that maketh me think upon you both day and night when I would sleep. Yours M P.

(Paston Letters, no. 923)

A few years further on, this next letter raises problems of dating. Gairdner dates it from 1484, following Margaret's death in early November that year. Family mourning circumscribed the Christmas festivities, further marred by John's absence. Margery was clearly torn between the desire to provide her household with some form of jollity while not scandalising the neighbourhood with inappropriate activity. Her two sons were still very small to be sent on the kind of errand on which she despatched them, though their presence, presumably in the company of a responsible servant, added dignity to the visit. Elizabeth, Lady Morley, was the wife of Henry Lovel, Lord Morley, and herself the daughter of John de la Pole, Duke of Suffolk, and Elizabeth, sister of Edward IV and Richard III, and thus a social arbiter of the highest level. Elizabeth is the only candidate as Lady Morley, because her mother-in-law had died in 1476 (before Margery Paston was married), but her husband, Henry, did not die until 1489. By this date Margery's husband had been knighted, yet she addresses her letter only to John Paston, so its date remains a mystery. Lady Stapleton was the widow of Sir Miles Stapleton, who retained the use of her first married name when she remarried Sir Richard Harcourt. The complaint about the servant at Caister who will not keep the buttery accounts as ordered is an illustration of the perennial problem of unsatisfactory servants. Again, as a counter-balance to the formal greeting she gives her husband, Margery ends with a very loving sentiment. In at least one later letter she addresses him as 'Mine own sweetheart'.

Margery Paston to John Paston, 24 December (?1484)

Right worshipful husband, I recommend me unto you. Please it you to know that I sent your eldest son to my Lady Morley, to have knowledge what sports were used in her house in Christmas next following after the decease of my lord, her husband; and she said that there were no disguisings, nor harping nor luting nor singing, nor none loud disports, but playing at the tables, and chess and cards. Such sports she gave her folks leave to play and none other.

Your son did his errand right well as you shall hear after this. I sent your younger son to the Lady Stapleton, and she said according to my Lady Morley's saying in that, and as she had seen used in places of worship there as she has been.

I pray you that you will assure to you some man at Caister to keep your buttery, for the man you left with me will not take upon him to breve [make up accounts] daily as you commanded. He says he has not been used to give a reckoning neither of bread nor ale til at the week's end; and he says he knows well that he should not containeth [give satisfaction] and therefore I suppose he shall not abide, and I trow you shall be fain to purvey another man for Simmond, for you are never the nearer a wise man for him.

I am sorry you shall not be at home for Christmas. I pray you that you will come as soon as you may. I shall think myself half a widow, because you shall not be at home, etc. God have you in his keeping.

Written on Christmas Eve. By your M.P.

(Paston Letters, no. 999)

In the next letter, Margery's position is reversed: this time she is in London and John is in Norfolk. The main topic is the beaching of a whale at Thornham. Whales were legally regarded as royal fish or spoils of the Crown, so John had dashed back to deal with the matter in his capacity as head of an Admiralty commission for Norfolk and Suffolk. 'My lord' was John de Vere, Earl of Oxford, the Lord Admiral, whose instructions, issued to her brother-in-law, William Paston, Margery was passing on. Having dealt with the issue of the whale, Margery went on, perhaps with some degree of pleasure, to fill her husband in on all the news of the capital. The forthcoming dissolution of Parliament which she announces in fact took place on 27 February, but as she again reports, various dignitaries were leaving early. The Archbishop of York was Thomas Rotherham, former Bishop of Lincoln, while the Earl of

Northumberland, Henry Percy, was riding to his death in Yorkshire. He was murdered there in April, partly because of opposition to his collection of the tax just voted in by Parliament, but partly because of his local unpopularity; he had failed at Bosworth to support Richard III, who was closely identified with Yorkshire. Margery refers to the tax, which was levied to pay for a military expedition to Brittany. Henry VII had reluctantly agreed to it as part of the Treaty of Redon to aid Brittany against France, signed four days after Margery wrote. He had spent much of his exile in Brittany, but Duke Francis, the last independent Duke of Brittany, had died a few months earlier after a disastrous military defeat by France, leaving a twelve-year-old heiress, Anne. Henry sent 6,000 men under Giles, Lord Daubeney, to aid Brittany, and while the force was militarily successful, there was little that could be done in the long term, and two years later Charles VIII of France married the Duchess Anne, incorporating Brittany into France. Margery lists some of the more prominent men whom she had learned were to form part of the expedition. These included her mother's brother, Sir Gilbert Debenham, which is probably why she was so well informed. She refers to a member of the Audley family as her brother and makes a similar reference to Heydon; in neither case was she related to them; this is an example of the use of the term in a much wider context than we are familiar with, and should be taken to imply a close association only. John Heydon had been a notorious enemy of the Pastons in earlier generations, but Margery was referring to his son, Henry. Her 'sister Anne' was indeed a Paston, the younger sister of John II and John III, who was married to William Yelverton.

Margery Paston to Sir John Paston, 10 February 1489

Right reverend and worshipful sir, in the most humble wise I recommend me unto you, desiring to hear of your welfare, the which God long continue.

Sir, my brother William recommends him unto you. And as for the letter that you sent unto him, he has shown my lord [Oxford] the intent thereof, and he thinketh himself, that it is no part of his duty to have any part of the fish, or any money that should grow thereof. Nevertheless my lord, according as your desire was in the letter, had questioned John a Lowe of this fish, before the coming of John Daniel, what he had done withal; and he answered, as for the nether jaw thereof, he had put it in surety and laid it in a house, because your deputy seized it for my lord's use, til it might be understood whether the property was in the King or in my lord; and so my lord held him well content it should be so, in so much as the King and my lord have commanded John a Lowe that this foresaid jaw should be brought up to the King in all goodly haste.

Furthermore, my brother William perceived by your writing that you could make the remnant of the fish worth £4 to my lord. My lord would that you should not trouble yourself no more with all, because he thinks the property is not in him. And also another, my brother William hears say in the court, that the King and my lord be content that the remnant of the fish be to the use of them of the country, the which you shall hear the more certain thereof hereafter.

Also my brother William says, that my lord willed you that you should send the return of the commission as hastily as you can, and marvels that you have not sent it up ere this.

As towards the breaking up of the Parliament, many likelihoods there be, that it should continue no while, and these be they. My lord the Archbishop of York departed as yesterday, and my lord of Northumberland shall go as on Friday; and also all such folk as shall go into Brittany shall be at Portsmouth on Saturday come fortnight, and the Monday after on seaboard, at which season the King intendeth to be there to take the musters.

And as for those gentlemen that took shipping to go over into Brittany upon a fortnight ago, that is to say, Sir Richard Edgecombe, the Controller [of the King's Household], Sir Robert Clifford, Sir John Turberville and John Motton, serjeant porter, be arrived again upon the coast of England, save all only Sir Richard Edgecombe, which landed in Brittany and there was in a town called Morlaix, which anon upon his coming was besieged with the Frenchmen, and so escaped hardly with his life, the which town the French have gotten, and also the town called Brest; howbeit the castle holds, as we hear say.

And there be appointed certain captains at this season, which be Lord Brooke, Sir John Cheney, Sir John Arundell, Sir John Beauchamp, Sir John Gray, my brother Audley, my uncle Sir Gilbert Debenham and Thomas Stafford and many other knights and esquires.

And, sir, I thank you for the letter that you sent me. Also, sir, I have fulfilled my pilgrimage, thanked be God.

Also, sir, we understand it is enacted of every ten marks of movable goods, 20d. to the King, besides the tenth of every man's lands.

And, sir, my brother Heydon shall send you the certain of all other things granted at this Parliament, for he hath caused John Daniel to tarry all this day for his letter, because he was with the King at Westminster, that he might not intend to write it til night.

Also, sir, Master Calthorp has paid one hundred marks to the King. Also, sir, I have delivered the £10 to Master Hawes and received of him the obligation. Also, I have delivered the twenty marks to Edmund Dorman, by my brother Heydon's commandment.

No more to you at this time, but God and the Holy Trinity have you in their keeping. And my sister Anne, with all the company, recommend them to you.

Written at London, the 10th day of February. By your servant, Margery Paston.

(*Paston Letters, no. 1030*)

Moving north from the Norfolk of the Pastons and the Oxfordshire of the Stonors, we come to the Yorkshire of the third of our families, the Plumptons. The Plumpton correspondence is rather later in date and lacks many of the personal touches which enliven the other two collections, but their main preoccupations were no different from those of southern gentry: the enrichment of their family, ruthless litigation and the use of marriage to maintain and extend their influence. The Plumptons were loyal supporters of the Percy Earls of Northumberland and Lancastrian in their political allegiance during the Wars of the Roses. Their family affairs were complicated by the extraordinary behaviour of Sir William Plumpton who died in 1480.

101

His son and heir by his deceased wife, Agnes Stapleton, also called William, died at the Battle of Towton in 1461, leaving two small daughters as their grandfather's heirs. Sir William, on this basis, arranged two advantageous marriages for them, with carefully phrased marriage contracts. In 1468, however, he revealed that his mistress, Joan Wintringham, was his legal second wife and that their son, Robert, aged about ten, was legitimate and therefore his heir. After Sir William's death this led to endless lawsuits from the husbands of Robert's nieces, who considered themselves defrauded of their wives' inheritances.

In 1477 Sir William had arranged for the marriage of Robert to Agnes, daughter of Sir William Gascoigne of Gawthorpe. The series of letters here from Dame Agnes to her husband Robert, who had been knighted by Northumberland in 1481 while campaigning against the Scots, all deal with legal matters. In 1496 the Plumptons were dismayed by the news that one of Henry VII's most powerful administrators, Richard Empson (see chapter 1), whose daughter was married to the son of one of Robert's dispossessed nieces, was taking up the legal battle against them. Not surprisingly, the Plumptons lost the subsequent lawsuit in 1501 and with it much of their ancestral lands. They spent the following years in fruitless attempts to have the verdict reversed, and a final negotiated settlement was not reached until 1515. During the intervening years, Dame Agnes struggled to defend Plumpton itself and raise money for her husband's litigation, which well-nigh ruined them. The exasperation she probably felt at his refusal to face reality may account for the brisk and business-like letter, which is hardly affectionate in tone. Her husband, on the other hand, was sometimes moved to address her as his 'best beloved'. The letter also illustrates the difficulties in collecting rents from disputed lands. In Cowthorpe some of the tenants had paid, while others, who refused, had their possessions distrained. The taking of cattle from tenants who refused to pay rent to a claimant could later be used in court as evidence of seisin. Sir Richard Goldsborough was a neighbour and husband of Robert's half-sister Alice. The term 'ragman' means a catalogue of complaints and 'replevy' was the recovery of distrained goods on security given for submission to trial and judgment. Thus it was not just the Plumptons who suffered but their loyal tenants as well.

Dame Agnes Plumpton to Sir Robert Plumpton, 16 November 1502

Sir, in my most heartiest wise I recommend me unto you, desiring to hear of your prosperity and welfare and of your good speed in your matters; certifying that I and my son William with all your children are in good health, thanks be Jesu, with all your servants. Sir, you and I and my son was content, at your departing, that my son should take the farms at Martinmas of his tenants, or else cast them forth and [ap]praise their goods and so my son hath done with some of them; and here are the names of them that have paid me: Robert Wood, Peter Cott, John Gloster, Robert Taler, William Bentham. Sir, it is to let us understand that there is other tenants that are cast forth each been at Cowthorpe, and make one ragman to complain on my son and you, that you take their goods from them; and it is not so, for my son hath sent for the neighbours of Knaresborough and Harrogate and Spofforth to set price on their common and cattle, after their conscience, and my son has set strays some in their lays, for there is some that will not apply to his mind, and they purpose to get on discharge for my son, that they may be set in again and he not to occupy. Therefore I pray you to take good heed thereupon and they have set these names in the ragman that hath paid my son, that they know not of, nor will be counselled thereto.

Also Sir Richard Goldsburgh hath taken an ox of William Bentham that was driven over the water with their cattle of the town of Plumpton, that be caused to be put over for the safeguard of their cattle; and when he came for his ox, he answered him and said: Sir George Ratcliffe had written for certain tenants to be so tarried by him and spirre [?interrogated] him whose tenant he was, and he showed him whose he was, and he will not let him have them without a replevie; and I trow he will die in the fold, for I sent

William Skargill and William Croft and they cannot get him without a replevie; and therefore if you can find any remedy I pray you for. And also I pray you to send me some word, as you may, of your good speed. No more at this time, but I betake you to the keeping of the Trinity. From Plumpton in haste, the 16th day November. By your wife, Dame Agnes Plumpton.

To the worshipful Sir Robert Plumton kt be these delivered in haste.

(Plumpton Letters, no. 168)

Dame Agnes's next letter hardly contains comfort, either. Thomas Savage, Archbishop of York and the King's Lieutenant in the North, took a hand in the matter by writing to William, Robert's son, demanding that he restore their property to those tenants whose cattle he had distrained in lieu of rent and that William appear before him to answer for his actions. On top of all this, Dame Agnes was trying to satisfy her husband's constant demands for money to pay his legal bills.

Dame Agnes Plumpton to Sir Robert Plumpton, 27 November 1502

Right worshipful Sir, in my most hearty wise, I recommend me unto you, desiring to know of your prosperity and welfare; letting you understand that I and all your children is in good health, blessed be Jesu, with all your servants. Letting you to understand that my lord Archbishop sent one servant of his unto my son William, charging him in the king's name to set the tenants in again, and if he would not do it, he would send to the sheriff and cause him to appoint them in again; and so I sent one servant to the sheriff and the sheriff showed my servant that my lord had written unto him for to appoint them in again, but my son keeps them forth as yet, and therefore I trow the Archbishop will complain of my son and you, and saith that he will indict them that was at casting out of them.

And, Sir, I pray you that you be not miscontent that I sent not to you, for indeed I make the labour that is possible for me to make, and as yet I cannot speed, but as shortly as I can I shall speed the matter. No more at this time, but the Trinity have you in his keeping. Scribbled in haste at Plumpton, this Sunday, next after St Katherine's Day

By your wife Dame Agnes Plumpton

To the worshipful Sir Robert Plumpton kt be these delivered in haste.

(Plumpton Letters no. 170)

William attempted to defy the archbishop, which was not a wise move, since, as Dame Agnes reported to her husband, he then proceeded to indict William and sixteen of the Plumpton servants. So desperate was the Plumpton need for money that William was also guilty of selling timber from the disputed property, which brought another reprimand from the archbishop.

Dame Agnes Plumpton to Sir Robert Plumpton, 21 December 1502

Right worshipful Sir, in my most hearty wise I recommend me unto you, desiring to hear of your welfare and good speed in your matters. I and all your children is in good health, blessed be Jesu. And, Sir, so it is, as God knows, that I have made as great labour as was possible for me to make to content your mind in all causes; and now I have made the usance of £20 and sent you with Thomas Bickerdyke to content where you know; and I pray you to send some writing to Thomas Meering for the repayment of the money and your discharge. Sir, it is so that my lord Archbishop has indicted my son William and 16 of his servants a week last Tuesday. But Anthony Clifford gave in the bill of indictment against my son and his servants, but the inquest [jury] would not indict them. But my lord Archbishop caused them or else he bade them, tell him who would not, and he should punish them, that all others should take example; and I cannot get the copy of the indictment, for my lord has it in his hand. No more at this time. The Lord preserve you. From Plumpton in haste, this St Thomas Day.

By your wife, Dame Agnes Plumpton

To the worshipful Sir Robert Plumton knight be this bill delivered in haste.

(Plumpton Letters no. 171)

Dame Agnes died in 1504, and about a year later Sir Robert married Isabel, daughter of Ralph, Lord Neville, son and heir of the Earl of Westmorland, who had predeceased his father. Isabel must still have been in her mid teens, since her father did not marry her mother, Edith Sandys, until 1490 (see chapter 1). Isabel's brother Ralph had succeeded their grandfather to the Earldom of Westmorland in 1499, so Isabel's marriage after that date to a dispossessed and impoverished knight with an adult family seems a very bad bargain for the Nevilles. Young and untried as she was, Isabel was immediately plunged into the same problems which beset her predecessor, the main one of which was trying to keep her husband supplied with money. Since most of the county was aware of Sir Robert's needs, the majority of his neighbours had long since ceased to cooperate with loans. There is a note of desperation in Isabel's letter, which is hardly surprising. Henry VII reacted sympathetically to Sir Robert's pleas about the injustice of the court findings, by making him a knight of the body, which meant that as a member of the court he could not be arrested for debt, but this relief ended when Henry died in 1509. The result was that Sir Robert's creditors closed in and he and his wife spent several months in a debtors' prison.

Dame Isabel Plumpton to Sir Robert Plumpton, ?1506

Sir, in the most hearty wise that I can, I recommend me unto you; Sir, I have sent to Wright of Idell for the money that he promise you and he says he hath it not to lend, and makes choses; and so I can get none nowhere; and as for wood, there is none that will buy, for they know you want money, and without they might have it half for nought they will buy none. For your son, William Plumpton and Thomas Beckerdyke have been every day at wood since you went, and they can get no money for nothing, for that will buy none without they have timber trees and will give nothing for them. And so shall your wood be destroyed and get nought for it. Sir, I told you this ere you went but you would not believe me. Sir, I have taken of your timber as much as I can get of, or Whitsunday farm, forehand, and that is but little to do you any good, for there is but some that will lend so long before the time; and your Lenten stuff is to buy, and I wot not what to do, God wot, for I am ever left in this fashion.

Sir, there is land in Rybston field that Christopher Chambers would buy, if you will sell it, but I am not in a surety what he will give for it. But if you will sell it, send word to your son what you will do, for I know nothing else wherewith to help you with. Sir, for God's sake take an end, so we are brought to beggarstaff, for you have not to defend them withall. Sir, I send you my mare and 3s. 4d. by the bearer hereof, and I pray you send me word as soon as you may. No more at this time, but the Holy Trinity send you good speed in all your matters and send you soon home. Sir, remember your children's books. By your bedfellow, Isabel Plumpton

To Sir Robert Plumpton kt be this letter delivered

(Plumpton Letters, no. 199)

FOUR

'Son, I send you God's blessing and mine': Women and their sons

Relations between medieval women and their sons were naturally as complex as those of their modern counterparts, but for gently born women in the Middle Ages the system of inheritance added an extra dimension. In the first part of the period, the operation of the feudal system ensured that a man was succeeded by his eldest son to the lands he held of his feudal lord. Younger sons had to be provided for by other means: inheritance from their mother, the purchase of new estates, perhaps with the money that came as their mother's dowry, marriage to an heiress, a cash inheritance or through a career in the law or the church. Yet heirs could die and younger sons often ended up inheriting. Mothers have always worried about their sons: their obedience, their rebelliousness, their abilities, their marriage prospects: concerns reflected in the letters here. In many cases the relationship was complicated by the widowed mother holding a proportion of the family lands in dower. If an heir's grandmother was also alive, then his inheritance would be severely curtailed; for instance between 1391 and 1393 the Clifford estates were supporting three dowagers, the widows of the fourth, fifth and sixth lords. John Paston I had to wait for his inheritance longer than he might have anticipated because of the longevity of his mother, his wife's mother and his wife's grandmother. If the widow was not the mother of the heir, but his stepmother, then the situation became more fraught, particularly if she herself had sons.

In the event of her husband dying while her children were still young, the difference between the classes became marked. If the husband had been a member of the nobility, or held his land directly of the Crown, then the wardship of the heir, or heiress, became a royal reward, granted to another tenant-in-chief in favour with the Crown or to a successful royal servant. The child, at whatever age he or she might be, moved to the household of the guardian, who then administered all their lands which were not held by the widowed mother in dower. The guardian paid a fixed annual sum to the Crown for the wardship, but was then free to exploit the lands for what they were worth over and above that sum. An unscrupulous guardian could strip the lands of all saleable assets, leaving the heir to inherit an impoverished estate when he reached adulthood. It was more likely, however, that the guardian, who also had the right to arrange the marriage of the heir or heiress, would marry them to one of his own children or to another member of his family. The mother, having lost her husband, would effectively have lost her eldest son, and possibly his younger brothers as well. Lower down the social scale, at gentry level or below, the mother, with the help of male relatives, would have a much stronger chance of bringing up her children herself until they were old enough to enter service in another household. This mobility lessened the general problems of tension, authority and intimacy at home which were bound up with the cherished hopes mothers had for their sons and their daughters.

It is hardly surprising that surviving letters between mothers and sons are primarily concerned with estate business of one sort or another, but they do serve to illustrate how involved in the day-to-day running of estates women actually were. They are also dominated by the Pastons, which makes the section more unbalanced than is desirable, but nonetheless allows a more detailed picture to be built up of the problems of estate management and of the relationship of two particular women with their sons. Two of the last letters are not from a mother to her sons, but a woman to her future son-in-law.

The first letter is from Adela, the fourth daughter of William the Conqueror and Matilda of Flanders. She was born in Normandy four years before her father became king of England, and it is stretching the criteria somewhat to include her here; the decision is only justified by the fact that she and her sons had a marked impact on English affairs. She herself spent little time in England and married Stephen, Count of Blois, in about 1080. Stephen died in 1102 on crusade and his letters back to the wife he had appointed regent in his absence describe her as sweetest friend and wife, and address her as 'dearest' and 'beloved'. Following his death she remained regent until her son Theobald, who succeeded his father, came of age. Adela and Stephen had three remarkable sons. Theobald, the eldest, was Count of Blois, Champagne and Chartres, and followed his father's tradition of supporting Normandy in its struggles against the king of France. Stephen, the second son, spent a good deal of his time in England at the court of his uncle, Henry I, where he had found much favour and a marriage to the Queen's niece, Matilda, the heiress to the county of Boulogne. Henry, Adela's third son, entered the Church, where his uncle promoted him to Winchester, the richest see in England. When Henry I died without a male heir in 1135, many of his nobles honoured their promise to support the candidature of his only surviving daughter, the Empress Matilda, to be queen, but others looked towards his nearest male relations. The Norman nobles favoured Theobald, and were engaged in electing him their duke, when news reached them that Stephen had slipped across the Channel and had been crowned king with the approval of most of the English nobles, and the considerable help of his brother, Henry. With some grumbling, Theobald accepted the *fait accompli*.

Even after Adela handed over the reins of power to Theobald, she continued to live with him rather than retiring to her dower lands. She was a noted patron of literature and had both poetry and works of history dedicated to her, and she was also particularly pious and generous to the Church. Because she was a close friend of Ivo, Bishop of Chartres, a famous expert in canon law, she was able to play an influential part in helping to resolve the long-running dispute between her brother, Henry I, and the saintly Anslem, Archbishop of Canterbury, over lay investiture. This was the right of the king to have some say in the appointment of bishops and abbots, who held large estates burdened with military and financial obligations. The dispute lasted for years, many of which Anselm spent in exile, and was finally resolved in 1107, when Adela encouraged Henry to allow Ivo of Chartres to broker a settlement along lines similar to one he had arranged in France. In old age she took the veil, entering the convent of Martigny at some time after 1118, but it was a decision she had discussed with Anslem before his death in 1109. Nuns of noble birth, however, could rarely divorce themselves entirely from the secular world, as this affectionate letter shows. The monastery of Marmoutier had received a large benefaction from Count Stephen before he set out for the Holy Land and its monks were particular favourites of his wife also. Adela had more than once settled differences between them and the canons of Blois, as she here reminds Theobald.

Adela, Countess of Blois, to her son, Theobald, Count of Blois, 1130

To her dearest Count of Blois, Adela the nun of Martigny sends the affections of maternal love.

I remember, dearest son, that while yet I wore a secular habit, the canons of St Carilef complained about the tithe of the almsgift of Francville, which my consort, namely the Count your father, and I gave to the monks of Marmoutier. About which be it known to your grace, that these canons, in our presence, dismissed their complaints against the said monks, that this quarrel might be set to rest for ever without further renewal. Therefore I entreat you, dearest son, that our alms which we freely gave to the monks you will as freely keep for them, nor let the church of Marmoutier be teased with any further controversy about this affair. Farewell.

(Archives of Marmoutier, printed in Wood, I, pp. 7–8; Latin)

The long and anxious letter written by Hawisa de Neville to her son Hugh is a graphic example of the role of women in running estates in the absence of their husbands or sons. Clearly in this case Hawisa was having a difficult time. She was the daughter of Sir Robert de Courtney of Okehampton in Devon, and married John de Neville of

Essex. In 1235 John was appointed chief forester and justice of the whole of the king's forest in England, but was so rapacious and oppressive in office that following a commission of enquiry he escaped prison only by paying a very heavy fine. He retired in disgrace and died shortly afterwards in 1246. Within a few weeks, their young son Hugh was sent to Windsor to live with other children in the king's care, but his wardship was granted to his uncle, John de Courtney, until he came of age in 1256. Hawisa, after a few years of widowhood, remarried and became the second wife of Sir John de Gatesden in about 1254, by whom she had a single daughter, Margaret. Sir John died in 1262, so by the time of this letter, she was a widow for the second time and her son Hugh was in serious difficulties. Unlike his mother, who remained loyal to Henry III, he had joined the barons in the civil war, but had been taken prisoner by Prince Edward at Kenilworth, and imprisoned at Norwich. Escaping from there, he held out with the younger Simon de Montfort in the Isle of Axhome until Christmas 1265. His confiscated lands (which did not include his mother's dower lands, safely in the possession of her second husband) were granted to Robert de Walerand. Hugh submitted to the king in 1266 and received back two of his chief manors but was compelled to confirm Walerand in several others as the price of his submission.

Later in the year Hugh escaped from his troubles by leaving for the Holy Land, after making his mother and his younger brother, John, his attorneys to manage his lands in his absence. The fact that he was a crusader gave the family a chance to obtain the pope's support for their legal battle to regain the lands in Walerand's possession. Walerand, who was in royal favour, was clearly a formidable opponent. Hawisa and John were left to raise money for legal expenses as well as attempting to fund Hugh's crusading, because royal support for the crusade was inadequate. Hugh seemed to believe he had obtained a papal petition for the restoration of his lands, but had only succeeded in getting one for the payment of his crusading expenses. His mother, and all those who supported him, were anxious that he should go to Rome and get something more substantial. Hugh never left the Holy Land. Reports of his death were current in April 1269 at the time his mother died, but in fact he did not die until October 1269, leaving his brother, John, as his heir. John redeemed the family fortunes, becoming Constable of the Tower of London.

Difficulties of sending letters around England were as nothing compared with communicating with the Holy Land, and Hawisa's relief in having a first-hand report from a returning crusader, William FitzSimon, is transparent, but she is also anxious that money she was forwarding was not reaching Hugh and was desperate that he should return, via Rome, to press his claims in person. There is no clue as to why Hugh took on the responsibility of a debt owed by de Umfraville, which clearly exasperated his mother. The reference to his father-in-law is to Robert de Brewes, whose daughter Beatrice he had married. The term father-in-law was more loosely used in the Middle Ages and could equally well have applied to his mother's second husband, save that we know he was dead by this date. The letter is another instance of a woman either retaining the name of a first husband during a second marriage, or using it selectively when dealing with people or affairs relating to her first marriage.

Lady Hawisa de Neville to her son, Hugh de Neville, 1267

Hawisa de Neville to her very dear son, Hugh de Neville, wishes health and the blessing of God and her own.

Know, dear son, that I am well and hearty, thanks to God, and am much rejoiced at the news that William FitzSimon brought me of your health. God be thanked for it! Know, dear son, that our necessities of receiving returns from your lands can avail nothing, on account of the great rule your adversary has in the king's court, unless you yourself were present. Wherefore your father-in-law and I, and all your other friends, agree that you should come to England, and we pray and entreat you, by the faith and love that you owe us, that you will not by any means fail in this; since you ought once again to return. For we know well that it would be a very great dishonour, and we consider it a great sin, to suffer us and ours to be disinherited by your indolence. Therefore I anxiously pray you, dear son, that you will travel with all possible haste, and also, according to the counsel of all your friends, that you go to the court of Rome, and procure if you can the letter of the Pope, express and stringent, to the King of England, that he should restore your lands, and have them restored. And that you may make a proper understanding at the court of all your needs, without omitting or concealing anything; that is, how you are placed with the King, and that you are compelled by a writing to hold the [?obligation] without contradiction and without ever making an acquisition to the contrary. For wise persons have said the acquisition would be worth nothing, unless it made express mention of this, that it was through no fault of yours that you made this the aforesaid obligation when in war and through fear of prison. And know, good son, that the first acquisition you got at Rome for our lands was not such as you understood, for it was only a loving petition for your rights of the money which you ought to have had of the crusade allowance. The legate, thanks to him, has granted us that he would let us have it if we could espy out where it is, but we have not as yet found any, except what is in the hands of such as themselves would wish to go into the Holy Land; but as much as we may be able to acquire, now or henceforth, between this and St John's day, we will then send you by messengers of the Temple, who will bring their own money. And for God's sake, good son, guard against making such an obligation as you have made for Sir Ingelram de Umfranville; for I was grieved that it was proper to have it paid from our own demesne. And good, sweet, dear son, I anxiously pray you that you will send us word how much money you have really had by my command, for the thing is not in my power, for I could never spy a man who went to that part, that I might send you letters, which weighs no little upon me. For if it could be that I could often have good news of you, and comfort you again often by my messages, there would be nothing that could more rejoice me except it were to see and speak to you. And know, dear son, that my heart is grieved and alarmed night and day, since William FitzSimon brought me news that you were so poorly provided with money; but God, who is Almighty, if it please him, give you speedy amendment, and I will do it to my utmost power. Dear son, I pray you not to trust too much to the money of the crusade allowance, for they say that more great lords of England will take the cross; and they will take away as much as shall be raised for the crusade, as certain friends have given me to know. But do not ever cease, as you dearly love me, for no waiting for money, to borrow all the money that you can, and go to the court of Rome to acquire for our necessities, and to hasten to come to England to accomplish our needs. For I hope, by the help of God, if you could well accomplish what you have to do about the acquisition of our lands, that you will see such change in England, that never in our time could you have better accomplished your wish, or more to your honour. Wherefore cease not to solicit again about your coming, since you can here best serve God. I commend you to the true body of God, who give you life and health. Sir Walter de la Hide, Joanna your sister, and all our household, salute you. And know, dear son, that my counsel is that you obtain the letters of request of the legate of that country, and the letters of the Master of the Temple and of the Hospital, to the legate of England and to other rich men, for your needs, and in testimony of your deeds in that country on the occasion of your coming and ever take care of your house that you have there, if God give you courage to return.

(PRO DL 34/2; Wood, I, pp. 42–6; French)

The next letter presents several problems common to medieval letters. Firstly, there is no obvious clue as to the identity of the writer and her son. Next, the whereabouts of the parish of Cedeneye is hard to discover. Thirdly, why is Sir William described as the vicar of Cedeneye, when he is asking the Kirkbys to help him obtain the living, which is held by another priest? Amice's plea for money to help in running her son's affairs is a common one, but where was John and why was he ignoring her messages? The name Kirkby is not an uncommon one, and Tanquerey, when he first printed the letter, made no attempt to identify the correspondents. However, his dating of 'pre 1290' is a clue to the man he thought likely to be the recipient. The best known John de Kirkby of the period began his career as one of Henry III's chancery clerks, moving upwards until he was in effect deputy to the chancellor. In 1284 he was appointed treasurer. In this role he was extremely useful to Edward I, raising large sums of money for the king; he received his reward in 1286 when he was made Bishop of Ely. However, de Kirkby enjoyed his office for only four years, as he died in 1290. A little is known of the bishop's family background. His brother, William, was named as his heir in his will, and four sisters, all married and, like William, in their thirties, are also referred to, so it seems likely that Bishop John was not more than forty at his death. Bishop John is also known to have inherited land in Northamptonshire from Amice de Gorham. Amice is not a common name, so this may be our Amice, who had remarried, or it might possibly have been a grandmother of the same name.

Many letters, like the one above, provide examples of women who had remarried but retained the use of their first husband's name when the business concerned his affairs or those of their children. The last clue is the survival of the letter itself in official custody. If John received it during his time as a chancery clerk, what was more natural than for it to have slipped unnoticed in among his business correspondence. If the letter predates 1279, as it almost certainly does, then this was the period when John, as an ambitious young royal clerk, was more concerned about what was happening at Westminster than his family affairs. Therefore, although the identification of the son in this letter remains unconfirmed, its seems highly likely that he was the Bishop of Ely. The location of Cedeneye remains a mystery.

Amice de Kirkby to John de Kirkby, c. 270–86

To her very dear son, John de Kirkby, his own mother, Amice, sends greetings with her blessing.

Because, dear son, Sir William, vicar of Cedeneye, asked me in his letter to ask you to aid and help him in obtaining the ownership [incumbency?] of your church of Cedeneye, which Sir Peres le

Couple holds, as will be seen, if you please, in the letter which Sir William sent me; I ask you, dear son, and earnestly request that for love of me and my entreaty, for your virtue and honour, that you will aid and help him in the affairs which you will see in his letter, as you will see that it is an honour to God and the Holy Church and to your honour and claim of being a worthy man, and in so doing, if you please, he will acknowledge the advantage of my entreaty. Farewell ever in the name of God, and if you please, inform me of your health, may God keep it ever good.

Moreover, dear son, I ask that you receive on 2 March from Sir Nicholas de Martlefeld his account for my business, or if you arrange things with him, I will charge them from your purse. Farewell.

Moreover, dear son, I am much amazed that I have so often sent you of our need and our lack which we have of money in your affairs and we have no willing response from you.

(PRO SC1/8/78; Tanquerey, no. 62; French)

Turning now to the great Paston collection, Edmund Paston was the second son of Justice William and Agnes Paston, and was twenty when his mother wrote him this letter. His father had been dead for less than six months and Edmund was studying law at Clifford's Inn in London. By the time of his death, Justice William had raised his family to a position of wealth and influence in East Anglia. By marriage and purchase he had acquired considerable estates, but he knew that after his death his sons would struggle to retain them all from the inevitable enemies he had made in his rapid rise and from his judicial position. Not unnaturally, he regarded a sound knowledge of the law as one of the tools that would help them. His eldest son, John, had a Cambridge education before going to the Inns of Court in London, but Edmund was sent straight to London, probably because his father intended him to become a lawyer. It is clear from Agnes's letter that she felt her husband's judgment to have been, as ever, sound, and Edmund should follow in his legal footsteps. As she relates, men who had reached agreements with her husband during his lifetime were already reneging on them as a way of testing his widow and sons. That the wishes of William remained paramount to his widow is clear from the strict measurements he decreed for improvements to the parlour and chapel at Paston, which Agnes asked Edmund to pass on to his elder brother, together with the request for him to purchase the timber, since nothing suitable was available locally. The reference to Stanstead church is to the manor in Suffolk which the family owned. The news from overseas that she asks for probably relates to the truce with the French and the ceding to them of the county of Maine by the English following from the king's recent marriage to Margaret of Anjou. Edmund did not live long enough to follow his father into the law, for he died in 1449 after a short illness.

Agnes Paston to Edmund Paston, 4 February 1445

To my well beloved son, I greet you well, and advise you to think once of the day of your father's counsel to learn the law, for he said many times that whosoever should dwell at Paston, should have need to know [how to] defend himself.

The Vicar of Paston and your father, in Lent last year, were through and accorded, and dolestones set how broad the way should be, and now he hath pulled up the dolestones, and sayeth he will make a ditch from the corner of his wall, right over the way to the new ditch of the great close. And there is a man in Trunch [Norfolk], called Palmer, that had of your father certain land in Trunch over 7 or 8 years ago for corn and truly hath paid all the years; and now he hath suffered the corn to be set for 8s. of rent to Gimingham [a Norfolk manor held by the Pastons], which your father paid never. Geoffrey asked Palmer why the rent was not asked in my husband's time; and Palmer said, for he was a great man, and a wise man of the law, and that was the cause men would not ask him the rent.

I send you the names of the men that cast down the pits, that was Gynnis Close (in Paston), written in a bill closed in this letter.

I send you not this letter to make you weary of Paston; for I live in hope, and you will learn that they shall be made weary of their work, for in good faith I dare well say it was your father's last will to have do right well to that place, and that I can show of good proof, though men will say nay.

God make you right a good man, and send God's blessing and mine.

Written in haste, at Norwich, the Thursday after Candlemass day.

Know of your brother John how many joists will serve the parlour and chapel at Paston, and what length they must be, and what breadth and thickness they must be; for your father's will was, as I know verily, that they should be 9 inches one way and 7 another way. And purveyeth therefore that they must be squared there and sent hither, for here none such can be had in this country. And say you to your brother John it were well done to think on Stanstead church; and I pray you send me tidings from beyond the sea, for here they are afeard to tell such as be reported.

By your mother, Agnes Paston.

(Paston Letters, no. 62)

Agnes' next letter, to her eldest son, John, in London, is largely concerned with less weighty matters, although she is anxious to get arrears of rent from the farmer (tenant) of Orwellbury in Hertfordshire, which she owned. The unfortunate Philip Burney was an uncle of John's wife, Margaret, while Sir John Heveningham was a local landowner and Agnes gives a vivid, circumstantial account of his death. 'My cousin Clere' was Elizabeth (see chapter 3), a niece of Sir John Fastolf and the widow of Robert Clere of Ormesby. Elizabeth was presumably staying with Agnes, which is why her letter was sent under Agnes's seal, but there is no clue as to why John was not to let anyone see it, or whether it was personal or legal in its nature. It is not impossible that it concerned Agnes's unfortunate daughter Elizabeth (see below).

Agnes Paston to John Paston, 6 July 1453

Son, I greet you well and send you God's blessing and mine, and let you know that Robert Hill came homeward by Orwellbury and Gurney told him he had been at London for money and could not speeding and behested Robert that he should send me money by you. I pray forget not as you come homeward, and speak sadly for another farmer.

And as for tidings, Philip Burney is passed to God on Monday last past with the greatest pain that ever I see man; and on Tuesday Sir John Heveningham went to his church and heard three masses and came home never merrier, and said to his wife he would go say a little devotion in his garden and then he would dine; and forthwith he felt a fainting in his legs and sit down. This was at 9 of the clock and he was dead ere noon.

My cousin Clere prays you that you let no man see her letter which is in sealed under my seal. I pray you that you will pay your brother William for four ounces and one half of silk as he paid, which he sent me by William Taverner, and bring with you one quarter of one ounce even like of the same that I send you closed in this letter; and say your brother William that his horse hath one farseyn [?] and great running sores in his legs. God have you in keeping.

Written at Norwich on St Thomas' eve in great haste. By your mother, Agnes Paston.

(Paston Letters, no. 227)

In the next letter to her eldest son, Agnes is concerned with John's sister, Elizabeth. We know from other letters (see chapters 1 and 5) that the two women were getting on very badly, and that the whole family was anxious to find a husband for Elizabeth. For nearly ten years, from 1449 to 1459, there are continuous references to potential husbands for her. John took the search seriously and having found a good prospect in Sir William Oldhall, wrote home to his wife Margaret asking her to sound out Agnes and Elizabeth on whether he would be acceptable. Elizabeth, whose only wish was to marry and get away from her mother, was happy to leave the matter in John's hands and trusted his choice. Agnes, of course, was only concerned that Elizabeth would not oppose the match and that Oldhall's lands were sufficiently extensive to make him a suitable prospect. On the face of it, Oldhall was a good match. He was the

Duke of York's chamberlain, but at this date was a sixty-year-old widower. He went on to be speaker of the York-dominated Parliament of 1450–1, although when York fell out of power he spent a period in sanctuary and at one point was declared an outlaw. Although the marriage negotiations continued for some time, they were eventually abandoned and Oldhall never remarried.

Agnes Paston to John Paston, c. 1454

I greet you well and let you wete that this day I was with my daughter your wife, and she was in good health at the making of this letter, thanked be God! and she let your sister and me wete of a letter which you sent her, that you have been laboured to for Sir William Oldhall to have your sister, and desiring in the said letter to have an answer in short time, how she will be demeaned in this matter.

Your sister recommendeth her to you, and thanketh you heartily that you will remember her and let her have knowledge thereof, and prays you that you will do your devour to bring it to a good conclusion; for she sayeth to me that she trusteth that you will do so, that it shall be both for her worship and profit. And as for me, if you can think that his land standeth clear, in as much as I feel your sister well willed thereto, I hold me well content.

And as for the obligation of the parson of Marlingforth, which I sent you by John Newman, I pray you let it be sued; and as for the parson and Lyndsey, they be accorded. And God have you in keeping and send you His blessing and mine.

Written at Norwich on Pulver [Ash] Wednesday, by your mother A. Paston

This letter be delivered to John Paston, dwelling in the Inner Inn of the Temple at London, in haste.

(Paston Letters, no. 237)

More letters written by Margaret, wife of John Paston I, survive than for any other medieval woman. A great many of them are to her two eldest sons, John II and John III. Margaret was widowed in 1466, when her sons were twenty-four and twenty-two respectively, and like her mother-in-law, Agnes, she never remarried. Her eldest son had been found a place at the court of Edward IV and knighted when he came of age, while John III served in the household of the Duke of Norfolk. Both these moves were a means of providing the Pastons with influential friends in their twenty years or more of battling to retain the estates left to John Paston I by his patron, Sir John Fastolf. Soon after his father's death Sir John agreed a settlement of the Fastolf estates whereby the Pastons gave up claims to most of them, but retained Caister Castle, Fastolf's home, on which he had lavished large sums of money. Unfortunately for Sir John Paston, his father's disgruntled fellow trustees ignored the agreement and sold Caister to the Duke of Norfolk. The Pastons hastily garrisoned Caister, while Sir John sought help from his friends at court. Edward IV conceded the validity of the Paston claim, but the timing could not have been worse, for it coincided with the Earl of Warwick's rebellion and his capture of the king, which meant that in the ensuing political chaos, Norfolk could do much as he liked. Margaret's frantic letter to her son was based on very real fear. The Duke of Suffolk had sent a force of 300 against the Fastolf manor of Hellesdon while the Pastons held it and had broken and destroyed much of it. Norfolk was rumoured to be amassing nearly ten times as many men against Caister, and John III and his small force of Paston supporters and servants could not hope to hold out for long unless they received powerful aid from outside. Margaret suggests Sir John approach the Archbishop of York, who was Warwick's brother, or Edward IV's brother, Clarence, married to Warwick's daughter, but her greatest hope lay in the Earl of Oxford, whose family had long been Paston patrons. Her desperation was such that she even suggested that if he could resolve the situation, the family should let him have Caister for life. But the political situation meant that, however sympathetic to the Pastons they might be, nobody of influence was willing or indeed able to force Norfolk to give up his claim.

Margaret Paston to Sir John Paston, 12 September 1469

I greet you well, letting you know that your brother and his fellowship stand in great jeopardy at Caister, and lack victuals; and Daubeney and Berney be dead and divers others greatly hurt; and they fail gunpowder and arrows, and the place sore broken with guns of the other part, so that, but they have hasty help, they be like to lose both their lives and the place, to the greatest rebuke to you that ever came to any gentleman, for every man in this country marvels greatly that you suffer them to be so long in so great jeopardy without help or other remedy.

The Duke has been more fervently set thereupon, and more cruel, since that Wretill, my lord of Clarence's man, was there, than he was before, and he has sent for all his tenants from every place, and other, to be there at Caister at Thursday next coming, that there is then like to be the greatest multitude of people that came there yet. And they purpose them to make a great assault – for they have sent for guns to Lynn and other places by the sea's side – that, with their great multitude of guns, with other shoot and ordinance, there shall no man dare appear in the place. They shall hold them so busy with their great people, that it shall not lie in their power within to hold it against them without God help them or have hasty succour from you.

Therefore, as you will have my blessing, I charge you and require you that you see your brother helped in haste. And if you can have no means, rather desire writing from my lord of Clarence, if he be in London, or else of my lord Archbishop of York, to the Duke of Norfolk that he will grant them that be in the place their lives and their goods; and in eschewing of insurrections with other inconveniences that be like to grow within the shire of Norfolk, this troubled world, because of such conventicles and gatherings within the said shire for cause of the said place, they shall suffer them to enter upon such appointment, or other like taken by the advice of your council there at London, if you think this be not good, til the law has determined otherwise; and let him write another letter to your brother to deliver the place up on the same appointment. And if you think, as I can suppose, that the Duke of Norfolk will not agree to this, because he granted this before and they in the place would not accept it, then I would the said messenger should with the said letters bring from the said lord of Clarence, or else my lord Archbishop, to my lord of Oxford, other letters to rescue them forthwith, though the said Earl of Oxford should have the place during his life for his labour. Spare not this to be done in haste, if you will have their lives, and be set by in Norfolk, though you should lose the best manor of all for the rescue. I had liefer you lost the livelihood than their lives. You must get a messenger of the lords or some other notable man to bring their letters.

Do your devoir now, and let me send you no more messengers for this matter; but send me by the bearer hereof more certain comfort than you have done by all other that I have sent before. In any wise, let the letters that shall come to the Earl of Oxford come with the letters that shall come to the Duke of Norfolk, that if he will not agree to the tone, that you may have ready your rescue that it need no more to send therefore. God keep you.

Written the Tuesday next before Holy Rood Day, in haste, by your mother.

(Paston Letters, no. 724)

Sir John failed to send either men, money or negotiate a truce, and faced with overwhelming odds, the Paston garrison surrendered and were allowed to leave Caister unharmed. Sir John's immediate reply to his mother was tart and defensive – he was well aware of the situation but lacked money and means to help; the archbishop and Clarence were out of town and he had writen to the king in York, and when he had last heard, Berney and Daubeney were alive and well, but he would rather lose Caister than have any man lose his life for it. And he most emphatically did not need his mother telling him what the problems were and what his duty was.

Margaret's relations with her eldest son continued to be strained. In these years money, or the lack of it, were a constant refrain. Sir John's life at court was expensive and he was more interested in the money his estates would provide than in his business affairs, leaving his mother and brother John to run the Norfolk estates. He was perfectly prepared to sell land to raise money, a state of affairs that would have deeply shocked his father and grandfather. His mother retaliated by saying that if he sold any more she would subtract double their value from anything she might leave him. He then resorted to mortgaging them instead, but Margaret was only too well aware that he would never redeem them. He borrowed as much money as he could, largely from relatives and particularly from his uncle, William Paston. As Margaret's next letter indicates, the Clere family were another crucial source, but they could not lend indefinitely, and once again recourse had to be made to 'your good uncle'. It is noteworthy that it was John III who was expected to arrange matters and not his brother. William Paston's help is surprising because he had been shabbily treated by their father under Justice William's will. Agnes Paston as a widow lived with her son William in London for most of the time, though judging by Margaret's comment, she did not regard herself as his dependent, and indeed she was very well provided for. After her death in 1479, William quarrelled with John over her inheritance, but John was in the right, legally, and they came to an accommodation. The manor of Oxnead, to which Margaret refers in the letter, had been purchased by Justice William and formed part of Agnes' jointure, but she had to struggle to maintain the legal right to it after his death. For fifty years it was one of the family's favourite homes, but that does not seem to have stopped Sir John mortgaging it to a distant cousin, John Bacton. Margaret was in Mautby, her own inheritance, which was situated just three miles from Caister and served as her dower house, when she wrote this letter to her younger son, John III, who was on a visit to London. She wrote to Sir John on the same day. Margaret's health does not seem to have been of the best, since she complains of ill health, and three years later she had an illness serious enough to make her draw up her will. She died in 1482.

Margaret Paston to John Paston, 29 January 1475

I greet you well and send you God's blessing and mine, letting you know that my cousin, Robert Clere was here with me this week, and told me he was not paid of the money that you know that was borrowed of his mother and of him, but £80. The £20 that my pledges lie for is unpaid. He said that he was desired to deliver my pledges and to have been paid the £20; but he would not, til he had spoken with me, because of the promise that he had made for me before that he should deliver them to none without my assent. I said to him that I suppose verily that your brother is agreed with your uncle that he should pay all the whole, for I suppose he has a surety for all that and more. I would understand how it is, and how that my said cousin shall be content, for I were loth to lose my pledges; I know it well, your good uncle would be in possession with good will, but I will not so. I would that you should speak with your uncle therein, and send me word what he saith.

I marvel, by my troth, that I had no writing from your brother, ere he departed from London, as he promised in the last letter that he sent me, the which was written before the King's coming to Norwich; I expected, verily, to have heard from him ere this time. I would you should send him word of your uncle's dealing in this said matter, and send me an answer thereof.

Recommend me to your granddam. I would she were here in Norfolk, as well at ease as ever I saw her, and as little ruled by her son as ever she was, and then I would hope that we all should fare the better for her. It is told me that your uncle has made great means and large profits to John Bacton to make a release to him of Oxnead. Whether that be done or not, I know not yet, but I shall know in haste, if I may.

I would you should speak with my lord of Norwich [the Bishop] and assay to get a licence of him to that I may have the sacrament here in the chapel, because it is so far to the church, and I am sickly and the parson is often out. For all manner of 'casweltes' [causes?] of me and mine, I would have it granted if I might.

Send me word if you hear any tidings of your brother how he does of his sickness, and in other things, as farforth as you know, as hastily as you may. I think long til I hear from him for divers causes. God keep you.

Written in haste at Mautby, on the Saturday next before Candlemas Day.

Send me an answer of this letter in haste, and other tidings, etc.

By your mother.

My cousin Robert told me that there was more than £7 of the money that was paid him that was right on rusty and he could not have it changed. He was ungodly served therein.

(Paston Letters, no. 862)

Sir John Paston got round to replying to the January letter from his mother referred to above about a month later, and then as she complains in her next, she heard nothing more from him. The repayment of loans was still a pressing concern, as was her son's need for money. This was combined with a fall in agricultural prices, and her reference to the king probably refers to taxes. William Pecock was a senior member of the Paston staff, but Margaret was urging her son to make a formal appointment of a bailiff to oversee their property in the Caister area and to deal with the matter himself, since it would look better than her doing it on his behalf. The loss of Caister had concentrated Sir John's mind for a while and he negotiated ceaselessly for its return. Even the Duke of Norfolk's council and his duchess acknowledged the justice of the Paston claim but the duke remained immoveable. The deadlock was finally broken by his death in 1476 and after a gap of seven years, the Pastons returned to their castle. Selling his timber in Sporle Wood was one of Sir John's way of raising money, and Richard Calle, to whom Margaret refers, was the Pastons' chief bailiff. He was, moreover, a good deal more than this, for in 1469 he had married Margaret's elder daughter, Margery. The couple had fallen in love and had made a solemn pledge of marriage to each other. When they were found out, the rest of the Paston family was furious at such a prospective misalliance and tried to separate them, but the couple stuck to their guns and were supported in their vows by the Church. They eventually married and Calle remained bailiff, but he seems never to have been received into the family and Margery remained unforgiven.

In the summer of 1475 Edward IV took a huge army to France to revive the English claim to the throne of France and at least two of Margaret's younger sons had joined the army in a quest for excitement and experience. In her view they had no idea of what soldiering could entail, so she wanted their eldest brother to give them good advice. Luckily the expedition saw no fighting at all and Edward IV and Louis XI agreed on a settlement which in effect paid the English to go away and stay away. Which of the younger Pastons went soldiering is not clear, but probably Edmund and Walter, since the youngest, William, was still at Eton.

Margaret Paston to Sir John Paston, 23 May 1475

Right well beloved son, I greet you well, and send you Christ's blessing and mine, desiring to know how you fare. I marvel that I have heard no tidings from you since you sent me the letter of an answer of the £20 the which I have laid pledges for to my cousin Clere, the which letter was written the 22nd day of February; and as for that money, I can not get no longer day thereof than Midsummer, or fortnight after; and towards that money, and the £20 that I sent you besides to London by Sim, I have received no more money of yours, but as much as I send you written in this letter. And as for any discharge that I promised at the borrowing of the £20 when I laid the pledges therefore, I thought not but that your uncle should have borrowed them out, and I to have had my pledges, as well as he his; nevertheless, I shall be the warier how I shall deal hereafter. By my troth, I know not how to do therefore; the King goes so near us in this country, both to poor and rich, that I know not how we shall live, but unless the world amend. God amend it, when his will is. We can neither sell corn nor cattle to no good price. Malt is here but at 10d a comb; wheat, a comb 28d; oats, a comb 10d; and thereof is but little to get here at this time.

William Pecock shall send you a bill what he has paid for you for 2 tasks at this time; and how he has purveyed for the remnant of your corn; and also of other things that be necessary that should be purveyed for in your absence. Send me word also whom you will desire to do for you in this country or elsewhere in your absence; and write to them to do for you, and they will be the better willed to do for you; and I will do my devoir for you also, as well as I can.

The sum of money that I have received of William Pecock: – First, 40s of Runham. Item, of Baswick, 20s. Item, of Runham, 20s. Item, of him for barley at Runham, 20s. Item, of the fishing at Bastwick, 13s 4d. Item, for barley sold at Runham, 8s. Sum total £6 0s 16d.

Item, I have received of Richard Calle, of Sporle wood, 26s 8d, and more shall I hope hereafter within short time; as I receive for you, I hope to give you a true account; and this is all that I have received for you since you departed hence. God bring you well again to this country, to His pleasure, and to your worship and profit.

Written at Mautby, the 23rd day of May, and the Tuesday next after Trinity Sunday.

For God's love, an your brothers go over the sea, advise them as you think best for their safeguard. For some of them be but young soldiers and know full little what it means to be a soldier, nor for to endure to do as a soldier should do. God save you all, and send me good tidings of you all. And send you me word in haste how you do, for I think long to I hear of you. By your Mother.

Item, I would not in no wise that you should neither sell nor set in pledge that you have in Runham, what sum ever fortune of the remnant; for it is a pretty thing, and reasonable well paid and near this town. I would be right sorry that you should forbear that; I had leifer you forbore that your uncle has to mortgage than that.

(Paston Letters, no. 871)

The next correspondent is a delightful contrast to the serious and careworn Margaret. Elizabeth Brews was the daughter of Gilbert Debenham and the second wife of Sir Thomas Brews. She seemed to have been almost as charmed by John III as was her daughter Margery (see chapter 3), and, given the respectability of the Paston match, was certainly willing to do all she could to let her daughter have her way. There was a little dickering over the amount Sir Thomas would give his daughter and how much the Pastons could afford to offer as John's part of the settlement, but agreement was reached without too much difficulty. Margery declared that she would have John even if he had only half what was being negotiated and Elizabeth so clearly loved and valued her merry, witty daughter that she wrote to John suggesting that he come and stay for a few days with them over the period of Valentine's day so that he could speak to her husband. An earlier appointment had had to be cancelled because 'her cousin Derby' could not manage the day. There are several Derbys mentioned in the letters, but whether any of them were Elizabeth's 'cousin' is open to conjecture. When she addresses John by the term, this is merely an indication of the warmth of her feeling towards her prospective son-in-law.

Dame Elizabeth Brews to John Paston, February 1477

Right worshipful cousin, I recommend me unto you etc. And I sent my husband a bill of the matter that you know of, and he wrote another bill to me again touching the same matter; and he would that you should go unto my mistress your mother and assay whether you might get the whole £20 into your hands and then he would be more glad to marry with you and will give you £100. And, cousin, the day that she is married, my father will give her 1 mark. But, an we accord, I shall give you a greater treasure, that is, a witty gentlewoman, and if I say it, both good and virtuous; for if I should take money for her, I would not give her for £1,000. But, cousin, I trust you so much that I would think her well beset on you and you were worth much more. And, cousin, a little after that you were gone, come a man from my cousin Derby and brought me word that such a chance fell that he might not come at that day that was set, as I shall let you understand more plainly when I speak with you etc. But cousin, an it would please you to come again what day that you will set, I dare undertake that they shall keep the same day; for I would be glad that, and my husband and you might accord in this marriage, that it might be my

130

fortune to make an end in this matter between my cousins and you, that each of you might love other in friendly wise etc. And, cousin, if this bill please not you intent, I pray you that it be burnt etc. No more unto you at this time, but Almightly Jesus preserve you, etc. By your cousin, Dame Elizabeth Brews.

Unto my right worshipful cousin, John Paston, be this letter delivered, etc.

(Paston Letters, no. 895)

Dame Elizabeth Brews to John Paston, February 1477

Cousin, I recommend me unto you, thanking you heartily for the great cheer that you made me and all my folks, the last time that I was at Norwich; and you promised me that you would never break the matter to Margery until such time as you and I were at point. But you have made her such an advocate for you, that I might never have rest night or day, for calling and crying upon to bring the said matter to effect, etc.

And, cousin, upon Friday is St Valentine's Day, and every bird chooseth him a mate; and if it like you to come one Thursday at night and so purvey you that you may abide there til Monday, I trust to God that you shall so speak to my husband; and I shall pray that we shall bring the matter to a conclusion, etc. For, cousin

> It is but a simple oak
> That is cut down at the first stroke

For you will be reasonable, I trust to God, which have you ever in His merciful keeping, etc.

By your cousin, Dame Elizabeth Brews, otherwise shall be called by God's grace.

To my worshipful cousin, John Paston, be this bill delivered.

(Paston Letters, no. 896)

The following letters are taken somewhat out of chronological order, so that the letters from the Paston women to their sons may be taken together. As noted earlier (see chapter 3), Jane, the wife of Thomas

131

Stonor, was the illegitimate daughter of William de la Pole, Duke of Suffolk. Thomas died in April 1474, naming his wife as one of the executors of his will; this was customarily a sign of a husband's belief in his wife's abilities and good sense as well as affection. Jane's 'simple bill', however, masks considerable disagreement with William, the eldest of her three sons, over the settlement of her late husband's estate. They quarrelled over the costs of Thomas's funeral, over debts due to and by him, over income from the estate paid to Jane after his death and even over who should have ownership of a psalter from the family chapel. Things got so bad that eighteen months later the dispute was submitted to the arbitration of three disinterested local gentlemen. The letter here probably dates from this period of dispute, and certainly cannot be before the summer of 1475 when William was first married. The tenants referred to may be those of the manor of Penton Mewsey in Hampshire, which is referred to in the arbitration award. It was one of several whose issues Thomas willed should first be used to pay his debts and then provide marriage portions for his daughters. It was not part of Jane's dower and William claimed she was withholding money paid to her by the tenants after his father's death. A letter written by the parson of Penton to Sir William at the time describes how he had visited Jane and been called 'false varlet, thief and her traitor' for his pains. The parson's view was 'God give me grace that I never meet with her more'.

Jane Stonor to William Stonor (?1475)

Son, I send you God's blessing and mine. I understand by my tenants and yours that Master Lewis John desires for to have a letter from you for to understand your mastership and your favour towards your said tenants and mine. Wherefore I pray you to do after his desire in supporting your right, and I will do to the power that God has sent unto me my part with the grace of God, whom I beseech to be your guide, and that this simple bill may recommend me unto my worshipful and good daughter your wife. By your poor Mother, Jane Stonor

(Stonor Letters, no. 158)

Cecily Neville was the youngest of the numerous offspring of Ralph, Earl of Westmorland, and his second wife, Joan Beaufort (see chapter 2), daughter of John of Gaunt, Duke of Lancaster. Cecily was known as the 'Rose of Raby' (Raby was her family's main seat in Durham) for her beauty and was married to her father's ward, Richard, Duke of York, in 1424 when they were nine and thirteen respectively. They did not cohabit immediately and their eldest child was not born until 1439. Richard, their youngest child, was born in 1452. At the Battle of Wakefield in 1460 York and their second son, Edmund, Earl of Rutland, were killed; but a few months later the wheel of fortune had turned again and Cecily's eldest son, Edward, was crowned king at the age of nineteen. Her husband may never have occupied the throne he claimed, but Cecily routinely described herself as 'wife of the rightful inheritor of the realm of England', and her pride may perhaps be shown in her use of the first person plural in this letter to her son. Its use was not uncommon by great ladies, particularly queens, but rarely in letters to their children. The background to the case referred to in the letter is given later (see chapter 5), but here Cecily appears to be mildly rebuking her son for not have acted more promptly concerning it, and also perhaps for not visiting her as often as she thought he should. And in case he did not respond to her letter immediately, she wrote to Robert Chamberlain herself, telling him to refrain from interfering. Chamberlain, whose home was in Suffolk, was Richard's steward for his East Anglian lands. Her views on Richard's usurpation of her grandson, Edward V, are unknown, but during the period of the usurpation, Richard was a frequent visitor at his mother's London home, Baynard's Castle. In Cecily's later years, she was famed for her piety, and her life at Berkhamsted and in London was monastic in all save vows. She survived all her children, dying at the age of eighty in 1495.

Cecily, Duchess of York, to Richard, Duke of Gloucester, 15 March (?1474)

R ight trusty and entirely well beloved son, we greet you heartily well, giving you God's blessing and ours. And whereas it is come unto our knowledge that since our departing you have been sued unto by our wellbeloved servant, John Prince, as is according to his duty. By whose report we understand to the accomplishment of your promise made unto us at Syon you have showed him the favour of your good lordship and the more especially at our contemplation [*sic*], we thank you therefore in our most hearty wise, praying you that no man intromitt [meddle] with our said servant's matter, saving only our counsel learned and yours, as our faithful trust is in you. And whereas your servant Sir Robert Chamberlain, kt, intendeth to have interest therein, we pray you to commend him the contrary, remembering the said promise made between us and you, which we doubt not shall be observed on your part. Son, we trusted you should have been at Berkhamsted with my lord my son [King Edward IV] at his last being there with us, and if it had pleased you to come at that time, you should have been right heartily welcome. And so you shall be whensoever you shall do the same, as God knoweth, whom we beseech to have you in governance.

Written at our Castle of Berkhamsted, the 15th day of March.

To the Duke of Gloucester.

(Transactions of the Essex Archaeological Society,
new series, 5 (1895))

FIVE

'Trusty and wellbeloved cousin':
Women and their kinfolk

The term 'cousin' has changed its meaning since the Middle Ages. It is used much more precisely now, referring to the children of an uncle or aunt, or of a parent's first cousin's child. In the Middle Ages it could mean the same thing, but it was also used loosely to refer to anyone who was either a blood relation or linked by marriage, or as a courtesy title to someone who was related only in esteem or friendship. There are also examples of women addressing their husbands as 'cousin', which seems strange to the modern eye. Nonetheless, the use of the term was significant: family networks were the mainstay of medieval life in the village, in the county community or on a countrywide scale. Friendship as a concept should not be lightly dismissed, but the defence of landed possessions and very often their enhancement depended on the family. Conversely, some of the most virulent property feuds were between branches of the same family. Because many people married twice, three or even four times, with a variety of step-children involved, the extended family could be very widespread. Most families had relatives both above and below them in the social scale. Those above could be confidently approached to serve as patrons, those below employed as lawyers, stewards, agents and the like, or recommended as such to neighbours. However, then, as now, it was the nuclear family that was most significant. The maintenance of close relations, even with siblings, let alone aunts, uncles and cousins, depended to a large degree on propinquity. If relations lived within easy visiting distance, then the relationship was more likely to remain close and to be utilised more frequently. It was also more likely to occur where there was a more formal legal relationship, such as guardian or executor, and thus was more common when under-age children were involved in property inheritance.

Relationships brought with them both rights and obligations to seek and provide aid and support whenever required. Although people rarely sent their children to serve close relatives, preferring to broaden their horizons and networks, kinfolk were often useful in keeping an eye out for suitable spouses and in advancing matches. The maintenance of social and familial networks has always been seen as primarily a woman's role; Margery Hampton's postcript to her husband's letter to John Paston is a nice example. At the highest level, like that of Eleanor, Princess of Wales, women oiled the diplomatic wheels by keeping on good terms with their relatives at the English court. The family links were particularly important for women, who in the event of widowhood, might need all the help they could summon up. The letters in this section where 'cousinship' is involved are to people known to be tied by blood or marriage to the writer. Letters addressed to 'cousins' where it is clearly used as a courtesy title are included in the next chapter.

Eleanor, Princess of Wales, was the only daughter of Simon de Montfort, Earl of Leicester, and Eleanor, sister of Henry III. She was born in 1252 and during her father's brief political ascendancy in the 1260s was betrothed to Prince Llywelyn ap Gruffydd of Wales as part of her father's peace proposals. After her father's death at Evesham in 1265 followed by her brothers' flight into exile, the marriage ceased to be English policy, but both Llywelyn and the de Montforts maintained the betrothal. In 1275, ten years later, Eleanor, who had been living with her mother in France, took ship for Wales and Llywelyn, escorted by her youngest brother, Amauri, but they were captured off the coast of Glamorgan and brought to their cousin, Edward I, at Windsor. There Eleanor remained for three years, part honoured guest, part hostage. Edward did not oppose the marriage as such, but was determined that Llywelyn should first do homage to him for Wales. After three years of military struggle, Llywelyn submitted and in October 1278 he and Eleanor were married at Worcester under Edward's patronage.

Thereafter, as her letter shows, Eleanor fulfilled the diplomatic role of a princess, easing the tense relationship between her husband and her cousin.

Eleanor, Princess of Wales, to her cousin, Edward I, 8 July (c. 1279)

To her excellent lord and well-beloved cousin, the Lord Edward, by the grace of God King of England, Lord of Ireland, and Duke of Aquitaine, his devoted cousin Eleanor, Princess of Wales, Lady of Snowdon, with such sincere affection as becometh, sends health to so great and so near a kinsman.

Be it known to your excellency, that we desire to hear good and prosperous news concerning your state and condition: therefore we entreat your excellency, humbly and earnestly, for our love's sake, that you deign to make known to us, as your humble cousin, and one ready to do your good pleasures, your state; and whether you wish anything within our power which may redound to your honour, or may please your highness.

Although, as we have heard, the contrary hereto hath been reported of us to your excellency by some; and we believe, notwithstanding, that you in no wise give credit to any who report unfavourably concerning our lord and ourself, until you learn from ourselves if such speeches contain truth: because you showed, of your grace, so much honour and so much friendliness to our lord and ourself, when you were at the last time at Worcester.

Wherefore, whatever you shall demand from us in this, or other matters that you wish, we shall ever be ready, according to our ability, to execute and accomplish.

Given at Llanmaes, the 8th day of July.

(PRO SC 1/17/2; Wood, I, pp. 54–5; Latin)

While Eleanor was released from honourable captivity to marry the Prince of Wales, her brother Amauri continued a prisoner, first at Corfe Castle and then in the custody of the Archbishop of Canterbury. Amauri was a graduate of the university of Padua and a papal chaplain, but unfortunately he was also the brother of Guy de Montfort who had earned Edward I's undying emnity by the treacherous murder of their mutual cousin, and Edward's beloved friend, Henry, the eldest son of Henry III's brother, Richard, Earl of Cornwall. One pope after another urged Edward to release Amauri, Eleanor added her pleas in letters like that quoted below, and finally Archbishop Pecham got Edward and his lords to agree to Amauri's departure from the country in April 1282. The endorsement shows that her prayers were taken into consideration. In another letter she pleads the case for three of her men who were captured with her, and again the men were pardoned, at 'the instance of Eleanor Princess of Wales'. Eleanor died in June 1282 giving birth to her only child, a daughter called Gwenllian, and did not live to see the defeat of Welsh independence and the death of her husband later that year. The infant Gwenllian was placed by Edward I with the nuns of Sempringham, Lincolnshire, where she remained all her life, taking her vows as a nun and thus being excluded as a claimant to the Principality.

Eleanor, Princess of Wales, to her cousin, Edward I, 18 October 1280

To the most excellent prince, and also her very dear cousin, the Lord Edward, by the grace of God King of England, Lord of Ireland and Duke of Aquitaine, his devoted Eleanor, Princess of Wales, Lady of Snowdon, sends health, with such sincere affection as becometh to so great a lord and so near a kinsman.

We make it known to your excellency by these presents, that we, blessed be God, enjoy good health and prosperity; which same we not only desire, but long to learn, concerning yourself.

And whereas it has been reported to us by some that you propose to have it debated, in the present parliament, touching the relieving of the condition of our very dear brother, the Lord Amauri, therefore with clasped hands, and with bended knees and tearful groanings, we supplicate your highness that, reverencing from your inmost soul the Divine mercy (which holds out the hand of pity to all, especially to those who seek Him with their whole heart), you would deign mercifully to take again to your grace and favour our aforesaid brother and your kinsman, who humbly craves, as we understand, your kindness.

For if your excellency, as we have often known, mercifully condescends to strangers, with much more reason, as we think, ought you to hold out the hand of pity to one so near to you by the ties of nature.

May you long fare well in the Lord!

Given at St Anneir, on the feast of St Luke the Evangelist [18 October].

[Endorsed:] 'It was answered to her that the affair was treated of in that parliament and what could be done has been done, and it is believed that the liberation of her brother has been greatly forwarded by that which has been said'.

(PRO SC 1/17/3; Wood, I, pp. 56–7; Latin)

Maud Pantulf was the daughter and heiress of William Pantulf of Wem and married Ralph Boteler of Oversley, Warwickshire. Both Ralph and their son, William, were summoned to Parliament by individual writ and were regarded as being raised to the baronage thereby. Ralph died in July 1281 and Maud endeavoured to retain her own lands rather than have them escheat to the Crown with those of her husband before they were granted to her son. Clearly having the chance to seek help from a relation who was chancellor and who had constant access to the king was an opportunity not to be missed. Bishop Burnell responded to her application and her lands were returned to her. In this letter of thanks, Maud complains that the issues of her lands while they were in the hands of the escheator, the county official responsible for taking Crown lands into his posssession on the death of a tenant in chief, had not been paid to her, despite the promise that they should be. Maud remarried in the spring of 1283, and her new husband, Walter de Hopton of Hopton, Salop, retained her lands when she died in 1289, because Maud had already outlived her son William and her grandson, though technically those lands should have descended to her own family heirs. The case of Donkerbur, to which Maud refers in her letter, is obscure. It is noteworthy that she uses her own family name when writing to her cousin, possibly because the matter related to lands that had come to her from her own family, perhaps as a gentle reminder to a busy chancellor of the connection between them. Previous letters in this collection show that using a maiden name, or the name of a first husband during a second marriage, was not uncommon, particularly when the matter in hand related to the affairs of a natal family or dower from an earlier marriage. Robert Burnell came, like Maud, from Shropshire, having been born at Acton Burnell, where he later built a palatial home. He became a clerk in royal service and a close personal friend of Edward I, and after the latter's accession was made chancellor and raised to the see of Bath and Wells, despite objections from the papacy about the unfitness of his personal life: he had a large family of illegitimate children.

Maud Pantulf to Robert Burnell, Bishop of Bath, Chancellor, 1281

To her very dear lord and cousin, if it pleases him, lord Robert Burnell, by the grace of God, Bishop of Bath, his own cousin, if it pleases him, Maud Pantulf, lady of Wemme, widow of lord Ralph le Boteler, greets him with as much honour and reverence as possible.

Dear lord, thank you very much for diligently helping me at Badewc in the presence of the king, to take possession of my lands and holdings with all their issues. And now, dear lord, if it pleases you, in the letter which was sent to the sheriff by the escheator, we lack the issues. Concerning which the sheriff tells me, lord, that he is held to answer for some of the issues on his account, and I have a letter which includes the issues as well as the lands and holdings. For this I ask you, as lord and cousin, that you help me concerning this, and also conceal, if you please for the love of God and for your soul, that I have a great interest in the case of Donkerbur which is now about to begin, for the death of my lord and all my other needs which I have to see to, so I place myself in the wisdom of God and yourself.

Farewell, dear lord, may God protect you and grant you long life.

(PRO SC 1/22/124; Tanquerey, no. 27)

Eleanor, the author of the next letter, was the eldest of the many daughters of Edward I and Eleanor of Castile. She was born about 1269 and was therefore in her late teens when she wrote to her father's cousin, Edmund, Earl of Cornwall, who was acting as regent during Edward's three year absence in his province of Gascony. Sir Eustace de Hache, the subject of her letter, was a long-standing member of the royal household, serving both the king and Queen Eleanor, who appointed him to take charge of the princesses' household while they were away. He apparently took his duties so seriously that he refused to leave his post, even though the process of law demanded his attendance in court elsewhere. William Hamilton, Dean of York, was deputy to the chancellor, and neither he nor the Earl of Cornwall responded positively to Eleanor's request, for Sir Eustace's excuse was disallowed. He did not, however, suffer permanently for his attention to duty, since Edward later put him in charge of the building of Caernarfon castle and raised him to a barony. Eleanor had been married by proxy to Alphonso of Aragon in 1282, but her mother and grandmother objected to her being sent to Spain while she was still very young and Edward, always indulgent to his womenfolk, agreed. She was preparing to leave England to join her husband when Alphonso died in 1291. Eleanor eventually married Henry, Count of Bar, in 1293, when she was twenty-four, and died in 1297 after only four years of marriage.

Eleanor of England to Edmund, Earl of Cornwall, c. 1286–9

To her very dear cousin, Lord Edmund, Earl of Cornwall, his cousin Eleanor, daughter to the King of England sends health and dear friendship.

141

Dear lord, since our lord the King has left us with Sir Eustace de Hache, our knight, and he is impleaded on many sides, and is so careful of the service of our lord the King that nothing avails him, since he cannot by any means depart from us, except by the mandate of our lord the King, we pray you, dear lord, since you are lieutenant of our lord the King, that you will command Sir William de Hamilton, by your letter, to let him [de Hache] have his warrant of essoin, so that he may not lose his land in our service, while our lord the King is out of the land. Dear lord, consent to do this thing for the love of us, so that he may feel our prayer avails for him. Dear lord, know that his day to have his warrant is this Tuesday next to come.

(Everett-Green, vol. 2, pp. 298–9; French)

Again, after thirteenth-century letters, which have survived because of their royal connection, there is a gap until the fifteenth century. This first letter is a plea for help from Joan Brokeholes to a distant female relative. So distant that she appears to have been unaware of the connection until it was pointed out to her, and which it has proved impossible to trace. Joan, married to her third husband, Robert Armburgh, desperately needed influential help to counter her brother-in-law in a disputed law suit, the background of which she neatly sums up in her letter. It appears that Ellen Ferrers was a relative on her mother's side, and thence could be persuaded that she might have a residual interest in the property. The name Ellen is an interesting link; it was not that common in the late Middle Ages and it was born both by Lady Ferrers and Joan's mother, thus enhancing the likely connection. Ellen Ferrers was the daughter and co-heiress of Thomas Roche of Castle Bromwich, Warwickshire, and had married Edmund, Lord Ferrers of Chartley; she was probably ten years or so older than Joan. Although the main inheritance at stake was that of her mother's Roos family in Hertfordshire and Essex, Joan specifically refers to her father's inheritance in Warwickshire, since that is where Ellen Ferrers came from and thus where the Ferrers family had influence. The letter did not go unanswered, as the Ferrers provided a limited degree of good lordship to the Armburghs in their long legal struggle.

Joan Armburgh to Ellen, Lady Ferrers of Chartley, 8 February 1428

My right worshipful and gracious lady, I recommend me to you as lowly as I am or may desire, desiring of your honourable estate and prosperity pleasant tidings to hear, which Almighty Jesu you grant so good as you for yourself best can desire. My gracious lady, like it to your ladyship to know that John Sumpter of Colchester, the which was husband to my sister and had by her two daughters, the which be dead, and should have departed [shared] with me my mother Dame Ellen Brokholes' inheritance, sometime the wife of my father Sir Geoffrey Brokholes, heir to the third part of the manor of Mancetter in Warwickshire, hath kept up two bastard children of his own and defiled the death of those two muliereris [sisters], and maketh the country believe that they be the same children that he had by his wife, and now late had writs out of Chancery directed to the escheators of Essex, of Hertfordshire and of Warwickshire, and thus, unknown to me or any of my council, hath proved them right heirs and of full age and hath sued out livery of the two moities of mine said inheritance, and to strengthen him against me in his wrong, hath married one of the said bastards to Thomas Bernard, an esquire of the Chancellor's and another to the son of Ralph Bellers, the last year's escheator of Warwickshire, in disinheriting of me and my heirs without help of your gracious ladyship and succour. Wherefore liketh it to your right worthy and gracious ladyship to consider this great wrong done to me your meek and poor kinswoman, so as I am informed by my friends, and to see the disinheritance that might fall to you if I and my parceners [joint heirs, i.e. children] died without issue, and that you vouchsafe so to stir my gracious lord your husband that he show his gracious lordship and help in this case that my right may be saved at the reverence of God. And if any service be that my husband and I may do to my lord your husband and you in any wise, we shall be always ready to fulfill it with all our hearts and power. My right worshipful and gracious lady, that blessed son of Our Lady you have evermore in his keeping.

Written at Westminster the 8th day of February.

(Chetham Mun. E.6.10(4); The Armburgh Papers, pp. 92–3)

143

Eleanor, Duchess of Norfolk, was the daughter of William Bourchier, Earl of Eu and her mother was a granddaughter of Edward III. She married John Mowbray, Duke of Norfolk, in about 1424. Her letter to Viscount Beaumont is written on behalf of one of her husband's servants. It is somewhat ambiguous, because she does not divulge what office in Lord Beaumont's service Roger Hunt had agreed to hand over to Norfolk's William of the Ewery. The ewery was the section of the household that had responsibility for such things as table furnishings, linen and drinking vessels. It also seems unusual, to say the least, that the two servants had made the agreement apparently unbeknownst to Beaumont and were relying on the duchess to act as go between and provide a reference for William. Such movement of household members from one master to another was not a very common occurrence except following a death, and is here explained by the fact that Beaumont was married to Eleanor's mother-in-law, Katherine, Dowager Duchess of Norfolk. This close connection explains the use of the word 'cousin', although there was no blood tie between them. Beaumont was a distinguished royal servant both at court and in arms in France. He was the first man to be advanced to the rank of viscount in England (it was a French title), which gave him precedence over all barons. He was killed in 1460 at the Battle of Northampton on the Lancastrian side. Eleanor was widowed in 1461 and died in 1474; her mother-in-law lived to a great age and was last noted at the coronation of Richard III in 1485.

Eleanor, Duchess of Norfolk to Viscount Beaumont, 8 March (c. 1444–60)

Right worshipful and entirely well-beloved cousin, I commend me to you with all my heart, desiring to hear and verily to know of your worshipful estate, profit, health and good prosperity, the which I beseech our Lord Jesu ever to maintain and preserve in all worship, and to your heart's ease.

Please it you, cousin, to wit that your wellbeloved servant Roger Hunt, and a servant of my most dread Lord, my husband, one

William, yeoman of the ewery, have come together and been fully through and agreed that the said William should have his office, if it may please your good Lordship.

Wherefore, cousin, I pray you, as my special trust is in you, that you will, at the instance of my prayer and writing, grant by your letters patent to the said William the aforesaid office, with such wages and fees as the said Roger your said servant have it of you; trusting verily that you shall find William a faithful servant to you and can and might do you right good service in that office.

And, cousin, in the accomplishment of my desire in this matter, you may do me a right good pleasure, as God knows, whom I beseech for His mercy to have you ever in His blessed governance, and send you good life and long, with much good worship.
Written at Framlingham, the 8th day of March.
Eleanor, the Duchess of Norfolk

(Paston Letters, no. 382)

The following letter is a particularly well-known one from the Paston collection because it deals with the question of arranged marriages and the difficult relations between Agnes Paston and her daughter Elizabeth. The writer, Elizabeth Clere (see chapters 3 and 4), was the widow of Robert Clere of Ormesby and the niece of John Paston's patron, Sir John Fastolf. She seems to have been blood kin of Margaret Paston, though the exact link is not clear. She knew the Paston family well and was probably rather older than John and Margaret, though she did not die until 1492, and therefore must have been still young when she was widowed in 1446. She was very comfortably provided for and chose not to remarry, despite royal urgings (see chapter 3). For decades she was a good friend to the Pastons, particularly to Margaret, lending considerable sums of money in the difficult years after John's death, and here, much earlier, acting as a conduit between John and his unfortunate sister, Elizabeth. Stephen Scrope was the stepson of Sir John Fastolf (whose wife, Milicent, was the widow of Sir Stephen Scrope), and was about ten at the time of his father's death. Fastolf proved to be a hostile and uncaring stepfather, selling off the boy's wardship to

Chief Justice Gascoigne for 500 marks, 'through the which sale', Scrope later wrote, 'I took sickness that kept me a thirteen or fourteen years ensuing; whereby I am disfigured in my person and shall be while I live'. Although Fastolf later bought the wardship back he continued to treat Stephen ungenerously. Scrope's first marriage produced a daughter before his wife died, of whom he says 'For very need, I was fain to sell a little daughter I have for much less than I should have done'. The purchaser of the wardship and marriage was an unnamed knight. By then in his forties, Stephen looked about him for a second wife. The Pastons regarded him as a suitable husband for Elizabeth, and Agnes Paston wanted her daughter married and off her hands as soon as possible. Whether Elizabeth had objected at first to Scrope, by the time her cousin wrote to her brother, Agnes's treatment of her, graphically described, had made her decide that Scrope, whom she was not allowed to meet, was better than nothing. As a properly reared Paston, however, she would only take him if the settlement on her and any children of the match would benefit at the expense of his daughter by his first marriage. Her cousin Elizabeth was very dubious about the whole affair and urged John Paston to look about him for someone better, but at the same time she felt that Scrope was better than no husband at all. She also warned John not to let his mother Agnes have sight of her letter, presumably fearing the old lady's anger would be further vented on her unfortunate daughter. In the end the proposals collapsed and neither Scrope nor Elizabeth married for several years.

Elizabeth Clere to John Paston, c. 1448

Trusty and welbeloved cousin I commend me to you, desiring to hear of your welfare and good speed in your matter, the which I pray God send you to his pleasaunce and your heart's ease.

Cousin, I let you know that Scrope hath been in this country to see my cousin your sister, and he has spoken with my cousin your mother and she desireth of him that he should show you the indentures made between the knight that hath his daughter and him, whether that Scrope, if he were married and fortuned to have children, if those children should inherit his land or his daughter who is married.

Cousin, for this cause take good heed to his indentures, for he is glad to show you them, or whom you will assign with you; and he saith to me he is the last in the [en]tail of his livelihood, the which is 350 marks and better, as Watkin Shipdam saith, for he hath taken account of his livelihood divers times; and Scrope saith to me if he be married and have a son and heir, his daughter that is married shall have 50 marks and no more; and therefore, cousin, meseemeth he were good for my cousin your sister, with[out] you might get her a better. And if you can get a better, I would advise you to labour it in as short time as you may goodly, for she was never in so great sorrow as she is nowadays, for she may not speak with no man, howsoever come, nor not may she speak with my man, nor with the servants of her mother's but that she beareth her on hand otherwise than she meaneth. And she has since Easter the most part been beaten once in the week or twice and sometimes twice on one day and her head broken in two or three places. Wherefore cousin, she hath sent to me by Friar Newton in great counsel and prayeth me that I would send you a letter of her heaviness, and pray you to be her good brother, as her trust is in you; and she saith if you may see by his evidences that his children and hers may inherit and she to have reasonable jointure, she hath heard so much of his birth and conditions, that an you will, she will have him, whether that her mother will or will not, not withstanding it is told her his person is simple, for she sayeth men shall have the more duty of her if she rule her to him as she ought to do.

Cousin, it is told me that there is a goodly man in your Inn, of the which the father died late, and if you think that he were better for her than Scrope, it would be laboured, and give Scrope a goodly answer that he be not put off til you be sure of a better; for he said when he was with me but unless he had some comfortable answer of you, he will no more labour in this matter, because he might not see my cousin your sister, and he saith he might have seen her and she had be better than she is; and that causes him to deem that her mother is not well willing, and so I have sent my cousin your mother word. Wherefore cousin, think on this matter, for sorrow oftentimes causes women to set them otherwise than they should do, and if she were in that case, I wot well you would be sorry.

Cousin, I pray you burn this letter, that your men nor none other man see it; for and my cousin your mother knew that I had sent you this letter, she should never love me. No more I write to you at this time, but Holy Ghost have you in keeping. Written in haste, on St Peter's Day, by candlelight, by your cousin Elizabeth Clere.

To my Cousin, John Paston, be this letter delivered.

(Paston Letters, no. 94)

In the following letter, Elizabeth Clere gives John Paston a detailed, circumstantial account of her confrontation on the Sunday before Easter with William Stiwardson, one of her tenants who was behind with his rents. The matter was complicated by the fact that Stiwardson was a servant of Lord Scales, a local peer; Scales had taken Elizabeth to law over an alleged attack on his servant by her men. What upset Elizabeth most, however, was the attack on her good name and honour, since her reputation as a good landlord, once lost, might never be regained. John Paston's reputation as a lawyer who could be trusted to arbitrate honestly between two sides is emphasised by the fact that even as Elizabeth was writing to him for advice, so was Scales, suggesting that he intercede with Elizabeth and get the matter settled. Such detailed recorded speech is rare and makes it possible to hear the authentic voice of ordinary people from the fifteenth century.

Elizabeth Clere to John Paston, ?1460

To my worshipful cousin John Paston be this letter delivered in haste.

Worshipful cousin, I recommend me to you. Like it you to know that Stiwardson came to me on Easter Even to church and prayed me to be his good mistress, and would put himself in my rule to do as I will bid him; trusting, he said, that I would take him to grace the rather for his submission, for if Judas, he said, would have asked grace of God he should an had it, and for His sake that I had received that day [Holy Communion] that I would take his submission. And I let him know that I was in charity, for I would to him no bodily harm, and I said, if a thief come and robbed me of all the goods I have and come and asked me for forgiveness on the other day, were it reason that I should forgive it without satisfaction? And he said nay; and I said he had done his endeavour in that in him was to noise me and slander me, the which I am worse pleased withal that with any money I have spent, and as for that I gave little force of. And he swore he said nothing that should noise me, and I said if it had been another day I should have rehearsed many more things, but that is openly known among my tenants in this country, and that is when I sent to his place to distrain for my duties [rents], where he hath said untruly that he was beat, upon which untrue language his master hath taken an action against me and my men. And he swore that he never said he was beaten, but he said he was never so sore afraid, for he knew not what my men would do to him. And I asked him if he would abide by that, that my men came into his place with force and arms, or not, and he answered again with many crafty words; but at the last he was a-know that he had said them and it was untruly said, and that he would no more say so; and this I bade my tenants should record for all that was said was said openly among the most part of all the parish. And for he said truth in this and for his own seeking should have fared the better, and if he had come with his master I would not have spoke with him, and for his maintenance he shall fare the worse; and [I said] if he had come to me in the beginning ere the law was attained I would have made therein an end myself. And since that time by his own desire to put it in my council learned [her legal advisers] the which I agreed at that time, the which now I will be advised, for he has caused me to spend money for his untruth and my friends have laboured for me; therefore I will give him no answer, but be advised by my friends the which have laboured for me in this matter. And I said his master should leave his maintenance, whereof I should have right good surety or else we should not go through easily; and he desire an answer the same day, and I said, nay, he should have his answer on Saturday on Easterweek. And he has told another man that Heydon hath promised his master that it should be put in award by Palm Sunday, for he is double both to him and to me, and so is William Jenney and more of my council; but he rehearsed no name, wherefore he said to the man that he will not be bound neither to me nor my council, but if I will bid him to bring in his deed and make a release he will do it. And as for his barn where my men went in to distrain, it is frank fee, he saith, wherefore he may give the rent where he please. Wherefore, cousin, I beseech you that you send me a bill, what answer is best to give, my worship saved, by the bringer hereof.

No more I write you at this time, but the Holy Ghost have you in His keeping. Written in haste the Monday next before Easter Day.

By your cousin Elizabeth Clere.

(Paston Letters (Davis), no. 600)

Elizabeth Clere wrote to Margaret soon after John's death, presumably after having paid a visit of condolence, about legal deeds of hers which John had held. The precise details she gives of each indicate a good head for business – either her own or one of her household or council. At the time the letter was written, Margaret's youngest son, William, was six or seven, and probably the only one of the children left at home.

Elizabeth Clere to Margaret Paston, ?1466

Worshipful cousin, I commend me to you, desiring to hear of your health and heart's ease, which I beseech God send you. And as for my little cousin, your son is a fair child and a merry, blessed be God.

Cousin, the cause of my writing at this time is for certain evidences of Frethorp that I delivered my cousin your husband for to have made award betwixt Rammesbury and me, and 1 book of paper of the customs of Ormesby and 1 roll called 'domesday' and certain other evidences belonging to the said manor and 1 deed of

St Anne teaching the Virgin Mary to read. (*Royal Commission on Historical Monuments for England*)

Women carding, spinning and weaving wool. (Roy. 16. G.V. f. 56. *British Library*)

Ladies hunting, from Queen Mary's Psalter, *c.* 1320. (MS. Royal 23. vii. f. 152v. *British Library*)

Music-making in a garden. (Harl. 4425. f. 12v. *British Library*)

'He maketh follies amerous': an embrace. (Cott. Tiberius MS. A VII f. 78v. *British Library*)

Marriage: the exchange of rings and vows. (f. 19r Dd. 4.17. *Cambridge University Library*)

Childbirth. (MS. 25241, f. 36. *Trustees of the National Library of Scotland*)

A lady dictating to her clerk. (MS. Royal 10E. IV. f. 307. *British Library*)

Playing backgammon. (Add. MS. 42130. f. 76v. *British Library*)

A lady offering the hospitality of her house to pilgrims. (Cott. Tiberius MS. A. VII. f. 90. *British Library*)

Poor Clares singing in chapel. (BL 51162 Cott. Dom. A XVII. f. 74v. *British Library/Bridgeman Art Library*)

entail of Reynthorp the which I delivered him, and certain evidences of Cleydon and Burgh. And also, cousin, your father-in-law [Justice William Paston] was of council with my mother and my mother-in-law wherefore I suppose there might be left some evidences or copies of evidences of my livelihood, that is to say, Tacolneston, Therston, Reynthorp, Rusteyn in Wymondham, Kesewik and Stratton, with him. Wherefore, cousin, I beseech you heartily that when you look among your evidences that you will lay them apart for me, as my very trust is that you will, for I hear say that you have right well and concientiously delivered certain persons the evidences belonging to to them and I trust verily you will the same to me. Cousin, there came a man from Norwich to me and found by the way certain rolls and took them . . . belong to you and not to me, wherefore I send them by the bringer of this bill.

No more to you at this time, but the Holy Trinity have you in His blessed keeping.

By your cousin, E. Clere.

(Paston Letters (Davis), no. 724)

Alice Crane was a member of a family distantly related to the Pastons through Agnes Berry. The Cranes held the manor of Norton Hall in Wood Norton, Norfolk, but they, unlike the Pastons, were slowly declining in the world. John Paston I lent small sums of money to John Crane, who was probably Alice's father, and who seems to have been a government servant of some sort. Simon Crane, probably Alice's brother, sometimes performed small services for the Pastons and was paid for them. It was through networks of family connections and friends like the Cranes and the Pastons that much of the day-to-day life of a county was conducted. Alice's ties to the county of her birth are expressed in her request for Norfolk thread. She was almost certainly quite a lot younger than Margaret Paston, who was a friend of her mother's, and Alice is clearly appreciative of the help and friendship both Pastons had shown her parents and herself. In return, Alice had sent medicine to Margaret when she was ill and this was a follow-up letter to see if it had proved effective. It is clear that she was in the household of an unidentified lady, possibly a member of the court, but whether the need for friendship and support she expresses came from her service there or quite another cause, will never be known. It may even have been the same problem which was causing her such concern a year or so earlier (see chapter 3).

Alice Crane to Margaret Paston, 29 June (c. 1455)

Right worshipful cousin, I recommend me unto you, desiring to hear of your welfare; and if it like you to hear of my welfare, at the making of this letter I was in good health, loved be God. The cause of my writing to you at this time is this, praying you to send me word of your welfare and how you do of your sickness, and if the medicine do you any good that I send you writing of last; thanking you of the great friendship that you have done to my mother with all my heart.

Also I pray you that you will be good meyn [?] to my cousin your husband, that he will see that my father be well ruled in his livelihood for his worship and his profit.

Also praying you to hold me excused that I have written no oftener to you, for, in good faith, I had no leisure; for my Lady hath been sick in London, ner hand this quarter of this year, and that hath been great heaviness to me; but now, blessed be God, she is amended and is in the country again.

Also thanking you of the great cheer that I had of you when I was with you last with all my heart, praying you of good countenance, for I had never greater need than I have now, and if I had leisure and space, I would write to you the cause.

No more at this time, but the Holy Trinity have you in his keeping.

Written at Windsor, the 29th day of June, by your poor bedewoman and cousin, Alice Crane.

Also, cousin, I pray you send me some Norfolk thread to do about my neck to ride with.

To my cousin Margaret Paston, be this letter delivered.

(Paston Letters, no. 296)

Elizabeth Mountford, who addresses John Paston I as her nephew, was not a blood relation. Her first husband was Thomas Berney, brother of Margaret Paston's mother, so she was technically an aunt by marriage-in-law to John Paston. These networks of kinship and marriage were of great importance for medieval families, and John Paston recognised the kinship, even after Thomas Berney died. This was in 1441, soon after his niece, Margaret, married, and his widow then took as her second husband Sir Osbert Mountford of Hockwold, near Thetford. Osbert was a correspondent of Paston's, who legally acted for him on at least one occasion. The Mountford family spent some years in Calais in the 1450s, where Osbert was Marshal of Calais, the last remaining possession of the English Crown in France. In 1460 the civil war reached Calais and the Yorkist Earl of Warwick captured a force led by Osbert and promptly beheaded him at the Tower of Ruysbank, part of the Calais fortifications. Elizabeth's letter to Paston for help over the seizure of one of her jointure manors is an illustration of the vulnerablity of the families of those killed during the war if they happened to be on the wrong side. The fact that Edmund Rous, having seized East Lexham, Norfolk, promptly made Warwick a trustee made Elizabeth doubly vulnerable. Walter Gorges and John Curde, the other two trustees, both held land in nearby Fransham. The recovery by assize to which she refers was an action taken by her husband's grandfather to ensure his legal title to the manor he had exchanged. It is not clear whether the dispute over East Lexham began before or after Osbert's death. In the short term, Paston could do nothing to shift Warwick, and it was not until after the earl's death in 1471 that the widow finally regained her manor.

Dame Elizabeth Mountford to John Paston, c. 1460–6

Right worshipful sir and my right good nephew, I recommend me unto you with all mine heart. Please it you to understand the great necessity of my writing to you is this, that there was made an exchange by the grandsire of my husband Mountford, on whose soul God have mercy, of the manor of Gressenale with the ancestors of Rous for the manor of East Lexham, the which is part of my jointure; and my grandfather Mountford recovered the said manor of East Lexham by assize against the ancestors of Rous and so made it clear. And now one Edmund Rous claims the said manor of East Lexham by virtue of an entail, and hath taken possession and made an enfeoffment to my lord of Warwick and Walter Gorges and to Curde; and on Friday before St Valentine's Day Walter Gorges and Curde entered and took possession for my said lord of Warwick. And so both the foresaid manors were entailed, and at the time of the exchange made the entails and evidences of both foresaid manors were delivered unto the parties indifferently, by the advice of men learned.

Wherefore I beseech you that it please you to take the great labour upon you to inform my lord's good lordship of the truth in the form above written, and that it please you to understand whether that my lord will abide by the feoffment made to him or not; and that it shall please my lord that I may have right as law requires, for I trust to God by such time as my lord shall be informed of the truth by you that his lordship will not support the foresaid Rous against my right.

And if I had very understanding that my lord would take no part in the matter above said I would trust to God's mercy and to you and other of my good friends to have possession again in right hasty time, beseeching you to pardon me of my simple writing, for I have no leisure.

Right worshipful and my right good nephew, I beseech the Blessed Trinity have you in His gracious keeping. Written at Norwich in great haste the Tuesday next after St Valentine's Day.

Your own Elizabeth Mountford.

(Paston Letters (Davis), no. 657)

It was not until ten long years after Elizabeth Clere wrote to John Paston about Stephen Scrope that his sister Elizabeth was finally married. As will be seen, in worldly terms the Pastons finally found her a good match. Sir Robert Poynings, second son of Lord Poynings, owned substantial lands in Kent, and when she wrote to

154

her mother Agnes immediately after her marriage (see chapter 1), Robert was busying himself about her jointure. This was prescient. The marriage lasted a brief two years, during which a son, Edward, was born, before Robert was killed in 1461 at the Battle of St Albans. He had left his widow as well provided for as he could, not just in way of dower and jointure, but by bequeathing her control over all his property during the minority of their infant son. However, a widow like Elizabeth was in a weak position at a time of political flux and changing dynasties. Her brother-in-law, Sir Edward Poynings, persuaded her to assign him some of the manors for the purposes of paying off her husband's debts; and other predators, such as Sir Robert Fenys, moved in on her vulnerable estates. Even the fact that they were in the hands of feoffees (trustees) does not seem to have deterred Fenys, and neither did direct orders from the king. Elizabeth hoped that her courtier nephew, Sir John Paston, might persuade the king to do more on her behalf. Other property had been occupied without any justification at all by the Earl of Kent, who had made it over to the Earl of Essex. Since both these men were in the favour of Edward IV, she had rather less hope of Paston being able to do anything about that part of her property. A final favour she asked was on behalf of one of her servants, whom Fenys had had charged with felony. At the time of writing, Elizabeth was living in the Poynings' town house in Southwark.

Dame Elizabeth Poynings to Sir John Paston, 15 December (?1468)

Worshipful and with all my heart, entirely wellbeloved nephew, I recommend me to you, desiring to hear of your prosperity and welfare, which I pray Almighty God maintain and increase to His pleasure and your heart's desire, thanking God of your amending and health; furthermore, certifying you that Sir Robert Fenys hath done great hurt in the livelihood which pertained to my husband and me in the shire of Kent, wherein William Keene and other persons are enfeoffed, and greatly trouble it, and receiveth the issues and profits of great part of them. And as of my said husband's livelihood, as well in the same shire as in other shires, besides my jointure, my said husband, when he departed towards the field of St Albans, made and ordained his will, that I should have the rule of his livelihood, and of Edward his son and mine, and to take the issues and profits of the said livelihood, to the finding of his and my said son, to pay his debts, and to keep the right and title of the same livelihood, which I might not according occupy for Sir Edward Poynings, my said husband's brother; and so since my said husband's departing I have assigned that the said Sir Edward for certain years should have and take the revenues of the manors of Westwood, Eastwell, Leveland, Horsmonden, Totynddon, Eccles, Staundon and Combesdon, parcel of the said livelihood, which are clearly yearly worth £76 13s 4d, to the intent that the said Sir Edward should pay my husband's debts, for he would not suffer me to be in rest without he might have a rule in the livelihood; and after the said assignment made, the said Robert Fenys, contrary to truth, and without cause of right, interrupted me and the said Sir Edward, as well of and in the said manors as of other manors underwritten; whereupon the said Sir Edward sued unto the King's Highness, and had the King's honourable letters under his signet, directed to the said Sir Robert Fenys, the tenor of which I send you herein enclosed; and as for the residue of the livelihood of my said husband and mine, within the same shire of Kent, wherein the said William Keen and others are enfeoffed, that is to say, the manors of Tyrlingham, Wolverton, Halton, Newington, Bastram, Rolesley, and Northcray, with appurtenances, I of them, by my said husband's will, should have residue and take the issues and profits of them, contrary to right and conscience, taking away my right and breaking my husband's will, the said Robert Fenys hath done great waste and hurt there, and long time hath taken up the revenues and profits of the same, where through I have not my right, and the said will may not be performed.

Wherefore I heartily pray you that you will labour unto the King's Highness, that it liketh him address his honourable letters to be directed to the said Robert Fenys, discharging him utterly of the menuraunce [occupation?] and receipt of the revenues of the said manor of Tyrlingham and others, according to the tenor of the letters laboured by Sir Edward, for the manors assigned to him from the King's Highness, directed to the same Robert Fenys, or straighter if it may be, and that I and my assigns may peaceably enjoy them; and if any would attempt to do the contrary, that a commandment, if it please the King's Highness, might be given to my lord Chancellor to seal writings sufficient with his great seal, in aiding and assisting me and my assigns in this same.

And as for the manors of Easthall, Faukham Asslie and Chelsfield, with their appurtenances in the said shire of Kent, whereof my husband at his departure was seized and my son since then, unto the time that the Earl of Kent without any inquisition or title of right from the King, by colour of the King's letters patent, entered into them and him thereof put out, and now my lord of Essex occupieth them in like manner and form; if any remedy therein will be had, I pray you attempt it.

Also, furthermore, I heartily pray you that if any general pardon be granted, that I may have one for John Dane my servant, whom the said Robert Fenys of great malice hath indicted of felony, and that you secretly labour this and send me answer in writing in as goodly haste as you may. As soon as that may please you to send me parcel of costs and expenses you bear and pay for the said causes, I will truly content you it of the same, and over that reward you to your pleasure by the grace of Jesu, who have you in His blessed keeping.

Written at Southwark, the 15th day of December, by your aunt, Elizabeth Poynings.

(Paston Letters, no. 692)

Elizabeth Paston, who earlier wrote first as a happy new wife and then as an embattled young widow, married again some ten years after the death of Robert Poynings. Her second husband was Sir George Browne of Bletchworth. The following is a curious letter, written at the behest of her nephew, John III, and giving her recollections of the circumstances surrounding the death of her father, Justice William, and the whereabouts of her brother, John's father, at the time.

Dame Elizabeth Browne to John Paston, 23 September 1485

Right worshipful and my right heartily beloved nephew, I recommend me to you. And whereas you desire me to send you word whether my brother John Paston, your father, was with my father and his, whom God assoil, during his last sickness and at the time of his decease at St Brides, or not.

Nephew, I ascertain you upon my faith and poor honour that I was 14, 15 or 16 years old and at St Brides with my father and my mother when my father's last sickness took him and til he was deceased; and I dare depose before any person honourable that when my father's last sickness took him, my brother, your father, was in Norfolk and he came not to London until after that my father was deceased and that can Sir William Cooting and James Gresham record, for they were both my father's clerks at that time. And I remember and wot well that James Gresham was with my father at St Brides during all his sickness and at his decease, and this will I witness while I live for a truth, as knoweth God, whom I beseech to reserve you and yours.

And, nephew, I pray you recommend to my niece your wife, whom I would be glad to see once again in London, where this bill was written, signed with my own hand and sealed with my seal the 23rd day of September the first year of the reign of King Henry the 7th. Your loving aunt, Elizabeth Browne

To my right worshipful and heartily beloved nephew, John Paston, esquire.

(Paston Letters, no. 1003)

Margery Hampden, daughter of Sir Stephen Popham and wife of Thomas Hampden, wrote a couple of short notes to her husband's first cousin, Thomas Stonor, and his son William, which, while not of much significance in themselves, were surely typical of thousands of similar missives despatched around the countryside by gentlewomen to their friends and relations whom they saw fairly frequently and with whom they had regular dealings. The second note, though separate from that of her husband, also accompanied a letter from Thomas to William, which related to one of Thomas's sisters. It is possible that a match between William and the sister had been suggested; if so, nothing came of it.

Margery Hampden to Thomas Stonor, c. 1465

[At the end of a letter by her husband concerning a benefice, Margery added the following postscript:]

Cousin, I recommend me unto you, and I beseech you of your good cousinhood in performing of my husband's desire etc. Cousin, and you had desired me or mine so often as I have desired you and my cousins, your sons, I would have seen you oftener. I wiss, cousin, it grieveth me. There may no man hold that will away; and therefore I must take it as well as I can, and thinketh this dealing under wisdom nor kindness all things to be considered to be so strange etc.

(Stonor Letters, no. 75)

Margery Hampden to William Stonor, c. 1477

Worshipful Cousin, I recommend me unto you, and I pray you heartily, cousin, to come hither this night or tomorrow betimes, both for the matter of my nephew, and also for the matter that I desired you, as my trust is in you, or as I may do anything to your pleasure, the which to do I would be glad, God knoweth, who have you in his keeping. Yours M. Hampden.

(Stonor Letters, no. 186)

Margaret Stephen's letter to her grandson, Thomas Perrott, is one that has survived in isolation, but like so many others, relates to the ownership of property, to which Thomas was her heir. Letters to grandchildren are rare, since most people died before their grandchildren were adult. The exceptions to this rule were almost invariably women and Margaret Stephen was a member of that small but influential group of long-lived landed dowagers. The relationships referred to in her letter, though obvious to her grandson, are obscure to the modern reader: John Eliott and Thomas Perrott seem to be related in some way, though not through Margaret. The Perrotts of Haroldston were a long-standing Pembrokeshire family, though Margaret herself does not seem to have been one of them; the connection was probably through the marriage of her daughter into the family. Margaret claimed that the manor of Ludchurch, Pembroke, was her own property and did not belong to her husband, and that John Eliott knew this perfectly well, since his grandfather had been her receiver [financial official] for years and had never made any claim upon it. Indeed he had apparently admitted the weakness of his claim to their lord, the Earl of Pembroke. It may be that Eliott hoped that the old lady was senile and could produce no proof of her right, but Margaret, or her attorney, John Okir, was certainly on the ball and she could produce documentary evidence to prove her ownership. The evidence was supported by Walter Devereux, Lord Ferrers, and his brother, who were perhaps more familiar with the situation, since William Herbert, King Edward IV's powerful lieutenant in Wales, had only been advanced to the Earldom of Pembroke a month before.

Margaret Stephen to Thomas Perrott, 27 October (c. 1468)

R ight reverend and worshipful, I recommend me to you, willing heartily to hear of your welfare and certifying you that I have received your letter the which sent with your messenger, the which letter specifieth that John Eliott and ye be in variance of Ludchurch and he [has] taken a distress of the same, the which your nevy [nephew?] have repleved the said distress and saith that your grandsire gave me none estate neither writing. Well it is that his grandsire had never estate in that said livelihood, the estate made unto me was after the custom and law of the country that time being, Sheriff David Perrott of the said shire of Pembroke and I endowed of the same. And not interrupt thereof as you knew well and your father afore you. And John Eliott when he was last with me acknowledged himself that he had wrong being at Hereford with my lord of Pembroke and would yield it up. And also where that Eliott his grandsire was my receiver long time and if his had been the right, he would not receive and account make to mine avail, which account of that years I have of writing of his hand. And I send you at this time one of them to prove the same of my title and right and to embarrass him of his unlawful interruption as the country knoweth well and you shall have credence by mouth by the bearer hereof and I will send unto you my trusty and wellbeloved friend John Okir, mine attorney, soon upon this writing, the which my will was to have it with you afore this time and shall give you credence by another or writing from my lord Ferrers and Master John Devereux, his brother, unto the steward of Pembroke that you be not wronged, as far as I can or may. And as for to say I am not willing at this time to hurt you or your heirs of any title or right or grant to any man otherwise than if your writing and endenture made be fulfilled at the coming of my wellbeloved attorney above rehearsed. And our Lord have you in his keeping.

Written at Hereford the 27th day of October by your granddam Margaret Stephen.

(PRO SC 1/51/104)

When Katherine Chiddiock married Sir John Arundell of Lanherne, Cornwall, Thomas Stonor, Sir Richard Harcourt and Edward Grimston became trustees for a number of manors jointly settled on the couple and their heirs. In her letter to Stonor, the widowed Katherine urged her trustees to implement an agreement already made by them for investing two small Cornish manors in one of her servants or advisors, Richard Tomyowe, to provide him with an agreed income for life. The trustees eventually did as she requested, for Tomyowe was noted as holding the manors in 1481, two years after Dame Katherine's death. She addresses Stonor as 'cousin', but whether they were in fact kin by blood or marriage is unclear; she refers to Harcourt, who was married to her step-daughter, by the same term.

Dame Katherine Arundell to Thomas Stonor, 27 January (?1473)

Right trusty cousin, I commend me to you; and where as it was agreed by you and my council at your being at Dorchester before Christmas that Richard Tomyowe, considering the good service that he has done for my husband and me in days passed and the charges that he must do for me hereafter, should be made sure of lands and tenements to the yearly value of 20 marks. And he is agreed to take two little manors in Cornwall, one called Winnington and the other called Kennall, of the value by year of £12; of the which, I pray you, cousin, to speak to my cousin, Sir Richard Harcourt, and Edward Grimston that between you to seal a deed that William Menwynnek or other Richard Reynolds shall bring you, of the said manors term of his life; for he will proceed no further in my matters unto the time he be made sure of the same, which were to me a great hurt, as you understand. And that this be done as my special trust is in you; and Our Lord have you in his blessed keeping. Written at Exeter the 27th day of January by your cousin Dame Katherine Arundell.

To my right worshipful Cousin, Thomas Stonor, Esquire.

(Stonor Letters, no. 125)

Lucy Prynce was the wife of John Prynce, a servant of Cecily, Duchess of York, and heir to the manor of Theydon Garnon, and its sub-manor, Theydon Gregories, in Essex, but while we know that Prynce had two wives called Lucy – Westbroke and Wrothe – we do not know which of them wrote the following letter. John Prynce was involved in a dispute over the legal ownership of Theydon Gregories. When his rivals, Thomas Withiale and Thomas Averey, found their case did not succeed in the courts, they technically made over their rights to Richard, Duke of Gloucester (Cecily of York's youngest son), Sir Robert Chamberlain, Walter Wretyll and others, and themselves resorted to physical violence. When Prynce attempted to show his title to Gloucester in London he was assaulted and then attacked at the manor on horseback with the aid of twenty men wearing Gloucester's livery. John hid in nearby woods while Lucy defended her home with sharp words rather than blows. She was particularly scathing of the suggestion that if Prynce were to die she could marry Withiale and settle the dispute that way. However, common sense finally prevailed; in 1474 the two antagonists sought help from their patrons in settling the dispute by arbitration. It was brought before their respective councils (see chapter 4) where Cecily's lawyers persuaded her son's council of Prynce's title, but when one of Prynce's advisors in the dispute complained to the duchess that he had not been paid, she also ensured that Prynce settled his debt. The dispute over Theydon is a good example of the practical working of the patron/client relationship, which was a combination of protection and loyalty, coupled with service and respect. The recipient of this letter, Lucy's cousin, Thomas Clifford, was a London scrivener, who acted as her husband's business advisor. Most families preferred to use family connections where possible, since they could then be reasonably sure that their advisors would act in their best interests. Lucy does not specify the urgent business on which she was summoning him, and it is not clear whether it had anything to do with the Theydon dispute, but the reference to Sir Thomas Montgomery, a leading courtier, suggests that it might be. Master Wretyll was Walter Wretyll, a prominent Essex man, who in 1468 was sheriff of the county.

Lucy Prynce to Thomas Clifford, c. 1474

Right worshipful cousin, I recommend me unto you and my cousin your wife, praying you and my Master Wretyll prays you, that you will come a spell with him on Monday next ensuing, for to speak with him and them that will be with him; for you must come in any wise, and not fail. Also you must come, for Sir Thomas

Mongumbere [Montgomery?] has sent letter and bill unto my Master Wretyll. Also, cousin, I pray you send me word when you will have your horse sent to you, on Saturday or else on Sunday, by the bringer of this bill.

No more at this time, but Jesus have you in his keeping. Written at Theydon Garnon, Wednesday last past, in haste. By your own cousin, Lucy Prynce

(Moriarty, pp. 232–3)

The following letter from Agnes Plumpton is an example of countless notes sent from women to friends, relatives or business contacts, simply requesting a visit to discuss some matter that is not named in the note. Thomas Everingham was a younger son of Sir John Everingham of Birkin, near Selby, Yorkshire, and may have been a cleric. It is not clear whether he was indeed a relative of the Plumptons or whether the term 'cousin' was used out of politeness.

Dame Agnes Plumpton to Thomas Everingham, 15 January 1503

Cousin Thomas Everingham, I recommend me unto you, thanking you of your good mind and will at all times, praying you that you will take the labour and pain upon you to come and speak with me betwixt this and Tuesday next, as my special trust is in you; and that you fail not thereof, as I may do for you as much in time to come. No more at this time, but the Trinity keep you. From Plumpton in haste, this St Maurus Day.

By yours at my power, Dame Agnes Plumpton

To Master Thomas Everingham be this bill delivered in haste.

(Plumpton Letters, no. 172)

SIX

'I recommend me to you in my most hearty manner': Women and their patrons, friends and servants

It is hardly surprising that the largest selection of surviving letters are to recipients who were not related to the writer; the same would be equally true today. None of the letters are written for purely social reasons, though social matters might enter one written primarily for business reasons; if social letters were written, then they were not deemed worthy of preservation by their recipients. Because women were so closely associated with their husbands' business affairs, they were familiar with the latters' business contacts and shared their friendships. If a woman's husband was absent and the need to entertain a business contact or social patron arose, then she and their household provided hospitality; in the cases where we have household acounts for widows, then it is clear that they entertained as many men, both lay and clerical, as women. For business convenience, most families who could afford it had town houses, either in London, or, more likely, in the local county town, and women benefitted from the increased sociability of town life. Manors could be isolated from friends and neighbours, whereas in town it was much easier for women to meet their female friends and relax in agreeable company. Many widows therefore chose to live in towns for much of the year rather than remain permanently on their dower manors, while others chose to live within, or close to, a local religious community, which provided like-minded companionship.

The use of patronage and influence was a key factor in the life of the shires. For example, the impartiality of the law was practised more in the breach than in the observance and for a law suit to prosper it was, if not essential, then at least advantageous, to have the ear of one of the leaders of county society. In many cases, expensive legal action could be avoided if patrons mutually agreeable to the parties involved could act as arbitrators. The leaders of county society were also responsible for making recommendations for offices and appointments in the gift of the Crown. In return, such patrons earned status from the number of clients seeking their favour, and the influence those clients could themselves wield lower down the social or political chain. At the end of many letters asking for assistance, the hope was expressed that if there was any service the writer could do the recipient, it would be willingly undertaken. This was not a meaningless gesture but a serious offer that the writer would expect to be taken up. Such interdependence was the bedrock of local society. Most members of the gentry would aim to place their sons or daughters in the households of possible or actual patrons, thus reinforcing or nurturing crucial links. On the death of the Duke of Norfolk who had so harried the Pastons over Caister castle, the Pastons placed John III in the household of the new duke, who was much the same age as John. The family clearly felt that they would benefit from the protection of such a great noble, and that in his train, young John would come into contact with other influential men. A new patron was particularly vital for the Pastons, because the Earl of Oxford, in whose circle they had previously moved, had recently been executed for treason. Marriages within the client circles were common, as were friendships and business associations. It was among this group of friends, neighbours and associates that most of the gentry sought help and support in times of emergency, but sometimes, as Robert Plumpton discovered, when they asked once too often and could give but little back, they were gradually frozen out from local society.

Medieval people were extemely conscious of social status, and their tone and address altered according to their social relationship to the addressee. The letters here have been classified into three groups: those from patrons to clients, those between equals, and those from clients to patrons, and the client/patron relationship has been taken to include servants and household members. It is perhaps inevitable that clients preserved more letters from their patrons than vice versa, and that the exception to this rule was the efficient civil service. While a number of the letters are from widows, others are from wives acting as their husband's partner in business or family affairs, and there is no indication that any less attention was paid to the letters because they came from women. Indeed, Margery Paston quoted her cousin Gurney (a member of the Duke of Norfolk's council) as saying 'if I [Margery] would go to my lady of Norfolk and beseech her good grace to be your good and gracious lady, she would so be; for he said that one word of a woman should do more than the words of twenty men'. Women's networks were as strong and usually as effective as those of their menfolk.

LETTERS FROM PATRONS TO CLIENTS

This anxious letter from Henry II's granddaughter to a number of leading Bretons is part of a sad story. Eleanor and her brother, Arthur, were the children of Geoffrey, third son of Henry II, and his wife, Constance, the heiress of Brittany. Geoffrey predeceased his father, but on the death of his elder brother, Richard I, without children, Arthur, though still a boy, was the senior male heir to the throne of England. Richard I's youngest brother, John, viewed things differently. At this date the rule of primogeniture was not absolutely fixed, and most of the English nobles preferred a resident adult royal male whom they knew, to an unknown foreign child, and John was crowned with virtually no opposition. After he had been on the throne for three years, however, a rebellion in favour of Arthur broke out in the Angevin continental possessions in 1202 and it was supported by King Philip of France. A military victory by John at Mirebeau led to all the leading rebels, including Arthur, being captured. Once in John's hands, Arthur simply disappeared and was never seen again, and before very long rumours were circulating that John had had him murdered.

Arthur, who was born a few days after his father's death, was about fifteen at the time of his capture, and his sister Eleanor two or three years older. Eleanor was also taken into John's custody, though her fate in his hands was different from her brother's. From the time of Arthur's death, whenever that was, she became John's nearest hereditary rival and he could not let her go. She was therefore kept in honourable captivity for the rest of her life until she died in 1241. She was given a generous allowance from the exchequer, the king sent her gifts from time to time and she even spent periods at court, but she was never allowed to marry, nor return to Brittany. Eleanor was recognised as the hereditary duchess when Arthur's fate became well known, and it was in that capacity that she wrote her letter. At the time she was still hoping that arrangements could be made for her release and return to Brittany. Once it was clear that John would never free her, the Bretons ensured that her rights passed to her younger half-sister Alice, daughter of Duchess Constance's second husband. The new duchess was married to a cousin of King Philip, Peter of Dreux, who became *de facto* Duke of Brittany in her right.

Eleanor, Duchess of Brittany, to her subjects in Brittany, 27 May 1208

Eleanor, Duchess of Brittany and Countess of Richmond, to her dear and faithful lords the Bishops of Nantes, Vannes and Cornwall, and to Eudo de Poule and Geoffery Espine and Oliver de Rugy and Pagan de Mal-Estrail, and all her other barons and faithful subjects of Brittany, greeting.

We give you manifold thanks concerning the things of which you have informed us, and earnestly entreat you that you, the above-named, come to England to my lord and uncle the King of England; and know you, certainly, that your advent will, God willing, tend to your and our great honour and convenience, and, by God's grace, to our liberation.

We have spoken with our said uncle about affording you a safe-conduct, and he is glad of your coming, and sends you his letters patent of safe-conduct; and you may all come safely by means of those letters – or as many of you as can, if all cannot come.

Witness myself, at Sarum, the 27th day of May

(Patent roll 10 John; Wood, I, p. 27; Latin)

Eleanor Despenser was the daughter of Gilbert de Clare, Earl of Gloucester and Joan 'of Acre', daughter of Edward I. She was born at Caerphilly Castle in 1292 and was married in 1306 to the younger Hugh Despenser, carrying with her a valuable inheritance of lands on the Welsh Marches and in South Wales. The marriage was one mark of the favour that her uncle, Edward II, showed her new husband and his father, and meant that local officials were eager to retain her support. The years of Edward II's reign saw a lengthy struggle between Despenser and other Marcher lords in order to extend his estates and influence in the area. When the revolt against Edward II led to the death of both Despensers in 1326, Eleanor was initially imprisoned in the Tower, but soon did homage for her lands to the new king, Edward III. Early in 1329 she was abducted from Hanley castle and married by William, Lord Zouche of Ashby. Abduction was not uncommon in the Middle Ages. Sometimes it was a genuine crime, carried out in order to gain possession of a widow's or heiress's estate, but more often was done in collusion with the abductee, when there was some family or political opposition to the match. Eleanor and William were both severely dealt with, which suggests that the king did not regard the abduction as a crime; they spent nearly a year in the Tower and were required to surrender to the king a substantial amount of her lands, which were to be redeemed by the enormous fine of £50,000, to be paid in a single instalment. In the event, when Edward III came of age, this sum was reduced to £5,000, and even that was never paid in full. Eleanor died in 1337 at the age of forty-four. The following letter was written before the deposition of Edward II and her first husband's execution. While the tone is both gracious and friendly, it is clear that the sheriff was expected to act in the Despensers' best interests at all times.

Eleanor Despenser to John Inge, Sheriff of Glamorgan, 6 March 1322

Eleanor Despenser sends greetings and love to our well-loved lord, John Inge, Sheriff of Glamorgan.

Because we know well that you are are always pleased to hear good news from us, we are letting you know that on the writing of these letters we were in good bodily health, thanks be to God, and we always want very much to hear the same of you. And we thank you very much and are very grateful because you are so industrious on our behalf in these parts. And we ask you, as far as we can, that you will aid and help Lessam d'Avesne, bearer of these letters, in the matters he will put to you; may the rights of my dear lord in every way be safe, so that we may be grateful to you. And send us your news in the meanwhile as soon as you can, for love of us.

May the Lord protect you. Written at Canterbury on 6 March.

(PRO SC 1/37/3; Tanquerey, no. 108; French)

Like the previous letter, this is also one charmingly requesting a favour that Eleanor does not expect to be refused. Since she had already taken the precaution of enlisting the aid of the queen, Isabella of France, it is unlikely that the chaplain failed to get whatever preferment his friends were seeking for him. The letter must have been written before the outbreak of war with France in 1324, when the queen was stripped of her possessions and treated as an enemy alien by the Despensers, who were ruling the country through King Edward. In that year, too, John de Stonor, Chief Justice of the Court of Common Pleas, a loyal royal servant, was knighted.

Eleanor Despenser to John Stonor, 7 February (c. 1323–6)

Eleanor le Despenser to our very dear and good friend John de Stonor, Justice of the Bench of our lord the King, greetings and honour. We pray you that when you receive the request of our dearest lady the Queen, you act on her letters for our chaplain, called John de Sadyngton, in as gracious a manner as you know and are able to do for the love of us, so that we may praise you and owe you thanks and gratitude. Because he belongs to those well loved by us, we have his interests much at heart. May our Lord protect you.

Written at Berkeley, the 7th day of February

(Stonor Letters, no. 3; French)

Margaret, the dowager Countess of Devon, was a first cousin of Eleanor Despenser, being the daughter of Humphrey de Bohun, Earl of Hereford and Elizabeth, daughter of Edward I. She married Hugh Courtney, Earl of Devon, in 1325, and the couple had eight sons and nine daughters, before he died in 1377. Only three of their sons had issue and by the time of Hugh's death, their heir and his only son were both dead and the earl was succeeded by the son of their third son, Edward. The manor of Ermington, near Plymouth, had been obtained by Sir John de Stonor and was held by the Stonors from the Earls of Devon. By 1380 it was in the possession of Sir John's grandson, Edmund, who was one of the leading Oxfordshire gentry, serving that county as sheriff, MP and JP. Ermington was one of the Stonors' most valuable manors, but there had been constant disputes with neighbours and difficulties supporting the tenants there, probably in part because it was so far from their main holdings in Oxfordshire. We do not know to what the royal warrant related, but it was clearly not unexpected, and by her letter, Margaret was keeping her promise to warn the Stonors. Margaret was another aristocratic lady who lived to a very old age, being at least eighty when she died in 1391.

Margaret, Countess of Devon, to Edmund Stonor, 13 January 1380

Greetings and good love. Please know that, as we have heard, there is a warrant of the King concerning the manor of Ermyngton; but we do not know for whom or in what name. For this be well-advised and prepared, and allow us to excuse our promise of former times to warn you in case we should hear about such a letter.

Written at Exmere the 13th day of January. The Countess of Devon, the mother.

To our dear and good friend Edmund Stonor

(Stonor Letters, no. 38; French)

Elizabeth Zouche was born a Despenser; she was great granddaughter of Eleanor Despenser. Her father, Sir Edward Despenser, had brought the family back into favour by loyal support to Edward III. Her brother, Thomas, was equally loyal to Richard II, and was created Earl of Gloucester, but lost the earldom and then his life for his continued support of Richard after the usurpation of Henry IV. In about 1384, while in her late teens, Elizabeth was married to John Arundel. He was the son and heir of John, Lord Arundel, but after his father's death in 1379 he was never summoned to Parliament and therefore was not held to be a baron. Elizabeth and John had three sons, but after about six years of marriage, John died of the plague. As a widow with three small children, it is hardly surprising that Elizabeth chose to remarry swiftly. Some time in 1392 she became the second wife of William, Lord Zouche of Harringworth, Northamptonshire, who was much her senior and already had at least seven children by his first wife. In 1396 Lord Zouche died, leaving Elizabeth, by then in her early thirties, a widow for the second time. With a comfortable income from two sets of dower and her sons growing up, she chose to remain a widow for the last twelve years of her life.

In the first of a series of letters to her trusted agent and receiver, John Bore, Elizabeth makes clear that there were tensions between her and her step-son, William, the new Lord Zouche, who was about ten years her junior; he had been angry with one of her officers or servants over a particular tenancy. Broke, the servant involved, is given the title 'Sir' by his mistress, which suggests that he was a cleric. Elizabeth seems to have made her main home at Eaton Bray, Bedfordshire, in which she held a half-share as part of her Zouche dower; Calston, Wiltshire, was another of her Zouche dower manors. Why her stepson wished to see deeds, or 'evidences' relating thereto, is not explained, but Bore is given very explicit instructions to look at the indenture between her and Zouche, and then to be sure and return it and other documents to her at Eaton. The bond between Elizabeth and John Tregoz from 1398 still survives: she agreed to pay him certain sums of money from her manor of Stopeham, Sussex, which was part of her Arundel dower; this was probably for the repayment of debts. That fact that Lord Zouche was requesting members of Elizabeth's council to visit him in London suggests that she was in the habit of consulting him on business affairs, but that does not explain why she should be requesting the release of Chichely and Scot, as Zouche had promised, though it seems to have something to do with the dispute with her servant Broke. The damask cloth that Bore was requested to purchase and present to Zouche was presumably intended as a 'douceur'.

Elizabeth, Lady Zouche, to John Bore, 18 March 1402

Right well beloved friend, I greet you well, and do you to know that the Lord la Zouche was at home with me at Eaton and so I spake to him of Broke and of the tenant also and so he hath raged at Broke right foul for his doing. And so I have spoke to him for Calston and he bid that my council should come and speak with him now at London and show him the evidences that I have thereof and therefore I pray you that you and Chichely will go and see the indenture that is between him and me. And also that you would see the indenture that is between Sir Thomas Yocflet and me of Bechesworth [Betchworth, Surrey?] and the bond that is between John Treygos and me and when you have all with the indentures that you will let put them altogether in the great coffer and send them home to Eaton. Also I pray you that you will go and buy a cloth of damask or two if it needeth of green or red or blue of the latest price and bear it to the good lord and pray him that he will make the release of Chichely and Scot as he behight me now at Eaton. I pray you as I trust you that you not fail me not of his cloth

for truly I would not fail Sir Broke at this time for more than it is
ten times worth. I write at Eaton the 18th day of March.
Elizabeth lady Zouche of Eaton.

[Endorsed in French:] By the commandment of this letter the said
John Bore bought I cloth of blue damask which cost 51s. 8d. and it
was delivered to William Lord la Zouche by the said John Bore. . . .
And also Thomas Scot prisoner of the said lord was delivered and
brought by the said John Bore to the said lady in the batailled
chamber at Eaton on the Sunday before St Philip and Jacob. The
third year of King H.

(PRO E 101/512/10 (2); Payne and Barron, p. 148)

It is clear from the terms in which she writes to him that Elizabeth
Zouche regarded John Bore as a close and trusted friend as well as a
business agent, but he still made every effort to obey her clear and
firm instructions as promptly as possible. Why she needed him to
put her house at Eaton in order is unclear, but she certainly spent
considerable periods of time in London. The particular interest in
the following letter is the request that he purchase some religious
jewellery for her mother, whom she was intending to visit. When
Elizabeth decided to remain a widow the second time, she was
following her mother's example because Elizabeth Despenser, in her
own right baroness Burghersh, had remained a widow since 1375
and in fact outlived her eldest daughter. Thanks to his meticulous
noting of expenses, we know that Bore fulfilled his commission and
Lady Despenser received her expensive gift. The pipe of wine,
presumably for consumption at Eaton, was an impressive 100
gallons.

Elizabeth, Lady Zouche, to John Bore, 31 August 1402

Right well beloved friend, I greet you well, and fain would hear
of your welfare, and I pray you that you will order a leisure
that Frome and you might come hither together and set, I pray, this
house in better governance, for I think to God it is ever longer the
worse; and that you would do it in haste, for I would shape me to

ride to my lady my mother. And also I would pray you that you would have ordered for me a pair of beads of gold for my lady my mother with the quaintest paternoster that you can find, whatsoever they cost; and I also pray you that you would order me a pipe of white wine as I spoke to you of; also I pray you that you will send me word what price a whole cloth of black velvet and as my trust is in you, fail me not, especially of my beads. I can no more but I pray God have you in His keeping. Written at Eaton on St Giles even. E. la Zouche

[Endorsed in French:] There was delivered by the said John Bore to Thomas, Chicheley's man, bearer of this letter, the fifth of September in the third year [of Henry IV] one pipe white wine, which cost 35s.8d.

And for barreling the same, 7d. And for drawing out of the cellar, 12d. And for carriage of the same between the cellar and Smithfield, 12d. And delivered to the said Thomas for his charges, 8d.

Item, sent to my Lady la Zouche by the said bearer one pair of gold beads, weighing one ounce and half.

(PRO E 101/512/10 (4); Payne and Barron, pp. 150–1)

The three following brief notes are from the wife of John Paston I's patron, John de Vere, 12th Earl of Oxford. Elizabeth Howard was a considerable East Anglian heiress and had married the young earl when he was still under age. Much later, the earl and their eldest son, Aubrey, were executed for treason in 1462 after rebelling on behalf of the deposed Henry VI. Their second son, John, who became the 13th earl, inherited both his father's Lancastrian tendencies and the Paston loyalties. Writing with the ease of familiarity and with the assurance that her wishes will be attended to, the countess's notes all concern James Arblaster and his wife Agnes, who seem to have been particular favourites of hers; it is possible that Agnes had been in her service. Arblaster's problems over the manor of Smallbergh in Suffolk were probably the perennial ones of disputed ownership. The letters make clear the rights and obligations of patronage. The countess could request Paston's service on behalf of one of her clients, and know that he would try hard to oblige her, but as she expresses in the third letter, if Paston needed help from her in return, she would supply it. It was presumably Paston's legal expertise she was seeking, and in fact he and Arblaster were already friends. When John died in 1466, Arblaster was one of the executors of his will. The reference to Margaret Gurney's language, which had so displeased the countess, may relate to a dispute the Gurney family had with the Pastons over the manor of Saxthorpe.

Elizabeth, Countess of Oxford, to John Paston, 7 August (c. 1454)

Right trusty and entirely wellbeloved, I greet you well. Praying you as I specially trust you that you will be good friend to James Arblaster in his matter touching the manor of Smallbergh, as I wot well you have ever been to him right especial friend; and though it be so that the said James had great troubles, losses and adversity here before, nevertheless he shall not be so bare of friends nor goods, but that I will see him helped with the mercy of God. In performing whereof the bearer of this shall inform you of my intent and disposition more largely than I will put in writing. And the Trinity have you in his keeping.

Written at Wivenhoe, the 7th day of August. Elizabeth Vere, Countess of Oxford.

(Paston Letters, no. 232)

Elizabeth, Countess of Oxford, to John Paston, 1 February (c. 1454)

Right entirely wellbeloved, I greet you well, and pray you that you will be good friend unto Arblaster in such matters as he shall inform you, and I thank you for the good friendship that you have showed to him. And I sent a letter to Margaret Gurney before Christmas of certain language that I heard, which pleased me nought, and so I prayed my lord to give me leave to write to her; and therefore an you hear anything, answer, as my trust is in you.

Right entirely wellbeloved, the Holy Ghost have you in his keeping. Written in haste the first day of February.

Elizabeth de Vere Oxford

(Paston Letters, no. 233)

Elizabeth, Countess of Oxford, to John Paston, 13 April (c. 1454)

Right entirely well-beloved, I greet you well, thanking you of the great gentleness that you have showed unto my right well-beloved James Arblast, praying you of continuance; and if there be anything that I may do for you, or any of yours, here or in any other place, I pray you let me wit, and I shall be ready to do it, with the grace of God, who have you in his keeping; and I pray you to be friendly unto my right well-beloved Agnes Arblast, which is to me great pleasure and heart's ease, an so you be. Written at Wivenhoe, the 13th day of April.

To my right entirely well-beloved John Paston of Norwich, esquire.

(Paston Letters, no. 234)

This next letter is a much-quoted one, referring as it does to the parliamentary election following the first battle of the Wars of the Roses at St Albans in 1455, when Richard, Duke of York, and his supporters gained the upper hand over a force loyal to King Henry VI. After St Albans the Yorkist party were out to make the most of their new ascendency. This meant ensuring as many of their supporters as possible gained seats in the new parliament. In the fifteenth century, parliamentary elections were managed rather than contested, and the expedients used (illustrated by the Paston Letters) included the recommendation of candidates, the persuasion of rivals to stand down, and the consoling of disappointed shire candidates with borough seats. A contested election meant that this system had broken down. John Mowbray, Duke of Norfolk, was York's nephew on his mother's side, but until 1455 had been politically eclipsed in East Anglia by the

177

power of the court party under the Duke of Suffolk. Now the tables had been turned and his wife, the Duchess Eleanor (see chapter 5), almost certainly wrote a large number of letters to influential men in Norfolk similar to this one to Paston. In Paston's case the letter cannot have been entirely welcome, because he had hoped to be a candidate himself. The two candidates Norfolk wished elected were members of his council: Sir Roger Chamberlain of Gedding, Suffolk, had formerly been chamberlain to Henry V's brother, Duke Humphrey of Gloucester, and in 1447 had been arrested with him, convicted of treason, but pardoned after being partially hanged. He had later become one of Norfolk's men. John Howard was a first cousin of Norfolk's on his mother's side (and was to become duke himself after the Mowbray line died out). Another of Paston's correspondents made it clear that while Chamberlain was acceptable to the Norfolk county community, Howard was not, for the simple reason that all his lands were in Suffolk and he held nothing in Norfolk. When this was put to the duke, he acknowledged the point and wrote to the under-sheriff agreeing to a free election provided that none of the Duke of Suffolk's men were chosen. In the end the community played safe and both Howard and Chamberlain were elected. This letter is a good illustration of wives playing a role in community affairs at the highest level, though doing so only as their husband's deputy.

Eleanor, Duchess of Norfolk, to John Paston, 8 June 1455

Right trusty and well-beloved, we greet you heartily well. And for as much as it is thought right necessary for divers causes that my Lord have at this time in the Parliament such persons as long unto him, and be of his menial servants, wherein we conceive your goodwill and diligence shall be right expedient, we heartily desire and pray you, that at the contemplation of these our letters, as our special trust is in you, you will give and apply your voice unto our right wellbeloved cousin and servants, John Howard and Sir Roger Chamberlain, to be knights of the shire, exhorting all such other as by your wisdom shall now be behoveful, to the good exploit and conclusion of the same.

And in your faithful attendance and true devoir in this party, you shall do unto my Lord and us a singular pleasure, and cause us hereafter to thank you therefore, as you shall hold you right well content and agreed, with the grace of God, who have you ever in his keeping.

Written in Framlingham Castle, the 8th day of June.

(Paston Letters, no. 288)

This letter from the elderly Margaret Paston is a glimpse into the role of the priest in gentry and noble families. The term 'Sir' was a courtesy title given to all priests, but in some contexts can be confusing. The ownership of a private chapel was a considerable status symbol, but even without that, the employment of domestic chaplains was an indication of gentility. Chaplains fulfilled many roles beyond that of priest: secretary, tutor, almoner and often estate manager as well.

James Gloys entered Paston service in the 1440s and may even have come from Mautby with Margaret when she married, and he remained with them until his death, six months or so after this letter was written. He became the friend and confidential agent of both John and Margaret Paston as they came to recognise his business competence, and John made him an executor of his will. In the years after John's death he became even more indispensible to his widow. Margaret's sons hated him and felt he came between them and their mother: John III described him as 'the proud, peevish and evil disposed priest to us all'. Gloys treated the younger Pastons with little respect and constantly criticised them and certainly seems to have stirred up trouble in a singularly unchristian manner. He encouraged Margaret's refusal of money to her eldest son, the head of the house, and when the Bishop of Norwich found in favour of her daughter Margery following her secret marriage to the family bailiff, Richard Calle, it was Gloys whom Margaret sent to tell Margery that she would never be received in her mother's house again. Somehow the impression is given that Gloys relished the task.

179

Yet his loyalty and devotion to Margaret's service cannot be questioned and the length of her letter and the range of subjects indicate the confidence she placed in Gloys.

The primary reason for writing was to instruct Gloys about taking her fourth son, Walter, then aged about seventeen, to Oriel College, Oxford, to start his undergraduate career. The dissatisfaction she expressed in her elder sons was an emotion Gloys had done much to foster, but nothing could be clearer than her affection for Walter. At this stage, there appears to have been the possibility that he would take holy orders, which presumably found favour in Gloys's eyes. In fact, by the time he graduated, Walter was planning a career in the law, which was terminated by his untimely death from the plague almost immediately after he left Oxford. It is a clear indication of Margaret's trust in Gloys, and an interesting light thrown on the formulation of letters, that she asks him to write to Walter in her name. Instead of dictating a letter to her son, she only tells Gloys what she wants said and leaves him to put it on paper. While this would be perfectly understandable in a business letter, it seems a trifle hard on a son.

Margaret also has some interesting things to say about the carriage of goods and letters. Robert, the son of Thomas Hollar of Moulton St Mary, Norfolk, who failed to deliver the expected letters, was to become a fellow student of Walter's and, despite Margaret's disapproval, became a close friend of her son and went on to have a distinguished academic career at Oxford. Lady Calthorpe, to whom Margaret also refers, was the daughter and co-heir of Sir Miles Stapleton and the wife of a distant cousin, Sir William Calthorpe of Burnham Thorpe, Norfolk. She was a good friend of the Pastons. From other references to her, it seems that as well as being an excellent maker of brews and simples, she was a good-looking woman. One of the more significant tasks of a medieval housewife was the creation of natural medicines, and some women became renowned for the efficacy of their cures. Certainly, Margaret hoped that her cousin John Burney's illness could be thus ameliorated, though her comment about him drawing up his will suggests she did not expect a cure in this case. William Pecock was one of the family's senior estate managers, but there is no indication that Margaret used him any less after 1473 despite her comments to Gloys. The letter, though it does not say so, was probably written at Mautby, where, towards the end of her life, Margaret spent most of her time, happy to have withdrawn from city life in Norwich.

Margaret Paston to Sir James Gloys, 18 January 1473

I recommend me to you and thank you heartily of your letters, and diligent labour that you have had in those matters that you have written to me of, and in all other, to my profit and worship, and in especial at this season touching the matter that I sent you the indenture of. You have lighted my heart therein by a pound, for I was in fear that it would not have been done so hastily without danger. And as for the letters that Thomas Hollar's son should have brought me, I see neither him nor the letters that he should have brought; wherefore, I pray you heartily, if it be no dis-ease to you, that you will take the labour to bring Walter there he should be, and to purvey for him that he may be set in good and sad rule. For I were loth to lose him, for I trust to have more joy of him than I have of them that be older; though it be more cost to me to send you forth with him, I hold me pleased, for I know well you shall best purvey for him, and for such things as is necessary to him, than another should do, after mine intent. And as for a horse to lead his gear, methink it were best to purvey one at Cambridge, unless you can get any carriers from thence to Oxford more hastily; and I marvel that the letters come not to me, and whether I may lay the fault to the father or to the son thereof. And I would Walter should be 'copilet' with a better than Hollar's son is, there as he shall be; howbeit I would not that he should make never the less of him, because he is his countryman and neighbour. And also, I pray you, write a letter in my name to Walter, after that you have known mine intent before this to him ward; so that he shall do well, learn well, and be of good rule and disposition, there shall nothing fail him that I may help with, so that it be necessary to him; and bid him that he be not too hasty of taking of orders that should bind him, til that he be of 24 year of age or more, though he be counselled the contrary, for often haste rueth. I will love him better to be a good secular man than a lewd priest.

And I am sore that my cousin Berney is sick, and I pray you give my white wine or any other thing that I have that is in your award, may do him any comfort. I let him have it; for I would be right sorry if anything should come to him but good. And for God's sake advise him to do make his will, if it be not done, and to do well to my cousin his wife, and to my aunt, and to all the gentlemen and gentlewomen there. And as for John Day, and he be dead I would be sorry, for I know not how to come by my money that he owes me; and I purpose that Pecock shall have less to do for me another year than he has had, if I may be better purveyed with your help, for he is for himself but not for me.

And as for any merchants to my corn, I can get none here; therefore I pray you, do you as well therein as you can; also I send you by the bearer hereof the bill of my receipts. And if you go forth with Walter, I pray you come to me as soon as you may after you be come home; and me liketh mine abiding and the country here right well, and I trust when summer comes and fair weather, I shall like it better, for I am cherished here but too well.

And I construe your letter in other matters well enough, whereof I thank you; and if it need not to send forth Walter hastily, I would you might come to me, though you should come upon one day and go again on the next day, than I should come with you in all matters; and I hold best if you have not the letters that Hollar's son should have brought me, that you send Sim over for them this night that I may have them tomorrow, and if you may come yourself, I would be the better pleased.

And I remember that water of mint or water of millefole were good for my cousin Berney to drink, for to make him to brook [able to retain food], and if they send to Dame Elizabeth Calthorpe, there you shall not fail of the one or of both, she has other waters to make folk to brook. God keep you.

Written on Monday next after St Hilary. I have no longer leisure at this time.

(Paston Letters, no. 825)

In another brief missive from a great lady to one of those enjoying her patronage, Alice Chaucer wrote to William Stonor, requesting his immediate attendance on her. Alice was the granddaughter of Geoffrey Chaucer, the poet, while her father, Thomas Chaucer, had amassed considerable riches in royal service. Alice, his only child, was born in about 1404. She was first married as a child to Sir John Philip and widowed before she was eleven. Her next husband was Thomas, Earl of Salisbury, who died in 1428, leaving Alice childless. She married William de la Pole, Duke of Suffolk, in 1430. As one of Henry VI's most powerful ministers, he was extremely unpopular and was murdered in 1450. In his will, he named Alice sole executrix, 'for above all the earth my singular trust is most in her'. In her powerful defence of their lands, she more than justified his faith in her. Alice remained a widow after Suffolk's death, and based herself at her own property of Ewelme in Oxfordshire, where she was responsible for magnificent tombs for herself and her parents; the duke was buried at Wingfield in Suffolk with others of his family. Alice spent many years in the service of Queen Margaret of Anjou and always remained a personal friend; after 1471, when the death of King Henry and Prince Edward removed the queen's political importance, Edward IV handed her over to the lenient custody of the duchess. A few months after Alice's death in May 1475, the queen's ransom was arranged with Louis XI of France and she left England for ever. The Stonors were near neighbours of the de la Poles in Oxfordshire and were linked by the marriage of Duke William's bastard daughter, Jane, to Thomas Stonor (see chapter 3). However graciously her letter was phrased, Alice expected an immediate response to her demand for Stonor's attendence.

Alice, Duchess of Suffolk, to William Stonor, 5 March (?1475)

Right trusty and entirely beloved friend, we greet you well, desiring and praying you, all excuses laid apart, that incontinent this letter seen, you come to us at Ewelme for certain great causes concerning our weal and pleasure, which at your coming you shall understand more plainly; and thereupon you to depart again at your pleasure, so that you fail not herein at this time as our perfect trust is in you; and as in greater case we will be glad to do for you, that knoweth Our Lord who have you ever in governance. Written at Ewelme the 5th day of March. Alice Suffolk

To our right trusty and entirely beloved friend William Stonor

(Stonor Letters, no. 148)

A similarly gracious demand to John Paston III came from Elizabeth, Duchess of Suffolk, sister of Edward IV and Richard III, so however unwelcome the request to give up his accommodation, it is unlikely that he refused her. That her need was urgent is clear from the fact that this is a holograph letter, not one written by a secretary and merely signed by the great lady. The lodging in question was wherever the court happened to be at the time, since outside Westminster, suitable accommodation was always in short supply, but because the letter is not dated, it is impossible to determine where. The lord chamberlain, officially responsible for this element of court life, was Edward IV's close friend, William, Lord Hastings. Elizabeth had been married to John de la Pole, son of Alice Chaucer, in 1460 at the age of sixteen, just before her brother became king. Despite Suffolk's attempts to wrest some of the Fastolf manors from the Pastons, the duchess had been more favourably inclined towards them, particularly after the land disputes were settled.

Elizabeth, Duchess of Suffolk, to John Paston (?1483)

Master Paston, I pray you that it may please you to leave your lodgings for three or four days til I may be purveyed of another, and I shall do as much to your pleasure. For God's sake, say me not nay; and I pray you recommend me to my Lord Chamberlain. Your friend, Elizabeth.

(Paston Letters, no. 993)

In the period of upheaval following Henry VII's usurpation, Francis, Lord Lovel, a friend and supporter of Richard III, who had survived the Battle of Bosworth, led a small rising in the north against Henry. It soon collapsed and he sought refuge in the Lancashire home of a supporter, Sir Thomas Broughton, from whence he escaped to Flanders, but the authorities were worried that he would seek to leave England via East Anglia. The Earl of Oxford, the senior military commander in the kingdom, was away from home, and his countess, Margaret Neville, sister of Warwick the Kingmaker, was exerting his authority locally and requested John Paston III, as sheriff of Norfolk and Suffolk, to ensure that all escape routes were watched. Although she almost certainly knew Paston well, the countess was writing formally, and this was probably one of a number of similar letters she sent out. The letter is made poignant by the fact that Margaret was a sister of Alice Fitzhugh (see below), whose daughter was Lovel's wife, and during her own husband's exile in the 1470s had suffered the disgrace and poverty which was currently afflicting her niece. Lovel had been attainted of treason after Bosworth and stripped of his peerage, hence the use of the term, 'late Lord Lovel'.

Margaret, Countess of Oxford, to John Paston, 19 May 1486

Right trusty and well-beloved, I recommend me to you. And for as much as I am credibly informed that Francis, late Lord Lovel, is now of late resorted into the Isle of Ely, to the intent by all likelihood, to find the ways and means to get him shipping and passage in your coasts, or else to resort again to sanctuary if he can or may.

I therefore heartily desire pray you, and nevertheless, in the King's name, straightly charge you in all goodly haste endeavour yourself that such watch or other means be used and had in the ports, and creeks, and other places where you think necessary by your discretion, to the letting of his said purpose; and that you also use all the ways you can or may by your wisdom, to the taking of the same late Lord Lovel. And what pleasure you may do to the King's Grace in this matter, I am sure, is not to you unknown. And God keep you.

Written at Lavenham, the 19th day of May. Margaret Oxford

(Paston Letters, no. 1009)

John Paston III was in the train of the Earl of Oxford at the Battle of Stoke in 1487 and was knighted in the field. Under the new Tudor regime he remained one of Oxford's most loyal lieutenants in East Anglia, hence the extraordinary mode of address that Countess Margaret used to him a decade or so later in a note requesting a favour; it was the ultimate expression of gracious patronage. The two were, in fact, much of an age.

Margaret, Countess of Oxford, to Sir John Paston, 15 January (c. 1494–8)

To my right trusty and heartily wellbeloved son, Sir John Paston, JP.

Right trusty and heartily wellbeloved son, I recommend me to you and send you God's blessing and mine. And where one John Malpas, mine old servant, bringer hereof, has purchased a writ directed to you and other justices of the peace in the shires of Norfolk and Suffolk, and also to the sheriff of the same, for to put him in possible possession in such certain lands of his according to the King's writ, I pray you therefore heartily and of my blessing charge you that at this my poor request and desire you will put you in your faithful devoir, with other justices associate with you, to see the execution done and performed according to the said writ.

And Almighty God ever more preserve you, mine own dear son.

Written at my lord's castle of Hedingham (Essex), the 15th day of January. Margaret Oxford

(Paston Letters (Davis), no. 837)

Elizabeth, widow of the last Mowbray Duke of Norfolk, was the daughter of John Talbot, Earl of Shrewsbury, and was an old lady at the time she wrote this letter to a number of influential Norfolk men of affairs, including John Paston III. Elizabeth was seeking the help of a group of powerful men on behalf of Thomas Martin, who was in her service. Although she states that Martin and his uncle, Sir Henry Grey, were blood relations to her late husband, it was only very distantly; Grey's grandfather had married Joan, sister of Thomas, Duke of Norfolk, great-grandfather of Elizabeth's husband. Elizabeth was right to be concerned about Thomas's prospects for inheriting his uncle's Norfolk manor of Ketteringham, for when Sir Henry died, soon after the letter was written, it was discovered that, despite the entail, he had left it to trustees for the use of his widow, Jane, and his step-daughter, Anne, wife of Thomas Heveningham.

Elizabeth, Duchess of Norfolk, to Sir William Knyvet, Sir John Paston and others, 14 September ?1496

Right entirely wellbeloved friends, I commend me to you. And for as much as I understand that Sir Harry Grey, that is the very owner and possessor of the manor of Ketringham, is now in great age and, as it is said, of right sickly disposition, and that after his decease the right and title thereof shall of right belong to my right wellbeloved servant, Thomas Martin, and his nephew and heir of blood, and his heir thereof by reason of entails. What the said Sir Harry intends to do therein, I know not, but it runs in report, that he is in purpose to disinherit the said Thomas Martin thereof, contrary to all right and good conscience. In eschewing whereof, I desire and pray you as heartily as I can, that it will please you to be so good masters to the said Thomas as, by your wisdoms and discretion, the said Sir Harry, by you or some of you, may be moved of conscience and of kindness to his blood to have regard to the said right, and not to do anything that should be disherison to his said nephew, and to have the more tender consideration to your motion, for that the said Thomas is to divers of you of kin and alliance, and to many other gentlemen of the shire in like case. And for the consideration that I have, that the said Sir Harry and Thomas his nephew, were of my lord's near blood, whose soul Jesu pardon and assoil, it were too great a pity to see him by disherison to fall to penury and poverty, where by your good exhortation in consideration of the premises and moreover by your wisdoms to be remembered, in the life of the said Sir Harry such inconveniences may be better remedied; wherein you shall not only do an alm's deed, and a great pleasure to God, but also to me for that blood's sake a singular pleasure, and cause me hereafter the rather to consider things that shall concern your reasonable pleasure, with God's grace, Who ever keep you.

At Earl Soham, this 14th day of September.

To my right entirely and wellbeloved friends, Sir William Knyvet, Sir John Paston, Sir Robert Clere, knights, the King's attorney, Philip Calthorpe, Richard Southwell, esquires and to each of them.

(Paston Letters, no. 1061)

Duchess Elizabeth had not asked for help from Paston and his fellows in vain, as her subsequent letter, written about six months later, shows. Paston in particular had been active on Martin's behalf and had reached an agreement with the widow and her trustees that the matter should go to arbitration. This latter was a favoured method of settling disputes because it avoided a costly lawsuit. It also had the advantage of settling matters to the satisaction of both parties rather than the win/lose situation inflicted by the law.

Elizabeth, Duchess of Norfolk, to Sir John Paston, 28 February 1497

To my right well beloved friend, Sir John Paston, knight. I commend me to you, thanking you as heartily as I can for your labour and substantial searching out of Thomas Martin's matter, praying you of continuance, and of your best advice therein, how he shall break the matter so as, by your help and wisdom, a friendly communication may be had, so as the matter may be had in examination by such gentlemen as shall be named with the assent of both parties, such as tender and love the weal of both parties, and also the peace and tranquility of the country, and love to eschew variance

188

and parties in the country, wherein you shall not only do a great pleasure to me, but a great deed of charity for the profit and ease of both parties, and also a pleasure to God, Who have you in his keeping.

At Earl Soham lodge, this 28th day of February.

(Paston Letters, no. 1064)

The following letter is not one that any man in his right mind would have wanted to receive during the reign of Henry VII. Margaret Beaufort, Countess of Richmond and Derby, was the king's mother (by which title she always described herself) and the most powerful woman in the kingdom. She had her son's total confidence and was a tough and determined businesswoman who pursued to the end the rights of her and hers. The letter was about a family matter. William Paston, the successful lawyer brother of John Paston I, had married Anne, daughter of Edmund Beaufort, Duke of Somerset, Margaret's first cousin. The king's mother arranged the marriage of their elder daughter, Mary, to Ralph Neville, son and heir of the Earl of Westmorland, who was in her custody as a guarantee of his father's good behaviour; he had been a close ally of Richard III. Mary died soon afterwards of measles, leaving her two sisters, Elizabeth and Agnes, as their father's co-heirs. William Paston died in November 1496 and named the countess as one of his executors, together with Cardinal Morton, Lord Daubeney and his nephew, Sir Edward Poynings. When he died neither of his two surviving daughters, who were in their teens, was married; as heiresses they were quickly snapped up. The countess may also have had a hand in the marriage of Elizabeth to Sir John Saville and Agnes to Gilbert Talbot. While John Paston III was undoubtedly his uncle's male heir, probably none of William's property was entailed and he had no serious legal claim on it, but it seems unlikely that the letter was addressed to anyone else. Paston probably entered the lands before the girls were married, as the senior male member of the family, but once they were married he had no justification to remain, which was presumably why he had reached an agreement with the countess's representatives; Bray was her receiver-general and senior man of business, while Lovel was a close associate, who was to be named as one of her own executors, and Heydon was the current representaive of an old Lancastrian family in Norfolk. Whatever agreement had been reached, Paston was being slow about fulfilling his side of the bargain. Where the king's mother was concerned, this was not wise.

Margaret, Countess of Richmond, to (?Sir John Paston) (c. 1497–1503)

By the King's Mother

Trusty and right wellbeloved, we greet you well. And where by the means of our trusty and right wellbeloved Sir Reynold Bray, Sir Thomas Lovell and Sir Henry Heydon, knights, there was a full agreement made and concluded, and also put in writing, between our trusty and right wellbeloved Sir John Savile, knight, and Gilbert Talbot, esquire, on the one part, and you on the other, for divers lands which they ought to have in right of their wives, daughters and heirs to William Paston, esquire, their late father deceased, which lands you by mighty power keep and withold from them without any just title, as they affirm; and albeit the said agreement was made by your mind and consent, yet you do not perform the same, to our marvel, if it be so. Wherefore we desire and also counsel you without delay upon the sight hereof now shortly to ride to the court to the said arbitrators, now there being, with whom you shall find your adverse party, or other in their names fully authorised, to abide such final end and conclusion in the premises as shall be consonant with the said agreement, without further troubles or business therein hereafter to be had; and that you will thus do in any wise, so as we be not driven (through your default) to put to our hands for further remedy to be had in the premises.

Given under our signet at our manor of Colly Weston, the 10th day of February.

(Paston Letters, no. 1063)

LETTERS TO EQUALS

The next correspondent, Agatha Mortimer, can be identified as the wife of Hugh de Mortimer of Chelmarsh in Shropshire. There were three or four branches of the Mortimer family which were baronial, but Chelmarsh was not among them. This is somewhat surprising because Agatha was the sixth daughter of William Ferrers, Earl of Derby, and his wife, Sibyl, sister and eventual co-heir of Walter and Anselm, Earls of Pembroke. In 1271 Agatha and her husband were assigned the manor of Cumbe as part of her portion of the inheritance of Earl Walter. Her reference to the royal court makes it clear that she was a woman of social standing, and she addresses the chancellor with confidence that her request will be granted and that Milicent will receive his writ. Hugh Mortimer died in 1275, and as a widow, Agatha held land in Ireland which she visited in 1279; this was probably also part of her Pembroke inheritance. Agatha died in June 1306, and her heir was her son, Henry, who was aged forty and more, so she died an old lady.

Agatha de Mortimer to Walter de Merton, Chancellor, c. 1272–4

To the prudent and discreet lord and her friend if it pleases, most dear lord Walter de Merton, Chancellor of the lord King. Agatha de Mortimer sends greetings with all reverence and honour. Whereas William Milicent of Ludlow, dear in Christ, while he was attending the royal court with me in my service, was disseised of his free tenement, I am led to intreat your discretion, reportedly worthy of full faith, that for my love you should of your grace grant him a writ of the lord King for this reason, so that which he lost less than justly in his absence on my service, he may recover by the gift of your grace mediating justice. You should if you please write back to me your will in all this. Farewell.

(PRO SC 1/7/165; Latin)

The following letter is a simple request by the Countess of Norfolk, in her husband's absence, for royal permission to transport wool overseas. Aline, daughter and heiress of Sir Philip Basset, a leading councillor of Henry III, was the widow of Sir Hugh le Despenser, and had married Roger Bigod, Earl of Norfolk in 1271. In 1272

Edward I began making his way home from the Holy Land, following his accession to the throne, but it was a very leisurely return and during it he spent a year in his French lands. While he was there, probably in early 1274, Bigod went out to visit him, leaving his wife to manage his estates and his affairs at home. Some pressing debts for the cost of his voyage needed to be settled and to do so Aline was applying for a licence to export some wool. This was not normally necessary but a trade dispute with Flanders, the main export market for English wool, had led to a temporary embargo. It was from this embargo that she was seeking a dispensation. On this occasion, the use of her first husband's name is inexplicable, given the much higher social status of her second. On the death of Henry III, Walter Merton, Archdeacon of Bath, was appointed chancellor, and following King Edward's return he was rewarded with the Bishopric of Rochester and replaced by Edward's own chancellor as prince, Robert Burnell. Aline died in 1281 and she and Roger had no children; on her death Roger tried to claim that she had borne him a child in a desperate, and unsuccessful, attempt to hold on to her lands during his lifetime (see introduction).

Aline de Despenser, Countess of Norfolk, to Walter de Merton, Chancellor, c. 1272–4

To her dear and good-willed friend, Walter of Merton, Chancellor of our lord the King of England, Aline le Despenser, Countess of Norfolk, sends greetings of dear friendship.

Know, dear lord, that my husband, the Earl, has ordered his bailiffs to have wool transported abroad to pay for those debts which he has incurred from his passage to meet our lord the king. Which is why, lord, that I ask that you will give us letters patent of safe conduct by land and sea to send abroad the wool, which amounts to thirty sacks or a little more. If it pleases you, lord, to do this at our entreaty, then my lord will be grateful and thankful on his return.

(PRO SC 1/7/84; Tanquerey, no. 10; French)

Like the letter written on behalf of one of her knights (see chapter 5), this letter from Edward I's eldest daughter, Eleanor, and her next sister, Joan (born in Acre while her parents were on Crusade and later married to Gilbert de Clare, Earl of Gloucester), was on behalf of one of their household. Ellen, Lady de Gorges, was the gentlewoman who had charge of the king's children in their infancy, and was probably still with the princesses. She was daughter and co-heir of Sir Ives de Morville, the wife of Sir Ralph Gorges of Wraxall, Somerset, whom she married in about 1255, and the mother of the Ralph de Gorges referred to in the letter. Ellen's husband appears to have gone on crusade with Edward I before he became king, and since he died in 1271, may have met his death in the Holy Land. The dispute that is the subject of the letter almost certainly concerned land in Somerset, but its ramifications are obscure. The Lovel family were lords of Cary, close to Wraxall and the two Johns may have been part of a cadet branch; a John Lovel was a trustee of Maud, the wife of the younger Sir Ralph Gorges. He may well be the Master John Lovel, who was an extremely active royal clerk during Edward I's reign. The Hugh le Despenser named may have been the son of the man of the same name who died at Evesham with Simon de Montfort and forfeited his lands, and whose widow, Aline, married the Earl of Norfolk (see above). If so, the Hugh of the letter went on to become a favourite of Edward II and Earl of Winchester before being hanged as a traitor in 1326. At this date, however, he had not regained his father's forfeited lands. There is no obvious connection with Somerset, since the main Despenser estates were in the Midlands. John de Kirkby, the chancellor, has also appeared before (see chapter 4).

Eleanor and Joan of England to John de Kirkeby, Bishop of Ely, 1286

To the honourable father in God, Monsieur John, by the grace of God, Bishop of Ely, Eleanor and Joanna, daughters to the King of England, send health and true love.

Dear sire, since we understand that peace is not yet made between Monsieur Hugh le Despenser and Monsieur John Lovel the heir, and

Monsieur Ralph de Gorges and Sir John Lovel the bastard, for whom we have aforetime prayed you, we pray and require you again, as earnestly as we can, that you, if you please, will take trouble to keep accord among them. And because we see our good friend, Lady de Gorges, is so ill at ease in her heart that we have great pity for her, and should be most glad if she were alleviated of the great grief of heart that she has on account of the contest that is among them – therefore, dear sire, we pray you, if it please you, that you will make exertions that good peace be made, and that the thing be brought to a good end; and since we know well that you are empowered to adjust the fines of each party, we beg that you will do it, for the love of us. We commend you, dear sire, to God, who keep you, body and soul.

(PRO SC 1/25/94; Everett-Green, vol. 2, p. 300; French)

The next letter is another example of a woman continuing to use the name of her first husband during a second marriage; in this case almost certainly because the property her letter concerns was part of her dower from her first husband. Margaret de Clare was granddaughter of an Earl of Gloucester, but her father was Lord of Thomond in Ireland and her mother a daughter of the Lord Justice of Ireland. Margaret was married to Gilbert d'Umfreville, son and heir of the Earl of Angus. She was widowed in 1303 while still very young and childless and five years later married Bartholomew Badlesmere; she was twenty-two and he was thirty-three. He was a successful royal servant and had been governor of several royal castles before he became steward of Edward II's household and was granted the lordship of Chilham and Leeds castles in Kent in 1318.

Despite the royal favour he enjoyed, Badlesmere joined the baronial opposition to Edward and his favourites, the Despensers, which resulted initially in the exile of the latter. In tackling the opposition, Edward decided to pick them off one by one, and in 1321 the first target was Badlesmere. Before Leeds castle had been granted to him, it had been promised to the queen, and Edward sent Isabella to Leeds to demand hospitality there. Bartholomew was absent, but Margaret refused the queen entry; to have admitted her would have been a form of recognition of her claim to the castle.

With this excuse, Edward beseiged the castle in the summer of 1321, and although it held out until November, Margaret was finally forced to surrender. As a result she was sent to the Tower. Bartholomew was attainted and hung as a traitor a year later, following the defeat of the rebels at the Battle of Boroughbridge.

After her husband's death, Edward released Margaret from the Tower, but sent her to be confined at the London Minories, a convent very popular with aristocratic women, where he paid 2s a day for her keep. She was not allowed to leave there and join her friends until 1324. Although Bartholomew's attainder was not reversed in favour of their fourteen-year-old son, Giles, until 1328, this should not technically have affected Matilda's own inheritance in Ireland, nor her Umfreville dower lands; but Matilda herself had been guilty of treasonable conduct, and when she inherited her family's Irish lands she was still under royal displeasure and the lands remained in royal hands for a year or so. In May 1327 she was granted safe conduct for two years to go to Ireland and later appointed two attorneys for her Irish lands. Even after their lands were restored to them, the Badlesmeres were still in a weak position until Giles came of age; any low ebb of fortune brought legal attacks on a family's property and the common form taken was the writ of 'novel disseisin'. The writ claimed that the plaintiff had been recently disseised or dispossessed of his freehold unjustly and without the judgment of a court. Although the assizes of novel disseisin were heard before justices, a jury answered on the matter of fact. In this instance, Margaret was very wisely seeking the assistance of one of the most senior royal lawyers; Henry de Clyf was the Keeper of the Rolls of Chancery. Margaret died two years later, in 1333, aged forty-six, and Giles, though not quite of age, had livery of all his parents' lands. He died married but childless when he was only twenty-four.

Margaret d'Umfreville to Henry de Clyf, 1331

To the honourable and wise master Henry de Clyf, Margaret d'Umfreville, Lady of Badlesmere, sends very dear greetings as much as we know and are able.

Dear lord, we thank you as earnestly as we can for all the friendship and great help that you always give in answer to our needs, for which we will forever be indebted to you. And because, lord, Piers Russell is issuing an assize of novel disseissin against us over property in Milton and Paston in the county of Northamptonshire, before Robert de Thorpe, Henry de Fenton and Roger de Bakewell, justices of these assizes, we beg, sir, if it pleases you to issue a letter that Thomas de Wympton or Thomas de Bergh may be our legal representatives to win or lose in the abovementioned assize.

May the Holy Spirit watch over you.

(PRO SC 1/36/112; Tanquerey, no. 131; French)

Marie de St Pol was one of the younger daughters of Guy de Chatillon, Count of St Pol, and his wife, Mary of Brittany, granddaughter of Henry III, and was connected to most of the ruling families of northern France. In July 1321 at the age of seventeen she was married to the recently widowed Aymer de Valence, Earl of Pembroke, who was three times her age and her grandmother's first cousin. Aymer's father was a son of Isabella of Angoulême, widow of King John, and her second husband, the Count of La Marche, and he came to England at the invitation of his half-brother, Henry III. Aymer's mother was a co-heiress of the Earldom of Pembroke, and on her death he was created earl. He was an immensely influential figure in English politics: as a soldier, an ambassador and finally as guardian of the realm during Edward II's absence overseas in 1320. In June 1324, three years after he married Marie, he died suddenly while on an embassy to France. At twenty, childless, she was an extremely wealthy widow, with a dower worth approximately £2,000 a year and was thus a great matrimonial catch. Somehow she persuaded the king, perhaps with a financial inducement, to allow her to remain single. For the rest of her long life (she died in 1377) she devoted herself to the memory of her husband and to good works. Early in her widowhood she had considerable trouble over her lands; as one of the executors of Aymer's will she complained that thanks to the ill will of the king's favourites, the Despensers, and their ally Robert Baldock, then chancellor, she was deprived of all her husband's personal possessions which were valued at £20,000 and had been seized to satisfy a non-existent debt to the exchequer.

The background to the transaction outlined in her letter to the chancellor probably relates to Holand lands. Maud Holand and William Zouche were first cousins, Maud being the daughter and co-heiress of Alan, first baron Zouche, while William, who inherited the title, was his nephew. Zouche was a companion in arms of Aymer and both he and Maud's husband, Robert Holand, had been involved in the baronial opposition to Edward II; for this, Holand had been deprived of his lands, and in 1327, at the queen's request, Maud had been granted £65 a year from lands for the support of herself and her children. The Holand lands were granted to Aymer and Marie, and two years later, after both Aymer and Holand were dead (Holand being murdered in 1328 in revenge for an act of treachery), Marie was granted a licence to demise some of the lands, including the castle and manor of Thorpewaterville, to Maud and her young son, Thomas. The sums specified in the transaction are large, and while a recognisance could be set up as a financial penalty to be exacted only if a specified action was not taken, in this case it looks more like a straighforward repurchase of most, if not all, of the Holand lands. The fact that it was made in the presence of the chancellor, Henry Burgersh, Bishop of Lincoln, emphasised its significance and the fact that it was done with royal approval. The reason for the involvement of Ralph, Lord Basset, is unclear, as there is no obvious family connection.

Marie de St Pol, Countess of Pembroke, to Henry Burgersh, Bishop of Lincoln, Chancellor, 1329

To the honourable father in Jesus Christ, Lord Henry by the grace of God, Bishop of Lincoln and Chancellor of England, Marie de St Pol, Countess of Pembroke, Lady of Wexford and Montignac brings all honour and respect.

Dear lord, you will well recall how Lady Maud, who was the wife of my lord Robert de Holand, and my lord William la Zouche of

Harringworth bound themselves to us in £1000 by a recognisance made before you at your residence on the Friday before St Martin last. And the said Maud and my lord Ralph Basset of Drayton for another £1000 by recognisance made before you. Of which £2000 we have received 1000 marks by the hand of the said Maud, of which we have made remission to her; the manner of the payment of the aforesaid 1000 marks is more fully shown. Lord, we beseech that you are willing to allot these 1000 marks to the said Maud, William and Ralph in part payment of the £2000 above written, according to the tenor of the said remission. May Our Lord preserve your soul and body. Written at Denny on the 16th September.

(PRO SC 1/38/203; Jenkinson Archeologia; *French)*

The following letter, which has only recently been published, is an astonishingly vituperative attack on the recipient. It uses vivid imagery drawn from nature and accompanies it with serious threats and accusations. As in so many other cases, it relates to a legal dispute. The occasion was the support given by John Horell, an Essex landowner, to Joan Armburgh's opponents in a lawsuit over property, but since Horell had been brought up and given his start in life by Joan's mother, Ellen Brokholes, she had expected him to remain loyal to her and his defection was bitterly felt. Part of Horell's betrayal was to prevent the proper execution of Ellen's will. The inability to execute the last wishes of a testator was a dereliction of duty which usually caused acute distress to the family and executors.

The estates in Essex, Hertfordshire and Warwickshire came into the family of Brokholes through the marriage of Ellen Roos to Geoffrey Brokholes. The couple had two daughters who became co-heiresses. At the time of Ellen's death, her elder daughter, Margery, the wife of John Sumpter, was already dead; so, too, were Margery's only son and her two daughters. Ellen's second daughter, Joan, married first Philip Kedington, by whom she had two children (see chapter 1), then Thomas Aspall, and finally, Robert Armburgh, a younger son who seems to have had little property of his own. Joan and Robert assumed that on Ellen's death the estates would descend in total to Joan in default of heirs to Margery. They were therefore dismayed and angry to discover that John Sumpter was claiming that he and his wife Margery's two daughters were still living and had a right to their mother's half share. Joan was sure that the girls were in fact Sumpter's two illigitimate daughters and not Margery's children at all. Unfortunately, the county escheators, carrying out Ellen's *Inquisition post mortem*, found for the girls, largely, according to the Armburghs, because of the influence Sumpter and his friends were able to bring to bear. In the years of legal wrangling that followed, the Armburghs sought to obtain their own influential friends (see chapter 5).

Joan Armburgh to John Horell, c. 1429–30

Bare friend in such manner wise as you have deserved, I greet you. For as much as it is not unknown to you and openly known in all the country, that your chief making has been through the manor of Radwinter, first by my lady mother's day and since in my time and notwithstanding that you, as a cuckoobird devouring the hedgesparrow when she hath bred him up and as an unkind bird that fouls his own nest, have laboured from that time unto this with my adversary John Sumpter and with them that have wedded his two bastard daughters, noising them all about the country for sisters and right heirs, there as you know well the contrary is true, so far forth that you as the devil's child, father of falsehood, whose kind is always to do evil against good, has forsworn the divers times before escheators and justices to give the country false information that should pass between us in disinheriting of me and of my heirs of the moiety of the mother's inheritance in all that ever in you is, the which with the grace of God shall never lie in your power nor in no worthless fellows that have wedded those false bastards. And besides this you have stirred mine adversaries to do strip and waste within my ground and to throw down my hedges and woods and especially the timber that groweth about in the garden, the which grieves me more than all the wrongs that they have done to me to this time, and have counselled them not to leave so much standing as pear trees nor apple trees nor any manner of trees that bear fruit and have a rejoicing in your heart to see the place at the utmost devoured and destroyed. In so much that when you sit in taverns among your fellows you have a common byword in manner as a false prophet, saying that you hope to see the day that a hare sits upon the hearthstone of Radwinter hall, but I trust to God ere that manor that has been a habitation and dwelling place for many a worthy man of my ancestors from the Conquest to this time, and a long time before, be so desolate as you desire, that you will see my husband set up a pair of gallows within the same franchise for your neck, for those you curry be more able to dwell upon a bond tenement as their kin asks, not upon a real lordship, the which well shows by the destruction that they have done in the said manor, leaving not a stick standing upon the ground; I thank God I am strong enough to buy timber for a pair of gallows to hang you upon, and that you have well deserved it by the same token that you robbed two women of Sampford, which is well known, of the which, one of them you set upon a tree and that other you lay with against her will in the porter's house within the manor of Radwinter, for she should discover you.

Wherefore I trust to God that he will vouchsafe to give me power to serve you as the eagle serves his birds which he finds unkind and that will smite the dam with the bill and contrary to his own kind, for when an eagle has kept up his birds til they be somewhat mighty of themselves, he dresses their heads even against the sun when it shines most bright and such as have been found kind to the dam and that look warily in the sun without any twinkling or blenching of their eye as their kind asks, he breeds them up until they be mighty enough of themselves to fly where they choose. And such as he has found unkind to the dam and that may not look against the sun without twinkling of their eye, as their kind would, he draws them out of his nest and throws them against the ground and breaks their necks. This eagle in holy writ is likened to Christ who is father and mother to all Christian people. These birds are likened to the people here on earth, who ought all to be his children, the sun is likened to righteousness and truth and, like the eagle serves his unkind birds in manner and form as it is before rehearsed, right so the good Lord shall serve the unkind children of this world that will not look in the sun of righteousness nor go in the way of his commandments but rob and riven and do extortions and deprive men of their goods, their livelihoods and their lives with false fore swearing, he shall shorten their days and draw them out of their nests that they have been brought up in, that is for to say out of this world and throw them into the pit of hell. And therefore by leave of that good Lord I take example of the eagle and for as much as you are like the eagle's bird that may not behold in the sun of righteousness, that is to say that you have made yourself blind through bribery and mead [mede?] that you have taken from my adversaries and will not know the truth, but like an unkind bird have fouled the nest you were bred up in of a knave of a nought, that is to say, you have counselled my adversaries to distrain the manor of Radwinter as within rehearsed, the which manor was the cause of your trust and like a false cuckoobird you have laboured to devour your dam, that is to say, my mother and me, who have been mothers of your trust and your bringers up. For anon after the death of my mother you stole away the moveable goods from Radwinter, that is to say, 'nete' and sheep and swine and household goods that should have been sold by her executors and used for her soul, and afterwards you had the management of Radwinter and Thycko and had as much of my goods as drew to the value of xl marks and falsely feigned general acquittance under my husband's seal and would never cease from that time to this with your false records, in hope to have disinherited me of my livelihood. And therefore I give you my word that it shall not be long, though it costs me £40, but that I shall get me a judge to sit under commission on the franchise of Radwinter as I may and, if law will serve, with the grace of God you will be pulled out of the nest that you have gotten in your trust and laboured so sorely to destroy, and made to break your neck on a pair of gallows. I can say no more at this time, but I pray God send you what you have deserved, that is to say, a rope and a ladder.

(Chetham Mun.E.6.10(4); The Armburgh Papers, pp. 120–3)

While the lesser gentry operated a network of friends and neighbours within a few miles radius of their homes, families with estates scattered more widely around the country had a more extensive range of neighbours and well-wishers. This is illustrated by a letter written by Alice, Lady Sudeley. She was the daughter of Sir John Beauchamp of Powick, Worcestershire, and in about 1385 married Thomas Boteler of Sudeley, Gloucestershire. He died in 1398 and she retained Sudeley as part of her dower, as well as holding two Warwickshire manors. A few years later, but before 1406, she took as her second husband, Sir John Dalyngrygg of Bodiam, Sussex, who also predeceased her. Alice therefore held widely dispersed property in Gloucestershire, Warwickshire and Sussex. At some point she wrote to Thomas Stonor as one of her feoffees, asking him to seal the necessary deeds for a resettlement of her estates, either because some of the feoffees needed to be replaced, or possibly following the death of one of her sons. She and Thomas Boteler had at least three sons; the eldest, John, died in about 1410 unmarried, his next brother William, died in 1417, childless, and it was the youngest, Ralph, who finally became his parents' heir and Lord Sudeley. How Alice became acquainted with the elder Thomas Stonor, we do not know, but although he was a prominent member of the Oxfordshire gentry, he had estates in Gloucestershire as well, so she probably met him while married to her first husband, a point underlined by her use of her first husband's name in the letter to him, despite her subsequent remarriage.

Alice, Lady Sudeley, to Thomas Stonor, 4 April (c. 1420s)

Right trusty and entirely well beloved friend, I commend me unto you; and whereas I, of singular trust in you, have enfeoffed you with others in my manors, lands and tenements within divers shires, will and heartily pray you, for great considerations and causes touching my worship and great profit, that you seal the deeds, made in your name and others, of the said manors to such persons as be named in the same, which said deeds the bearer of this shall show unto you, as my full trust is and hath been unto you, like as this bearer shall inform you: to whom I pray you give credence. And, sir, if there be anything that I may do for you in any matter in time coming, I will do it with all my heart, and that knoweth God, who have you in his blessed keeping. Written at Sudeley the 4th day of April, Alice, Lady Sudeley.

To the worshipful and my trusty friend Thomas Stonor

(Stonor Letters, no. 53)

The next letter harks back to the marriage of John Paston I and Margaret Mautby in 1440 (see chapter 3). The writer was Margaret's grandmother, whose son, John Mautby, Margaret's father, had died a decade or so previously. Eleanor Mautby was herself an heiress and held the manor of Sparham in her own right. At the time the marriage was arranged between Justice William Paston and Margaret's family, it was acknowledged that Sparham would, on Eleanor's death, form part of the bride's inheritance. This agreement was complicated when Eleanor contracted a second marriage, to Thomas Chamber, probably early in 1442. It appears from the letter that the newly married Chambers had agreed to pay the young Pastons an annuity from Sparham until such time as Margaret inherited. All that was needed was the formal legal agreement to the arrangement by Justice William.

Eleanor Chamber to William Paston, *November* c. 1442

Right worshipful and reverend sir, I recommend me unto you and thank you of your great labour that you had to me at Sparham the last time that we spake together. And for as much, sir, as you had no leisure at that time you desired I should send to you now after this Hallowmass, and there you said you should have better leisure and granted me fully that you should order that I should have lawful estate term of my life in the departison that was granted between you and me heretofore such that was there for my husband and for me at that time; praying you that it may be done now and delivered to my brother John Chamber or to John Cook our servant, bringer of this letter.

And, good sir, that this may be done in as goodly haste as you may, as my trust is in you, for they have not long leisure here for other occupations that they must have of ours; and also, sir, I send you here by him the deed of annuity sealed under my husband's signet and mine that I must pay yearly to your children. And therefore I pray you that they may be delivered under scripture and your seal, like as they shall deliver you that belonging to us; for I trust to God all that ever we made you promise on our part it is and shall be performed, and therefore I pray you, as our trust is fully in you, that you will perform the promise that you said to me that belonged to your part.

No more I write at this time, but the Holy Blessed Trinity have you in His keeping body and soul. Written at Welouby [Willowby?] on Sunday after St Martin's Day. Your Eleanor Chamber

(Paston Letters (Davis), no. 426)

Alice Ogard was probably not related by blood to John Paston (the title 'cousin' is used here as a courtesy), and it was as a lawyer that she had need of his services. John Radcliffe was almost certainly her cousin by blood, for the two were contesting the right to present a priest to the parish church at Attleborough. This right, referred to as the 'advowson', usually belonged to the lordship of the appropriate manor, in this case Attleborough. Alice was the widow of Sir Andrew Ogard of Bokenham Castle, while her cousin, John Radcliffe, was actually Lord Fitzwalter in right of his heiress wife, Margaret; he was killed at the Battle of Ferrybridge in 1461. Alice was unable to attend the ecclesiastical hearing to determine the legal ownership of the advowson, so her advisers were very anxious that she obtain Paston's services. With or without his services, she won her case, for Thomas Fairclowe was presented to the church in August of 1456, with Dame Alice as his patron.

Dame Alice Ogard to John Paston, 30 March 1456

R ight worshipful and entirely beloved cousin, I commend me to you heartily; letting you know that there is a controversy moved betwixt my cousin John Radcliffe of Attleborough and me for the advowson of the church of Attleborough, the which is now void, whereof the title is mine verily as God knows, the which shall be opened unto you; and upon Thursday next at Wymondham, there shall be taken an enquiry *de jure patronatus* before Master Robert Popy and Master Simon Thornham, at which day I may not be myself as God knows, and though I might, it were not convenient.

And therefore, right trusty cousin, considering I am a widow impotent as of body, tenderly and heartily I pray you, if it like you, to be there assisting my council in my right as reason and law will, upon Thursday next, by 8 of the clock; and Fincham, Spelman and others of my council shall be then there waiting upon you. And, gentle cousin, have me excused though I write thus briefly and homely to you, for in truth I do it of a singular trust and affection which I have in you, considering the good name and fame of truth, wisdom and good conduct, the which I hear of you. And therefore, and you may to your well, I beseech you heartily to be there, and you shall nought lose thereby with the grace of Almighty Jesu, the which ever preserve and promote you, gentle cousin, in much worship to your heart's ease.

At Bokenham Castle, on Tuesday in Pascal week, in haste. D.A. Ogard.

(Paston Letters, no. 327)

The following letter is well known and was written a few weeks after the Battle of Bosworth. Although the Countess of Surrey and John Paston were not, strictly speaking, social equals, the circumstances of the letter and the fact that she knew him well, meant that she addressed him as a friend from whom she could seek help. Elizabeth Tylney of Ashwellthorpe was an East Anglian heiress and was first the wife of Sir Humphrey Bourchier, son and heir of

Lord Berners. Bourchier was killed in 1471 at the Battle of Barnet, fighting on the Yorkist side. John Paston III was eager to marry the widowed Elizabeth, but in April 1472 he wrote to his brother, Sir John, 'this day . . . my lady and yours, Dame Elizabeth Bourchier is wedded to Lord Howard's son and heir'. John, Lord Howard, was an influential royal servant and one of the most powerful men in East Anglia under the Yorkist kings. Elizabeth would have been a good match indeed for the younger Paston, but Thomas Howard, as heir to a baron, could have done better. Although Elizabeth was an heiress, she had a son by Bourchier who would inherit her lands on her death, as well as the Berners title and estates, so Thomas would hold her property only during her lifetime. Since he had been badly wounded in the battle that killed her husband and probably knew Elizabeth personally, some degree of personal preference may have been at work here. The Howards made the best of it by marrying her son John, the future Lord Berners, to Thomas's young half-sister, Catherine Howard. When Thomas's father, as co-heir to the Mowbrays, was made Duke of Norfolk by Richard III, Thomas was granted the courtesy title of Earl of Surrey. At Bosworth, the duke was killed and Thomas, who survived, ended in the Tower under attainder.

Immediately after the battle Elizabeth had taken refuge in the nunnery at Minster with her young children, but the Surrey family home at Ashwellthorpe was part of her own inheritance and thus not included in the Howard attainder and confiscation. Once the political dust had settled, she wanted to return home, so it was at this juncture that Elizabeth wrote to her former suitor for help in lending her the horses she needed for the journey. She then heard that at Ashwellthorpe Lord Fitzwalter had been overzealous on behalf of the new king, Henry VII, and dismissed her husband's servants. John Radcliffe, Lord Fitzwalter (son of the man referred to in the previous letter), was a personal friend of Paston's, so she wrote to Paston again asking him to intercede with Fitzwalter, and more importantly, with the Earl of Oxford, on the subject. Although Oxford and the Howards fought on different sides during the Wars of the Roses, they were cousins and seemed to have remained on good terms when politics permitted. Elizabeth's father-in-law, Lord Howard, had helped Oxford's wife when her husband was in exile, and in turn Oxford had clearly promised to protect Elizabeth. Since Oxford had suddenly become one of the most powerful men in the country under the new king, it was unlikely that Fitzwalter would stand out against him. The Earl of Surrey, by loyal service, gradually worked his way back into royal favour, and in 1514, after winning the Battle of Flodden against the Scots, he was granted his father's dukedom.

Elizabeth's letter is beautifully phrased and is likely to have been her own composition; it is also socially interesting in its comment that even as a lone woman, living quietly in disgrace with her children, a countess would expect to have a dozen men in her household. From her reference to Paston's wife and more particularly to his mother-in-law, it is clear that she knew the family well. It is also clear that Paston stood well with the new regime and was in favour at court, for he had been made sheriff of Norfolk and Suffolk, a key post at that particular political juncture.

Elizabeth, Countess of Surrey, to John Paston, 3 October 1485

My right worshipful cousin, I recommend me heartily to you, thanking you of your great kindness and loving disposition towards my lord and me at all times, which I pray God I may live to see the acquittal thereof to your pleasure, praying you of your good continuance.

Cousin, I showed you my mind that I would have my children at Thorpe, wherein, God yield you, it pleased you to say that I should have horse of you to help convey them thither; but now I understand my lord Fitzwalter hath discharged my lord's servants thence, affirming upon them that they should have had unfitting language of the King's grace. Cousin, I trust that you and all the gentlemen of the shire, which have had knowledge of my lord's servants can say that heretofore they have not been of that disposition to be lavish with their tongues when they had more cause of boldness than they have now. I would not have thought my lord Fitzwalter would have taken so much displeasure for the keeping of 10 or 12 men at Thorpe; I know well there exceeds not 3 messes, good or bad [a mess here means four servants who ate together]. I trust, although I were a sole woman, to maintain so many at least, whatsoever I did more.

I trusted to have found my lord Fitzwalter a better lord to me, saying when I was with my lord of Oxford, upon my desire and request at that time made unto him, he promised to be a good lord to my lord and me, whereof I pray you to put him in remembrance, trusting it be the means of you to find him better lord to me hereafter.

I have found my lord of Oxford singular very good and kind lord to my lord and me, and steadfast in his promise, whereby he has won my lord's service as long as he liveth, and me to be true bedewoman term of my life; for him I dread most and as yet as hitherto I find him best. I pray you, good cousin, the rather by your means, that I may have the continuance of his good lordship, and to my poor power I trust to deserve it. I pray you, cousin, that this bill may recommend me to my lady Brews and to my cousin, your wife.

From Minster, in the Isle of Sheppey, the 3rd day of October. I pray you give credence to the bearer of this and to Thomas Jenney, when he comes to you.

Your faithful cousin, E Surrey.

(Paston Letters, no. 1004)

Like the previous letter from the Countess of Surrey, this letter from Alice, Lady Fitzhugh, was seeking help from an old acquaintance at a time of family disaster following the Battle of Bosworth. Alice was the daughter of Richard Neville, Earl of Salisbury, and was thus a sister of Warwick the Kingmaker and Margaret, Countess of Oxford, and a cousin of Edward IV. She married Henry, Lord Fitzhugh, at some point in the 1450s. When Henry died in 1472, their son Richard was under age and Alice was given custody of all their lands during his minority. The letter, however, concerns her daughter, Anne. During her father's lifetime, and before 1470, Anne had been matched in her teens to the equally young Francis, Lord Lovel, who at the time was her uncle Warwick's ward. Lovel prospered under the Yorkist kings, and was raised to the status of viscount in 1482. He was particularly close to Richard III, who made him chamberlain of his household. He fought at Bosworth but, unlike his master, escaped with his life and took sanctuary in Colchester Abbey before moving on to Yorkshire and raising a small force, which nearly captured Henry VII at York in April 1486.

At the time Alice wrote to John Paston, Lovel was on the run in the north, but no one other than his closest confederates knew where (see above pp. 184–5). Sir Edward Frank, who went north to enquire about him was himself from Richmondshire. Anne Lovel had clearly been in touch with Paston, who was sheriff of Norfolk and Suffolk that year, seeking his influence over a pardon for her husband, who was under attainder with all his honours and possessions forfeit, and frantic because she could get no news of him. Alice was writing in support of her daughter's plea, probably because Paston had been acting on her behalf in a business capacity, though what the 'bargain' he had made for her was, is unknown. Alice makes it clear that she is short of money and could not afford to pay for it before her midsummer rents came in. William Capell was a wealthy London draper, who had been knighted, but whether Alice's payment to him was for a purchase or repayment of a loan is not clear. Her statement that she could not leave her daughter is a vivid expression of maternal concern for an adult child in trouble. The fact that Alice uses the terms 'son' and 'mother' in relation to herself and Paston is an indication that she knew him well and placed great reliance on him.

To complete the story, Francis Lovel fled from the north to Richard III's sister, Margaret, Duchess of Burgundy, and was subsequently sent by her, with a small force, to Ireland to support the cause of the pretender, Lambert Simnel. After defeat at the subsequent Battle of Stoke, in 1487, which turned out to be the final one in the Wars of the Roses, Lovel simply disappeared. His subsequent fate was never discovered, but it meant that with his estates confiscated and with no proof that she was a widow and

209

thus entitled to dower, Anne Lovel was left virtually destitute until the Crown granted her a small pension of £20 a year in 1489.

Alice, Lady Fitzhugh, to John Paston, 24 February (?1486)

John Paston, I recommend me to you in my most hearty manner. And where I understand by my daughter Lovel, you desire to know whether I will have the bargain you made for me at Norwich or nay, and if I will, I must content therefore now in marks. Son, in good faith it is so, I shall receive no money of the revenues of my livelihood before midsummer; also I have paid according to my promise to Sir William Capell a great payment, the which you know well was due to be paid, so that I cannot be of power to content therefore, for the which I am right sorry, for I know well that I shall never have such a bargain.

Also my daughter Lovel maketh great suit and labour for my son her husband. Sir Edward Frank has been in the north to enquire for him; he is come again and cannot understand where he is. Wherefore her benevolers willeth her to continue her suit and labour; and so I cannot depart or leave her as you know well; and if I might be there, I would be full glad, as knoweth our Lord God, Who have you in His blessed keeping.

From London, the 24th day of February. Your loving mother, Alice, Lady Fitzhugh.

(Paston Letters, no. 1008)

This next letter, while written by a woman living in the country, relates to urban property in Taunton, Somerset. Many members of the gentry owned property in local towns, and either received rents for it or made use of it themselves, and a considerable number of widows chose to move into town for the company as they got older. Little is known of Joan Trowe or her husband, John, who held the manor of Playnefield, but at the time of writing Joan was newly widowed, and she herself died in September 1496. The letter is written in a less assured style than many and suggests that she or her

210

amanuensis were not customary letter writers and, therefore, that they were probably at the lower end of the gentry scale. John Porter was a lawyer and a JP in Somerset, and for his enlightenment, Joan launches into the history of a house in Taunton High Street that she and her late husband owned and of which Porter was a trustee. In a period before land registration, owners needed to ensure the safety of their title deeds and hold in their heads the legal history of both their own property and that of their neighbours. Other land and property in Ashill, Somerset seems to have been the subject of disputed ownership, which left the Trowes, apparently, only as tenants. Joan, newly widowed, was hoping that Porter would handle all the legal difficulties for her. Less than a year after Joan's death, the family lost Playnefield and their other lands in Somerset when her son, Thomas, was attainted for his involvement in the south-west rebellion against Henry VII in favour of Perkin Warbeck.

Joan Trowe to John Porter, c. 1495

Right worshipful sir, I recommend me to you. Please it you to wit as for a burgage and a toft with a curtillage set in Taunton beside the east gate there in the south part of the high street with the appurtenances, the case thereof is such that one Robert . . . man was thereof seized in his demesne as of fee. And of such estate died seized thereof without heir of his body, which after whose death one William Hastings as cousin and heir of the same Robert, that is to wit, son of William, son of Isabel, sister of the said Robert, entered in and thereof was seized in his demesne as of fee, and of such estate thereof died seized without heir of his body, and after whose death one John Hastings, clerk, as brother and heir of the said William entered and thereof was seized in his demesne as of fee. And so seized thereof, enfeoffed John Trowe, late mine husband, on whose soul I beseech Almighty God to have pity and mercy, to have it to him and his heirs forever; by virute of the which enfeoffment he was thereof seized in his demesne as of fee. And so seized thereof, enfeoffed you and others in fee by his deed indicted of great trust as more plainly shall appear unto you by the same. By virtue of the which you and your co-feoffees certified in the same and were thereof . . . seized . . . by John Bishop of Taunton. Sithens the death of mine said husband and the which deed endented I have sent to you now by the bearer hereof. Not only for this matter, but as well to the intent that it may please you to know Henry Hull, esquire, for as much as he hath entered upon you and others contained in the same deed, pretending certain lands and tenements in Ashill specified in the same deed to be hold of him by knight's service as in right of Alice, his wife. Whereof he submitteth my said husband to die his tenant and contrary to the said feoffment. Upon the which there was due livery and seisin had and made long to for his death as is openly known. And if the said Henry submit that mine husband is tenant in Ashill attorned not by virtue of the said feoffment and the case thereof is such they had been tenants at will nor never had other estate and for as much as there was due livery had in other places in the same shire in name of all, I remit it to your wisdom, beseeching you right heartily to tender this matter for me now in my poor widowhood, considering the great faith and trust my husband had in you. And also that it may like you to entitle on the backside hereof such answer as either of the said John Bishop or Henry Hull make hereto, and send it unto me by my servant, bearer hereof, at the reverence of God and in the way of charity, whom I beseech to have you ever in governance. From Playnefield, the 25th July. Your bedewoman and widow, Joan Trowe.

To my right worshipful and heartily well beloved John Porter of Somerton.

(PRO SC 1/44/90)

The following letter from Elizabeth de la Pole to Sir Robert Plumpton must stand for thousands of others written by women, expressing affection and support to a member of their network at a time of particular trouble. Sir Robert's daughter, Anne, had recently married Elizabeth's young grandson, German. The de la Pole family came from Radbourne, Derbyshire, and Elizabeth's husband, Ralph, had been an extremely successful lawyer and administrator in royal service. When he died in 1492, their son, John, was already dead and his heir was therefore his grandson. Elizabeth administered German's estate until he came of age in 1504, in partnership with her younger son, Thomas, and when German married Anne Plumpton in 1499 at the age of sixteen, they lived at Radbourne in Elizabeth's household.

The lack of precision used by medieval women to describe their relatives is illustrated here by Elizabeth's descripton of German as her nephew. The second half of her letter, concerned with the payment of money towards Anne's jointure shows her to be determined and businesslike. The sympathy she felt towards Plumpton over the entry of the powerful and unpopular Sir Richard Empson into his tangled legal affairs is vigorously expressed.

Dame Elizabeth de la Pole to Sir Robert Plumpton, 26 November 1501

R ight reverend and worshipful and my singular good master, in the most humble and lowly manner that I can, I recommend me unto you and unto my good lady your wife, desiring to have knowledge of your prosperous health, worship and welfare, which I beseech Almighty Jesus long to continue, to his pleasure and your most comfort. Heartily beseeching the good Lord that redeemed me and all mankind upon the holy Cross, that he will, of his benign mercy vouchsafe to be your helper and give you power to resist and withstand the utter and malicious emnity and false craft of Master Empson and such other your adversaries, which, as all the great part of England knows, has done to you and yours the most injury and wrong that ever was done, or wrought, to any man of worship in this land of peace; and no more sorry, therefore, than I myself is. If it were, or might be, in my poor power to remedy the matter, or any parcel of the matter, in any manner, condition or deed, and whereas I may do no more, my daily [prayers] shall be and have been ever ready, with the prayers of Jesus.

And where it is so that I am bounden to pay to your mastership, or to your assigns, certain money by year to the sum of £10, at two times, for such lands as be assigned in jointure to my nephew,

German, and my cousin, his wife and your daughter, I have delivered and paid to his hands for this last past Martinmas rent, £5, trusting that your mastership is contented therewith. What part, or how much thereof, my said nephew, German, hath sent to your mastership, I am ignorant, saving that he showed me that he sendeth you but £10 towards the exhibitions of my niece, his wife. I required you, as my singular trust is in you, to send me a quittance for my discharge for the payment of this said £5; and moreover I beseech you send me word in writing, by the bringer hereof, how I shall pay my rent from henceforward, and to whom I shall pay it. And it pleaseth you, by your own writing to command me, I shall be ready to perform it by the grace of Jesus, who ever preserve your good mastership. Written at Radbourne, in haste, the morrow after St Katherine's Day. Your true and faithful bedewoman to her power, Elizabeth de la Pole.

To the right worshipful my singular good master Sir Robert Plumpton, knight this letter be delivered in haste.

(Plumpton Letters, no. 159)

Elizabeth's earlier letter is followed by one written at the time her grandson came of age. In it she discusses the problem many widows had to face: leaving their family home to the next generation and finding somewhere new to live. Elizabeth's decision had been postponed during her grandson's minority, and it would appear that German and his wife, with the support of other family and friends, were suggesting that she should remain with them. In the letter, however, she told Sir Robert that she had decided to make other arrangements. She seems to have taken the decision partly because she was tired of running the family estates, but also because her younger son Thomas's affairs were in a mess, and she could best help him financially by living very quietly. The choice of a house or lodging within a religious community was one that many pious older widows made, although they stopped short of actually taking the veil. The religious house chosen was usually a local one and did not need to be a nunnery. Elizabeth had decided to rent a house from the friars in her local town of Derby.

Henry Arden, entrusted with handing over legal documents from Elizabeth to Sir Robert, later went on to marry Sir Robert's daughter, Eleanor.

Dame Elizabeth de la Pole to Sir Robert Plumpton, 10 July (?1504)

Right worshipful and my singular good master, in the most humble and lowly manner that I can or may, I humbly recommend me unto your good mastership and unto my good lady your wife, desiring heartily to hear of your welfare, and also of your good speed in your weighty and great matters, which I have prayed for, and shall do daily. Sir, I received a letter from you which bear date the 8th day of June, and in that letter you wrote to me that it was my son German's mind and yours, with others his friends, that I should occupy still at Radbourne, as I have done in times, as long as we can agree, upon condition that I would be as kind to my said son German as he intends to be to me. I pray Jesus that I may find him kind to me, for it is my full intent and purpose to be kind and loving unto him and his, wheresoever I come. But thus the matter is now: that I have taken another house within the Friars at Derby, which is but of a small charge, and there I intend to dispose myself to serve God diligently and keep a narrow house and but few of means; for I have such discomfort of my son Thomas's unfortunate matters that it is time for me to get myself into a little corner, and so I will do. I will beseech you and him take no displeasure with me for my departing, for it will be no otherwise: my heart is so set.

Moreover, as touching the custody of all such evidence as I have now in my keeping concerning the inheritance of my said son German, a gentleman of your acquaintance, Master Henry Arden, has been in hand with me for them, and I have shewed him whensoever and to whom it shall be thought by you most convenient time of the deliverance of them, I will be ready to deliver them, for I will be glad to be discharged of them; for I will flit at this next Michaelmas, as I am full minded, or sooner with God's grace. I pray you continue my good master, and owe me never the worse will therefore, for it rises on my own mind to give over great tuggs of husbandry which I had, and take me to less charge; and with God's grace I shall be as kind to him and to my daughter, his wife, as ever I was in my life, as well for them as with them. With the grace of Jesu, who ever preserve you. Written at Radbourne, in haste, the 10th day of July, by your poor sister and true bedewoman, Elizabeth Pole.

(Plumpton Letters, no. 193)

The following elegantly phrased threat was written by Maud Roos shortly after the death of her husband, Thomas Roos of Ingmanthorpe. Like many others, she and her husband had lent Sir Robert Plumpton money, and at her widowhood she was determined to be repaid. Since Sir Robert kept avoiding the issue, she sent him a final ultimatum before taking legal action against him. In the days before anyone other than the Crown and the greatest lords used bankers, the borrowing and lending of money was one of the ways that neighbours helped each other.

Maud Roos to Sir Robert Plumpton (?1504)

Sir, after my duty of commendations remembering, in my most hearty manner I recommend me unto you. Sir, I desire you to bear in remembrance money the which you caused to be borrowed upon my husband and me, the which money I divers times sent for, and you have divers times appointed me to send for it, and when I sent for it at your appointment you break day ever with me, whereby I cannot get my money. Therefore I desire you to send me word how I shall be answered of it, by this bearer, for if I may have it I were loath to trouble you. If you will not send me word how I shall have it, I will take my next remedy, that you shall well know, it shall be to your pain and they that borrowed it. No more at this time, but Jesu preserve you to his pleasure. Written at Killinghall by your loving friend, Maud Roos.

To Sir Robert Plumpton of Plumpton kt be these delivered

(Plumpton Letters no. 191)

LETTERS FROM CLIENTS TO LORDS AND PATRONS

The following letter is one of the earliest ones in this collection, and was sent by a noblewoman whose position was one of the most significant in the thirteenth century. Maud was the eldest daughter of Isabel, heiress of the earldom of Pembroke, and her husband William Marshal, hereditary marshal of the royal household, who held the earldom in her right. In about 1207 Maud married Hugh le Bigod, Earl of Norfolk, by whom she had three sons. On Hugh's death in 1225 she immediately married William de Warenne, Earl of Surrey, by whom she had another son. In 1245 Anselm, the youngest of her five brothers, all of whom in turn had succeeded their father as Earl of Pembroke, died without heirs and the great Pembroke inheritance in south Wales and the Marches was divided between Maud and the heirs of her four sisters, who included most of the members of the higher nobility. As the eldest, Maud received as her share the honour of Striguil and with it the family's principal fortress of Chepstow, together with lands in Ireland and manors in England; she also inherited the office of marshal, which was confirmed to her six months after her brother's death, suggesting that, as a woman, her right to it may have been disputed. In the early spring of 1248 Maud was seriously ill and her eldest son, Roger, Earl of Norfolk, became extremely worried that at her death other Marshal heirs would lay claim to Chepstow. King Henry III, in whose company he was at the time, did not want a dispute over such a strategically important castle either, and royal messengers were sent to Maud on 9 March for confirmation that Earl Roger was to succeed her. The result was this letter from the dying countess; it is possible, though, that the messengers were sent on receipt of the letter to verify statements. Earl Roger received seisin of Striguil within a week of his mother's death. She died on 29 March and her body was carried by her four sons into the abbey church of Tintern in Gloucestershire, where she was laid to rest in the choir. She had outlived two husbands and five brothers, all of them earls, and counted two earls among her sons.

Maud, Marshal of England and Countess of Norfolk and Warenne, to Henry III, 1248

To the noble man and her most dear lord, Henry by grace of God illustrious King of England, Lord of Ireland, Duke of Normandy and Aquitaine and Count of Anjou, Maud, Marshal of England, Countess of Norfolk and Warenne sends greetings and much honour and obedience in all things. You should know that we have given Chepstow Castle with its appurtenances to our dear son and heir the Earl Roger as his right and inheritance. For this reason we ask for your gift that you should, if it pleases you, receive his homage for it. In testimony of which we are sending you these letters patent. Farewell in the Lord.

(PRO SC 1/4/65; Latin)

The letter from Cecily de Beauchamp to the king was doubtless replicated many times by mothers furnishing a declaration that their sons were of age and thus entitled to have their fathers' estates confirmed to them. Cecily was the widow of John Beauchamp of Hatch, Somerset who died in 1283, probably still in his thirties, when their son, also called John, was only nine. Although John senior was not a peer, he was a substantial landowner, holding directly from the Crown. Cecily was the co-heir of her father, William de Vionne, and her mother, Maud, who was one of the seven daughters and co-heirs of William Ferrers, Earl of Derby, so the lands she inherited were extensive. King Edward I seems to have retained John junior's wardship in his own hands, though his marriage was almost immediately granted to Ralph d' Albini. The custody of most of his lands, including Hatch, and worth more than £110 a year, was granted to John de Neele, Lord of Falevy in Ponthieu, in 1284, subject to an annual charge of £12 7s 9d from the manor of Shepton, payable to Peter, Lord Corbet. Corbet also received additional Beauchamp manors worth £47 a year during the minority. Falevy in turn sublet his share of the estates to Robert Burnell, Bishop of Bath and Wells, the former chancellor. King Edward accepted Cecily's testimony, and John was granted seisin of his lands without further proof of age on

218

17 September. At that time he was serving as a king's yeoman, but four years later he was regarded as having been made a baron by writ of personal summons to parliament. Cecily was writing from Enmore Castle in Somerset, which formed part of her dower. In 1301 she was given a licence to grant to her son, Robert, her lands in Luton, Bedfordshire and others in Ireland; like his elder brother, Robert was also serving as a king's yeoman. At about the same time, Cecily's daughter, Beatrice, was married to the son and heir of Lord Corbet. Cecily died in 1320 without remarrying.

Cecily de Beauchamp to Edward I, 24 August 1295

To the most excellent prince and her revered lord, if it pleases, lord Edward by the grace of God, King of England, Lord of Ireland and Duke of Aquitaine, his devoted subject, Cecily de Beauchamp sends greetings and whatever she can of reverence and honour.

Whereas John de Beauchamp, my son, who is in your wardship, has given me to understand that it would please you to confirm to him the lands and tenements of his inheritance, out of the custody of Robert [Burnell] former bishop of Bath and Wells of good memory, who held them of the noble Lord John de Neele, to whom you granted them, and out of the custody of Lord Peter Corbet who held certain lands and tenements of the inheritance of the said John my son, should I by my letters declare him to be fully of age and that we wish those lands and tenements to be restored. I have been led by these presents to intimate that the said John my son was twenty-one years old on the Friday after the feast of St Peter ad Vincula [1 August] last past, in the twenty-third year of your reign. On this account I ask humbly and devotedly that if it please you, you would deign to return, of your remembered grace, the aforesaid lands and tenements to John my son. May your excellency fare well in the Lord. In testimony of these things I have caused my seal to be applied to these present letters. Given at Enmore in the county of Somerset on the morrow of St Bartholomew [24 August], in the year of your reign aforesaid.

(PRO SC 1/15/36; Latin)

Matilda de Braose was from a powerful Marcher family and she and her sisters were her parents' co-heiresses. She married Roger Mortimer, Lord of Wigmore, in 1247; he was loyal to the Crown during the Baron's War, helping Prince Edward escape from Hereford Castle after his defeat at Lewes. After the royal victory of Evesham, the head of Simon de Montfort, the barons' leader, was sent to Matilda at Wigmore. Roger remained a friend of Edward I for the rest of their lives and was a senior commander in the Welsh wars against Llywelyn the Great. He died in 1282 and Matilda remained a widow for nineteen years. Her own inheritance and her dower lands in the Marches were situated in a strategically important area for Edward I's campaigns in Wales, so she played an active role in supplying the king with men and provisions. Landholding widows like Matilda had all the responsibilities of their male peers and in some cases were known to have attended the king's court to hear legal pleas, though in general they would have sent a male deputy, as they did when providing troops. Roger and Matilda's eldest son, Ralph, had died unmarried in 1274 and their second son, Edmund, succeeded to the barony. William, their fourth son, the subject of this letter, died in May 1297, when all his lands were taken into custody by the royal escheators. It would appear from the letter that on his marriage to Hawise, daughter and heiress of Robert de Muscegros, his mother had settled some of her own lands upon him, and these, in the hands of escheators, were the ones she was seeking to be returned to her. They would, of course, exclude any her daughter-in-law, Hawise, was holding in dower and any that William had received from his father's holdings. In addressing her letter directly to King Edward, Matilda was taking full advantage of her husband's close connection with him. The result was an order from the king to his escheators not to occupy the castle and lands held by William in right of his mother. Matilda died shortly before 25 March 1301.

Matilda Mortimer to Edward I, 1297

To his very honourable lordship, my lord Edward by the grace of God, King of England, Lord of Ireland and Duke of Aquitaine, his very own liege, Matilda de Mortimer gives every honour and reverence to her very dear lord.

Because, lord, your escheators seized as you ordered lands that I had given to William de Mortimer, my son, to hold to him and the heirs of his body, and it is found by enquiry that the lands were given in this manner and that William is deceased without heir of his body, I ask, if you please, that you will command your escheators that possession of the aforementioned lands is given back to me according to the manner of the statute.

Lord, may your highness grow and prosper long in Jesus Christ.

(PRO SC 1/19/131; Tanquerey, no. 70; French)

At the time she wrote the following letter, Ela, Countess of Warwick, was a grand and elderly lady. She was the daughter of William Longespee, Earl of Salisbury, and had married Thomas de Beaumont, Earl of Warwick, some time in the early 1230s. Thomas died in 1242, and twelve years later she married Sir Philip Basset, thus becoming the step-mother of Aline Despenser (see above, pp. 191–2). After Philip's death in 1271, she became a vowess, that is, she took a vow of chastity and lived a religious life without actually entering a convent and taking the veil. This was an option favoured by a number of widows, especially those with considerable property and, like Ela, childless. Her dower and jointure from her two husbands would have been extensive, but it is unclear why the Crown owed her money; perhaps it was the repayment of a loan. Then, as now, the exchequer was slow to pay its debts, and Ela was taking advantage of her well-known position at the court of Edward's parents and the fact that she had presumably known Edward all his life. When she died early in 1298 she was at the very least in her late seventies; she was buried at Osney Abbey. The use of her maiden name in the letter is interesting; although most aristocratic widows who subsequently re-married into the gentry retained the use of their titles, it was less common to use a father's name unless the matter concerned lands inherited from him; here it indicates Ela's pride in her Longespee lineage.

Ela Longespee, Countess of Warwick,
to Edward I, c. 1272–98

To her dear lord, by the grace of God, King of England, his liege Ela Longespee, Countess of Warwick, greets him with as much honour and reverence as is possible.

Dear lord, I ask you earnestly and mercifully beg of you, by the great honour and virtue which is in you, do not suffer me to be kept waiting for the payment that you owe me from your Exchequer, which is in arrears from Eastertide. For to you, dear lord, this would be of little advantage, and it would cause me great trouble and harm. If it pleases you to do this, dear lord, for the great goodness which is in you, may your merit grow before the face of Jesus Christ.

Dear lord, may God grant you a good and long life.

(PRO SC 1/19/50; Tanquerey, no. 83; French)

Matilda de Bokeshull's husband, Alan, was one of the king's tenants-in-chief (he held the manor of Bryanston in Dorset directly from the king, though not his main holdings in Sussex) and in September 1324 he was sent to Aquitaine on royal business. He seems to have died in the course of the trip, and in November 1325 Matilda received her dower from the royal escheator. This consisted of the manor of Bokeshull and other lands in Sussex and one third of the manor of Bryanston, the whole worth about £21 a year. Since Alan's heir was declared to be his son, Alan, aged nine months, Matilda was obviously still a young woman. Although not rich, she was comfortably situated, and would normally have expected to remain at Bokeshull caring for her lands and raising her son. However, the fact that Alan had been a tenant-in-chief meant that Edward II had the right to use her remarriage as a form of patronage if he chose, and grant the wardship of her baby son away from her. That he intended to do so is clear from Matilda's letter to his chancellor, Robert Baldock, who for some reason, probably payment by Matilda, was acting on her behalf. Baldock was Archdeacon of Middlesex and as chancellor might have expected to be elevated to a bishopric, but the pope thwarted two royal attempts to appoint him to vacant sees. He was an ally of the hated royal favourites, the Despensers, and when they fell in 1326, so did he. He was caught and handed over to the custody of the Bishop of London, but a mob broke in and Baldock died of the ill-treatment he received at its hands.

Matilda de Bokeshull to Robert Baldock, Chancellor, 1325

To her very dear and honourable friend, if it pleases him, Master Robert de Baldock, Chancellor of our lord the King, his liegewoman Matilda de Bokeshull, willing and obedient to his commands, in all favour and honour.

Very dear lord, I thank you very much, which as your liegewoman I may and do venture to thank you, for all the favour and aid that you have often undeservedly shown me, and particularly, lord, for the great favour you have shown me as regards my marriage; because of which, lord, I am bound to you always to do anything which would be pleasing to you. For I have heard that nobody was ahead of you in court to obtain the marriage by the king's gift, but that you, lord, by your mercy were opposed to it. And so, while I am ever threatened from one day to the next, since I have your promise, I am keeping myself safe with your help, and I beg of you, lord, and request that it pleases you to order the issue of my letter to the invalidation of the existing one.

May the Lord watch over you and enrich you with honours.

(PRO SC 1/36/26; Tanquerey, no. 117; French)

As has been seen from an earlier letter, Marie de St Pol, widowed Countess of Pembroke, was both rich and very well connected in England and France. In 1331 she was stated to be abroad on the king's business. The young Edward III had just visited France to do homage a second time for his French lands after he had taken power and crushed the government of Roger Mortimer, lover of his mother, Queen Isabella. While she had some links with Isabella as queen dowager, Marie did not either live or serve at court on a regular basis. Her services were given to the king on specific occasions, such as this one, when he asked her to receive a royal visitor. The Spanish lady in question was almost certainly Maria, daughter of Ferdinand of Spain, Lord de Lara, a grandson of Alfonso X of Castile. Maria was contracted to marry King Edward's brother, John, Earl of Cornwall, in 1334, and apparently it was planned that she should travel to England a year later. Although Marie waited for months at her chief residence, Denny in Cambridgeshire, for news of Maria's arrival, it never came; indeed at about the time Marie wrote to the king, the marriage plans had clearly collapsed because Maria contracted a French marriage. Presumably the king was aware of the failure of the marriage plans but had forgotten he had put Marie on standby reception. She was thus released to attend to her legal business in the Court of Common Pleas.

Marie de St Pol, Countess of Pembroke to Edward III, 1335

To the most exalted, noble and excellent ruler, my lord the king of England. My very redoubtable lord, you ordered me by your letters around All Saints Day [1 November] that I was to await the arrival of the Lady of Spain. And that I was to go and meet her at Dover and accompany her to Yorkshire; my very redoubtable lord, may it please you to know that from that time until Shrovetide I remained in the one place without daring to move in order to carry out your command. And meanwhile I am brought by your service before your justices of your Court of Common Pleas in the case of the land relating to Eleyne, who was the wife of Thomas de Cleyton, the reversion of which land and portion of the manor of Temple Newsom in the county of Yorkshire now depends on you my very redoubtable lord, so I beg and request, if it pleases you, that you send a letter of delay to the Chancellor, so that I may have a letter of guarantee for your justices of the Court of Common Pleas in the aforementioned case. My very redoubtable lord, I recommend myself to you as humbly as possible and pray to sweet Jesu Christ that he may grant you a good and long life and maintain and augment your good estate. Written at your manor of Denny, 19th April, by your humble and obedient Marie de St Pol, Countess of Pembroke.

(PRO SC 1/38/137; Jenkinson Archaeologia, *66 (1914); French)*

In the twenty or so years between the two letters here that she addressed to Edward III, in 1339 Marie de St Pol had founded an abbey close to her main residence of Denny to which she continued to make grants during the rest of her life. She then turned her attentions to the planning of a Cambridge college. One of her close friends was Elizabeth, Countess of Clare, who established Clare College. Pembroke College was founded in 1349 and like Denny, continued to receive grants from its benefactress. In these and in a wide range of other charities she always associated her own name with that of her husband. After a period of economy in her early widowhood, she set about purchasing large amounts of land to form the endowments of Denny and Pembroke College and took a close personal interest in her land transactions. Although Marie de St Pol owned estates in France, and indeed spent long periods in that country, she successfully maintained a neutral position between her native and adopted countries. When what was to become known as the Hundred Years War finally broke out between them in 1337, she made the clear choice to settle her residence in England, where the bulk of her lands were situated. However, she did not abandon her French lands; English soldiers were given orders to respect her possessions, and when she could, she visited them. In 1353 there was a slight lull in hostilities, Edward III had won the Battle of Crécy, taken Calais and stabilised the English position in Gascony, and a series of truces served to maintain an uneasy peace. Marie had clearly seized the opportunity to attempt to visit France, but while waiting for French permission to come, her letter of safe conduct from Edward had been countermanded and she was left high and dry at Dover, trying to persuade Edward to change his mind and let her go after all. Eventually, in the early 1370s, the French confiscated her lands there, but despite that, Marie made provision for French scholars at her college and in her will left a bequest to the French king and queen.

Marie de St Pol, Countess of Pembroke, to Edward III, 1353

To the most exalted, noble and excellent ruler, her very dear and very honourable lord the King of England.

Very dear lord, for the great desire we have to know good news of your estate, which may Our Lord always wish to grant, as our heart desires and grants us the grace of seeing with joy, we write to you, asking, very dear lord, as earnestly as we can and dare, that by your humility you wish to inform us through the bearer of this letter, and as often as will be pleasing to you, for dear lord, we are always very much more at ease when we hear good news. And of our own estate, if it pleases you by your humility to know, dear lord, then thanks to Our Lord we are in quite good health when this letter was written, which may Our Lord always wish to grant.

Very dear and very honourable lord, when you had given your good permission to go overseas for our needs near Dover, where we stayed for 8 days or more awaiting our passage from the King of France; and we learned, very dear lord, that the date of the letters [of safe conduct] that you had us take to your officers at Dover allowing us to pass by your good leave, had been superceded by another command from you, such that we could not pass at all; which is why, very dear lord, we are emboldened to apply to you again. So we seek of you, very dear lord, as much as we can and dare, if it is still your wish that we pass, that if it pleases you . . . your officials of the port of departure that they allow us to pass, and the men who are in our retinue . . . our horses and our belongings without obstructing or stopping or searching any of our company of people. And will you please let us know by your letters and by the bearer of these what you would like us to do. And if you require anything from us that would please you, please command it. As she who is obedient and prepared to do what is in her power, may Our Lord watch over you . . . and body. Written at Wongham on the 8th day of Epiphany. From yours if it please you, Marie de St Pol, Countess of Pembroke.

(PRO SC 1/49/94; Jenkinson Archaeologia, *66; French)*

The author of the following letter is one of the most lowly correspondents in the collection, but the subject of her letter is one of the most political. She does not give her surname, but identifies herself as the former nurse of Philippa (see chapter 2), elder daughter of John of Gaunt, Duke of Lancaster, and his first wife, Blanche, daughter and heiress of Henry, Duke of Lancaster. John and Blanche married in 1359, when Blanche was only twelve. She died, probably of plague, in 1369, having borne three children, Philippa, Elizabeth and the future king, Henry IV, as well as two other sons who died in infancy. Philippa was the eldest, born in 1360, and thus sixteen when Maud wrote to her father. The letter indicates that Maud did not go on to become the nurse of either Elizabeth or Henry and this suggests that because the children were all born close together, each had their own nurse until they reached the age to leave the nursery. In 1365 Philippa graduated to the care of a governess. This was Katherine Swynford, wife of one of Gaunt's knights, who went on to become his mistress and ultimately his third wife. Maud was then almost certainly retired and given a pension or annuity by the duke; she may have been the Maud 'Godegibbeswyf" referred to in Gaunt's register as holding a messuage and market stall from him in Hertford, which was granted to another of his servants on her death in 1381. If this identification is correct, it does not explain how Maud knew of dissaffection in Canterbury, which worried her enough to pay for a letter to be sent to Gaunt, one, moreover, written in French, not English.

John of Gaunt was a controversial figure in 1376, the year that saw the death of the heir to the throne. His charismatic brother Edward, the Black Prince, left only a frail young son, the future Richard II, to succeed the senile and ailing king, Edward III, who died the following year. Gaunt, the senior surviving son of the king, was the throne's main prop. His diplomatic and military services overseas in the previous few years had been both expensive and unsuccessful, while in the factious politics of home, the Commons were flexing their muscles and demanding more control over the raising of taxes while attacking the corruption of the king's government. Since this was largely under his control, it was a covert attack on Gaunt himself. There was also a widespread fear, almost certainly unjustified, that Gaunt was planning to seize the throne on the death of his father. This political unpopularity was compounded by Gaunt's support for John Wyclif and his fellow Lollards in their attacks on the wealth and worldliness of the church, and their doctrine of the state's authority over the church rather than the reverse. The fact that the detractors of Gaunt in Canterbury were friars suggests that this was the element that had roused them. The rumour which they were disseminating, and which surfaced elsewhere, was probably one that claimed Gaunt was not the son of Edward III, but of a butcher of Ghent, substituted by Queen Philippa for a baby that died. This was manifest nonsense, but still hurtful to Gaunt, whose affection for his mother had been particularly remarked on.

Maud to John, Duke of Lancaster, 1376

To the very redoubtable and very powerful lord, my lord the Duke of Lancaster.

Most redoutable, excellent and powerful lord, I recommend myself most humbly to your exalted lordship, desiring especially to hear good news of your noble lordship, and pray to our sweet Lord Jesus Christ that he protects you out of His great pity; and because, very noble lord, the ancient proverb says in this manner, that he who is forewarned is not shamed, I wish to warn you of any enemies that I have perceived by my own experience; note that the brothers, Hugh Brandon and John Drynkestor, of the order of the Friars Minors [Franciscans] of Canterbury, and the brothers, John Pykeworth, John Robert and brother John Hill of the order of preaching friars [Dominicans] of Canterbury aforesaid, have wickedly and treacherously spoken of you, my very redoubtable lord, as I heard to the great misery of my heart, so I beseech you, my very powerful lord, that you protect yourself well from them and all others, in God's name and as an act of sacred charity. Very redoubtable and very powerful lord may the Holy Trinity protect your lordship for a long time and grant you victory over all your enemies.

Your humble suppliant and servant, Maud, former nurse to your very dear daughter, the very honourable lady Philippa.

(PRO SC 1/43/81; Camden 3rd Series, xxi, 355; French)

The following letter takes the form of a petition to Henry VI, but the writer, Lady Husee, was almost certainly known to him personally, because she had spent many years in the service of his step-grandmother, Joan of Navarre, queen of Henry IV. Her husband had been a knight in royal service also, and on his death Constance had retired with a pension of £25 a year granted her by the queen dowager. However, on Joan's death in 1437, the pension had ceased and four years later, presumably having exhausted her savings, Constance was asking for the Crown to reinstate the pension. Her plea was successful, and in May 1441 Henry VI granted her a pension of £25 for life in recognition of the services of her and her husband to his father and grandparents.

Constance, Lady Husee, to Henry VI, 1441

To the King our sovereign lord, beseecheth meekly your humble and continual oratrice Dame Constance, the wife of Henry Hussee, knight, the which was menial servant with the most worthy and Christian King your father, whose soul God assoil, and continued in his service as well beyond the sea as on this side the sea all the times of his noble reign, without any fee or reward; that whereas your said oratrice continued in the service of the noble Princess your grandame, whose soul God assoil, as well in the time of your full noble father and grandfather as in yours, unto the time of his dying, in recompense of which service it liked the Queen your grandame, of her grace special, for the term of her life, to grant by her gracious letters patent unto your said oratrice £20 yearly, to be taken of the issues and profits of the manor of Kingsthorp, in the county of Northampton; and also in likewise 100s. yearly, to be taken from the issues and profits of the manor of Odiham in the county of Southampton, as in the said letters patent openly appears; that it please you of your especial grace tenderly to consider the long service of the said Sir Henry and Dame Constance, that they never had other fee nor reward than the said £25, the which is now ceased by the death of your said grandame, and thereupon to grant unto your said oratrice, by your several letters patent, the said £25 in like form as she had it, term of her life, yearly to be taken of the issues and profits of the manors aforesaid. And your said oratrice shall pray God continually for you.

(BL Cotton MS Vespasian F xiii, art. 50, f .47;
Wood, I, pp. 92–3; English)

Like many other letters in the collection, the next two relate to property. They were written by an elderly widow called Joan Maryot to Justice William Paston and they concern the manor of East Beckham, Norfolk. The manor had been in the hands of the royal escheator following the death of William Maryot, the son of an immigrant from Friesland, and the Crown then granted its custody to William Paston in 1442 for seven years, backdated to February 1440, and thereafter at pleasure. Maryot's widow, Joan, and son, John, were apparently trying to sell it to Paston to help discharge John's debts of £200. Paston offered them 360 marks and the Maryots were asking 400 marks. They reached an agreement on the sale, and thereafter Paston leased the manor back to the Maryots. Some of the details in Joan's letters cannot be explained and it is not known what went wrong with the arrangements, or who were the enemies who caused her to lose her temper with William Paston. Joan died a year or so later, and her son, John, went off to Aquitaine in the train of its seneschal. Sir John Paston II sold the manor with other lands in the locality for a mere 100 marks in 1466 when he needed money badly after the loss of Caister.

Joan Maryot to William Paston, c. 1442

To my right worshipful and trusty master, William Paston, Justice.

Worshipful and right trusty master, I commend me unto you, desiring to hear of your worship and welfare, the which God keep to his pleasing and to your own heart's desire, praying you evermore of your good mastership and of your good continuance; praying you at the reverence of God to hold me excused of the lewd and uncunning language the which I answered you with at Cromer. For so help me God and holydom, I said it to you for no bad trust that I have in you, but only to let you know what temptations I have had by that same person that I told you of and by other many more that will avow it in the same manner, saving your reverence, as false men do and my bodily enemies. And, worshipful and trusty master, and as for that I should have the manor in farm in such form as you communed of before my neighbours at Cromer, I pray you at the reverence of God that you will do your good mastership therein as you have done before time; for as you do, I will stand thereto, for I have communed with our vicar and with other friends of mine, and they and I pray you evermore of your best counsel therein.

No more to you at this time, but Jesu keep you body and soul. By your poor bedewoman Joan Maryot.

(Paston Letters (Davis), no. 428)

Joan Maryot to William Paston, c. 1442

To my worshipful master Justice of the King, William Paston.

Worshipful master and reverent sovereign, I commend me to you ever as your poor bedewoman, desiring ever to hear of your good welfare with prosperity and good life to the pleasing of God, praying you evermore of your good mastership and counsel in the matter the which is for the manor of East Beckham, the which matter you and I communed of at Cromer the last time my son and

I spake with you. And I had liefer, and so had John, my son, to have an end and be in such possession within a year to the bare manor, without any reward of damages than longer abide to stand in doubt of law and of your life and ours also; and how the end be made and in what time I consent and am well pleased.

Nor more at this time, but the blissful Trinity have you ever in His keeping. Written at Cromer the Wednesday next before Corpus Christi day. By Joan Maryot your poor bedewoman.

(Paston Letters (Davis), no. 429)

The next letter is a considerable contrast, both in style and importance. In contrast to the simple and direct language favoured, with a few exceptions, by the gentry in their letters, this is intensely literary and florid. The emotions expressed are genuine enough, but there are numerous undercurrents which are not immediately apparent at first reading. In the early 1440s Cecily Neville (see chapter 4) and her husband Richard, Duke of York, lived in France, which York was governing in the name of Henry VI, and then in Ireland, where he was sent as lieutenant in 1449 as a form of political exile. In the factional struggles of the court in the 1450s, to which he returned after Cade's rebellion in an attempt to restore some form of good government, his position was strengthened by the fact that after the death of the king's uncle, Humphrey, Duke of Gloucester, in 1447, York became the king's heir presumptive; Henry VI had married Margaret of Anjou in 1445, but so far they had no children. York was descended from both Edward III's second son in the female line and his fourth son in the male line, and it could be argued that his hereditary claim to the throne was stonger than Henry's, descended, as he was from Edward's third son.

At the beginning of 1452, York's chief aim was to remove from power the king's favourite, Edmund Beaufort, Duke of Somerset, whom he blamed for the loss of France. However, an armed rebellion by York was met at Dartford by an unexpected show of force by the king, and since York did not attract much support from his fellow magnates, he was forced to capitulate and retire from court.

It was at this point that his wife approached the queen, seeking her intervention on York's behalf. Queen Margaret, though wary of York's ambitions, did not yet regard him as an enemy and gave Cecily a sympathetic hearing. It would appear from the letter that the two women met when the queen was on a pilgrimage to Our Lady of Walsingham. This was the foremost shrine for women in the country and was regarded as particularly efficacious for women trying to conceive; hence the queen's visit. And it worked. Her only son, Edward, was born in October 1453. Since the queen's pregnancy was known at the time Cecily wrote her letter, it must be dated to the summer of 1453. She also refers to her own state of health, talking of her sickness and trouble, which probably had a double meaning, first that she was physically unwell and secondly that she was sick at heart because of her husband's estrangement from the king. When she met the queen at Walsingham and sued in person, she implies that she herself was pregnant and had been ill since. The birth from which she had been slow to recover was that of her youngest son, the future Richard III, born in October 1452.

Three months before Queen Margaret was delivered of her son, Henry VI went mad. York then really felt his political isolation. As a leading peer, the king's cousin and still his heir presumptive, pending the queen's safe delivery of a son, together with the experience he had had in France and Ireland, he should have been closely involved in the decisions being made by the royal council. Instead, he was ignored. At this point Cecily again approached the queen, this time in writing. The intervention worked and York was recalled from the political wilderness. After Prince Edward was born, York was no longer heir presumptive, but he was appointed Protector of the Realm during the king's incapacity. When Henry recovered his wits, York was dismissed and the country descended slowly into civil war.

Cecily, Duchess of York, to Queen Margaret of Anjou, 1453

Beseecheth with all humbleness and reverence possible your lowly obeisant servant and bedewoman, Cecily, Duchess of York that, whereof the plenty of your good and benign grace it pleased thereunto in your coming from that blessed, gracious and devout pilgrimage of our Lady of Walsingham to suffer the coming of my simple person – replete with such immeasurable sorrow and heaviness as I doubt not will of the continuance thereof diminish and abridge my days, as it does my worldly joy and comfort – unto your most worthy and most high presence, whereunto than [you pleased] full benignly to receive my supplication to the same, made for your humble, true man and servant, my lord my husband, whose infinite sorrow, unrest of heart and of worldly comfort, caused of that that he heareth him to be estranged from the grace and benevolent favour of that most Christian, most gracious and most merciful prince, the king our sovereign lord, whose majesty royal my said lord and husband now and ever, God knoweth, during his life hath been as true and as humble, and as obeisant leigeman, and to the performing of his noble pleasure and commandment as ready, as well-disposed, and as diligent at his power, and over that as glad, as joyful to be thereunto commanded as any creature alive, being specified in the said supplication, I beseech your highness and good grace, at the mercy of our Creator now ready to send His grace to all Christian persons, and of that blessed Lady to whom you late prayed, in whom aboundeth plenteously mercy and grace, by whose mediation it pleased our Lord to fulfil your right honourable body of the most precious, most joyful, and most comfortable earthly treasure that might come unto this land and to the people thereof, the which I beseech His abundant grace to prosper in you, and at such as it pleaseth Him to bring into this world, with all honour, gracious speed and felicity, with also of furthermore supplication of blessed and noble fruit of your said body, for the great trust and most comfortable surety and weal of this realm and of the king's true liege people of the same, to call the good speed of the matters contained in this said supplication into the gracious and tender recommendation of your highness. Whereunto I should for the same have without sloth or discontinuance and with undelayed diligence have sued, nor had by the disease and infirmity that since my said being in your highness presence hath grown and groweth, upon me caused not only the encumberous labour, to me full painful and uneasy, God knoweth, that then I took upon me, but also the continuance and addition of such heaviness that I have taken, and take, for the consideration of the sorrow of my said lord and husband; and if it please your good grace not to take to any displeasure of strangeness that I have not diligently continued the suit of my said supplication unto your said highness, caused of the same infirmity not hid upon my wretched body. Wherefore I report me to God; and in reverence of whom, and of his said grace and mercy to you showed, it please [eftsones] unto your high nobility to be a tender and gracious mean unto the highness of our sovereign lord for the favour and benevolence of his hand to be showed unto my lord and husband, so that through the gracious mean of you, sovereign lady, he may and effectually obtain to have the same. Wherein I beseech your said highness that my said labour and pain may not be taken frivolously nor unfruitfully, but the more agreeable for my said lord unto your said good grace. Whereunto, notwithstanding my said infirmity, I should not have spared to have recontinued my said suit, if I could or might have done, that it should have pleased your nobility if that I should so have done the which, as it shall please thereunto I shall not let, not sparing pain that my body now suffice of any possibility to bear, or suffer, with God's grace, whom I shall pray to prosper your high estate in honour, joy and felicity.

(Rawcliffe, BIHR, 1987, pp. 237–8; Huntingdon Library, California, Battle Abbey MS 937)

The Greene family of Newby in Yorkshire were kin of the Plumptons and served them as stewards and feoffees; they were also, like the Plumptons, closely identified with the Percy Earls of Northumberland. In a letter written a few months later than this one, the earl describes Elizabeth Green's husband, Richard, as his servant, and addresses Sir Robert Plumpton as 'cousin'. The lands to which Elizabeth Greene's letter refers were in the honour of Knaresborough (for which Sir Robert was deputy steward for the earl), and for which he and the earl were feoffees. They belonged to the Aldborough family, who, like the Tancreds, were part of the Plumpton kinship network. William Aldborough was a member of a bastard branch of the family, and was later indicted at York assizes for having expelled Plumpton and another feoffee from the lands. As in so many other cases of disputed ownership of land, the tenants suffered from bullying and uncertainty, as Elizabeth's letter bears witness.

Elizabeth Greene to Sir Robert Plumpton, November 1487

Right worshipful Sir, I commend me to your mastership, certifying you that I have showed William Tancred your commandment that he should have warned the tenants to pay no farm to William Aldburgh; and he letting [them] pay farm to his mother and would not warn the tenants to pay none; and as for taking of William Aldburgh, he said he would not take him, for you let him alone and you might have taken him and you would, and may take him when you will. [I] beseech you be so good master unto me and set me and my husband tenants in rest of him, to God send my husband home so that I complain no further for no remedy, as my trust is in your mastership, as God knows who preserve you to his pleasure. From Newby, on Monday after All Souls Day. Your bedewoman Elizabeth Greene

Unto the right worshipful Sir Robert Plumpton, kt, deliver these.

(Plumpton Letters, no. 55)

The last two letters in this section are not really letters at all, but petitions. For the poor and despairing and those without influence, their last hope for justice was to beg for help from either the king himself, or someone very powerful. The act of mercy was approved by the Church, popular with the people and rarely costly to the Crown. In the case of John de Kynnesley, his wife's petition does not make it clear whose allegations had resulted in his incarceration in Norwich Castle, but it was someone with influence in official circles in Norfolk. *Habeas corpus* was a right that had been long established in England, but was honoured as much in the breach as in the observance. Joanna was asking either for John's release, or that he should be charged with a specific offence and tried for it. Royal justice came to her aid and ordered that John be brought to London by the sheriff of Norfolk and temporarily committed to the custody of the Fleet prison, while the cause of his arrest and imprisonment was investigated. The sheriff clearly could not provide sufficient cause and on 29 January 1406 an order was issued for John's release.

Joanna de Kynnesley to Henry IV, c. 1405

Supplicates most humbly a poor and simple woman, Joanna de Kynnesley; that whereas John de Kynnesley, her husband, by hate and malice, was put in prison within the castle of Norwich, where he has long lain through false suggestions, that it would please your most gracious lordship, for the love of God, and for the souls of your most noble father and mother, whom God assoil, to grant and give to your said suppliant your gracious letters, sealed under your seal, made in due form, directed to the sheriff of the county of Norfolk, charging and straitly commanding him to deliver up the body of the said John out of prison, that he may go at large, to answer before your royalty, in case any one should accuse him; and she will pray God for you and for your progenitors for ever.

(PRO Royal petitions; Wood, I, pp. 88–9; French)

In Joanna Conway's petition to the Duchess of York, she is appealing from one woman to another. Cecily was certainly an influential woman, both during the lifetime of her husband and the reigns of her sons, Edward IV and Richard III; the letter is not dated, but probably comes from the reign of Henry VI rather than later. Cecily was also noted for her piety, and, therefore, Joanna hoped she might be willing to perform the act of mercy requested of her. We do not know why Joanna was incarcerated in Ludgate, but Edward Neville, Lord Abergavenny, was the duchess's youngest brother. As in the case of Joanna Kynnesley, the survival of the petition suggests that Cecily responded positively to it.

Joanna Conway to Cecily, Duchess of York, c. 1450–76

To the most gracious and excellent princess the Duchess of York. Most piteously, and with incessant lamentation, complaineth unto your most gracious ladyship your continual and poor bedewoman Joanna Conway; foreasmuch as she has been long in the miserous [*sic*] prison of Ludgate, at the suit of the right noble lord, the Lord of Abergavenny, to her confusion and mortal destruction for ever, without your most merciable [*sic*] grace be benignly to her enlarged in that behalf. Whereof pleases it your most excellent gracious ladyship the premises tenderly to consider, and for the relief of your said beseecher to send of your most abundant grace to the said Lord of Abergavenny, and to will and desire him to release and withdraw all suits as he has willed to be done against your said beseecher, as conscience and law of God requireth. And your said bedewoman shall incessantly pray to God of his influent [*sic*] grace for to preserve your most benign and gracious estate, and to send your most royal estate many prosperous days.

(PRO SC 8/337; Wood, I, p. 108; English)

SEVEN

'May God save you in body and soul': Women of religion

How far did the lives and experience of women in religious life differ from those of their secular sisters? This is not a question that their letters can easily answer, because they deal with matters which were not spiritual. Their relationship with God was not discussed with lay people, but practical matters were. In many ways, the role of the head of a nunnery was not dissimilar to that of the widowed head of a gentry household. In the first instance, the women came from the same social class. Virtually without exception, nuns came from the higher social classes, since novices had to be able to read and sing, and were expected to enter the convent with a dowry, despite the fact that the latter was technically forbidden by the Church. Gently born women, too, were the only women whose social position made it impossible to stay single and earn a living. Many daughters of the gentry and aristocracy entered the religious life because they had a vocation; this is a vital fact that should not be overlooked. Others entered because they saw it as an alternative career to marriage, or as a refuge in widowhood, or occasionally from an unhappy marriage. These were all a result of decisions taken by the women themselves, but others found themselves behind convent walls following decisions taken by others. Convents were convenient dumping grounds for political prisoners, such as the baby daughter of the last Welsh Prince and Princess of Wales, or for daughters who were disabled or simple-minded, who were simply illegitimate or whose existence and possible claims to property were an inconvenience to relatives.

At the time of the Norman Conquest, there were about ten Saxon nunneries and in the succeeding few decades another seven or eight were founded, but from the beginning of the twelfth century there was a sharp rise in monastic foundations of all types, so that in the thirteenth and fourteenth centuries there were 138 nunneries in England. Half were Benedictine, the remainder Cluniac, Cistercian, Augustinian and Gilbertine, the latter an order founded in England specifically for women; of these convents, the most significant twenty-one were abbeys and the rest were priories. Most nunneries were small and poor, and only twenty (mostly, but not exclusively, the abbeys) had incomes of more than £200 a year, while thirty-nine had to manage on less than £50. All the richest ones were south of the Thames; only Elstow, in Bedfordshire, and Godstow, near Oxford, approached them in status and wealth. Even some of the greatest were daughter houses of continental foundations; in the case of Amesbury in Wiltshire, refounded in 1177 by Henry II, it was the great Plantagenet abbey of Fontevrault. The biggest English abbeys and priories had on average thirty to forty nuns, while the smallest houses had ten or less. Many nunneries were founded by women, whose females descendants continued the patronage and connection and sometimes entered the house itself. A number of the houses were urban, which facilitated the recruitment of novices, the teaching of local girls and the reception of a small community of lay widows, and meant that the house had a strong attachment to the local community and was more likely, therefore, to be the beneficiary of gifts and bequests. In the later Middle Ages, daughters of the merchant classes began to enter convents close to their towns in increasing numbers. This was at least in part because the religious life had begun to fall out of favour with the upper ranks of society. Such local ties meant that by the time of the Reformation, recruitment for nunneries was still holding up.

Unlike their male counterparts, women's religious houses could not be self-sufficient. Convents needed priests for spiritual guidance and the celebration of mass and lay brothers to perform the physically more demanding jobs about the buildings, but apart from this, all the other administrative and spiritual tasks could be performed as easily by nuns as by monks. Each nunnery's main link with the outside world was the head of the house. To become the head of an abbey or priory, a nun had to be over twenty-one, born in wedlock and of good reputation. As a rule, the nuns had the right of free election from among their number, but sometimes a mother house would impose a head from outside (see chapter 2). Once elected, the nun chosen remained in post until death or resignation from ill health, or unless deprived of office for incompetency or ill behaviour. If she resigned because of old age or ill health, then she remained in the same house as a simple nun, but retaining some of the advantages of office, such as a larger room. The administrative role of an abbess or prioress was similar to that of her secular sister who managed a large household and estate. She had to manage the convent's lands, ensure that it received its rents and dues, organise the repair of its buildings, pay its servants and lay administrative officials, such as bailiffs, and insure that the nuns were fed and clothed. In return, she had her own rooms and servants and frequently better food. The head of a house was permitted to entertain outside visitors, usually male, on business, but she had always to be in the company of another nun as witness to her behaviour; that nun often acted as her chaplain, and was supposed to be changed regularly to avoid favouritism. The head was also permitted to travel on the house's business. In terms of county society, the abbesses were the equivalent of peeresses and the prioresses of substantial members of the gentry; each also bore the courtesy title of 'Lady', just as a priest was addressed as 'Sir'. In theory, though, an abbess or prioress was only *primus inter pares*; major decisions were supposed to be taken communally in chapter. The head of a house was expected to work closely with her deputies, the sub-prioress and treasuress, together rendering annual accounts. In addition, the nuns chose from among their number to fill the offices of novice-mistress, infirmaress (responsible for the sick), chamberer (responsible for clothes), cellaress (food), sacrist (church fabric), chantress (services and library) and almoness (charity). It would be naive to suppose that in such a closed community there were no quarrels, power struggles, favouritism or autocratic government.

The first two letters here relate to the election of a new head of a convent. Such an operation was complicated and expensive. In the first instance, permission had to be sought from the convent's patron for the election to be held, and the result had to be confirmed by the patron and the local bishop and appropriate fees paid. All this took time, and while the vacancy lasted the lay patron of the nunnery was entitled to its temporalities, that is, the income from its lands. The nun chosen was often the best born, rather than the best personally qualified, on the grounds that her relatives would have the most influence when it mattered.

In the early Middle Ages many women from the upper ranks of society entered the religious life, and went on to become abbesses or prioresses, but in the fourteenth and fifteenth centuries, high-born women were less inclined to take the veil, leaving the lower gentry and women from the merchant classes to take their place. Sometimes the election as head of the house was unanimous, as seems to have been the case at St Mary's, Chester, where the deputy succeeded naturally. It is worth noting that the new prioress was a de la Haye, and almost certainly had an aristocratic background. The confirmation of Alice's election was merely a formality, but the nuns seized the opportunity to bring their poverty to the notice of the queen, acting as regent for her husband during his absence in France. Poverty was a serious problem for many nunneries and had a number of causes: litigation, taxation, extravagance, the loss of income during a vacancy, poor management and natural disasters all played a part, but the biggest cause was invariably insufficient endowment. St Mary's was a Saxon foundation, and had an income of only £66 a year in 1535, just before it was dissolved; earlier it might well have had less. What its 'multiplied desolations' were in 1253, we do not know, but it sounds as though a number of reasons played their part. For the dozen or so nuns to be reduced to begging for alms rather than granting them to others indicates that things were bad indeed. Queen Eleanor, noted for her piety (she was the only widowed queen in the period to take the veil herself), was a possible source of relief, though neither she nor the king were patrons of St Mary's.

The nuns of St Mary's, Chester, to Queen Eleanor of Provence, c. 1253–4

To the most excellent lady Eleanor, by god's grace Queen of England, Lady of Ireland, Duchess of Normandy and Aquitaine, Countess of Anjou, her humble convent of nuns of St Mary of Chester wishes her, if she pleases, health and happy success to her utmost desires.

When our prioress of happy memory, Lady Alice of Stockport, lately went the way of all flesh, we, having quickly sent a messenger about it to our most excellent lord Henry, by God's grace the illustrious King of England, according to the tenor of his benign reply, by a special letter of ratification sent to you on the morrow of St Lawrence the Martyr's day [11 August], having invoked the aid of the Holy Spirit, without any condition or reclamation, unanimously and cordially elected the Lady Alice de la Haye, our sub-prioress, a woman deserving commendation for her life and conduct, as our Prioress, all things thereto appertaining being canonically observed. Therefore it is that, mentally throwing ourselves at the feet of your excellency, since bowels of pity and mercy grow in you, we humbly and devoutly seek that you will deign, by the instinct of Divine compassion, to confirm the said Alice as Prioress to our miserable convent, amidst its multiplied desolations. For so greatly are we reduced that we are compelled to beg abroad our food, slight as it is. The very secret places of our afflicted hearts cry out therefore to you, expecting the wished-for effect of our pious petition. And we, each one of us, will, as is fitting, and as we formerly did, now in future much more devoutly, offer prayers to the Lord for you and yours. May your ladyship ever fare well in the Lord!

(PRO SC 1/11/18; Wood, I, pp. 34–5; Latin)

Like St Mary's, Barking abbey was a Saxon foundation, but there the similarity ended. It was one of the largest and richest nunneries and had had several abbesses of Saxon royal blood. This was an occasion when an abbess resigned because of age and ill health and her deputy immediately despatched this letter to the abbey's royal patron seeking permission to hold an election. Doubtless Prioress Matilda was hoping that natural progression would result in her own elevation to the office of abbess; in abbeys, the deputy head of the house held the rank of prioress. Until the increasing use of English in the fifteenth century, most correspondence from religious women was in Latin, but it is doubtful if many nuns were fluent in the language themselves. They would have been familiar with the service forms, but, like any secular lady, they had clerks to take care of their correspondence. The letter was to be carried by three of the nuns to the king. Nuns were, on occasion, permitted to leave their cloisters, but only for a specific purpose and with permission from their bishop.

Matilda, Prioress of Barking abbey, to Henry III, 3 December 1258

To her most excellent lord Henry, by God's grace illustrious King of England, Lord of Ireland, Duke of Normandy and Aquitaine, and Count of Anjou, Matilda, humble Prioress of Barking, and of the convent of the same place, wishes health, with due reverence and honour, and the suffrages of her prayers.

Since the lady our mother, venerable for her religion, the lady Christina, late Abbess of our house, did on the Monday next after the feast of St Andrew the Apostle, in the forty-third year of your reign [2 December 1258], of her own good and spontaneous will, yield up the government of the said abbey, on account of the infirmity and debility of her body, and was absolved from it by our venerable father Foulk, Bishop of London, we now, being destitute of the solace of an abbess, send to you our beloved sisters and fellow nuns, Roesia de Argentes, Joanna de Wantham, and Agnes Cotentin, humbly and devoutly supplicating that the bowels of your compassion may be moved towards us, and that the condescension of your mercy will grant us permission to elect some other as our abbess, so that henceforth you may receive from the highest retributor a worthy reward, and we may be henceforth obligated more specially to offer up the merited suffrages of our prayers for you and yours. Given at Barking the Tuesday after the feast of St Andrew the Apostle, in the forty-third year of your reign.

(PRO C 84/2/39; Wood, I, pp. 40–1; Latin)

Wherwell abbey was another Saxon foundation, this time in Hampshire, close to the even greater Amesbury and Wilton abbeys. In the years just before this letter was written, Wherwell had one of the truly great English abbesses of the Middle Ages. Euphemia of Wherwell was in charge for a very long time, 1226–57, and impressed everyone with her great piety and charitable works as well as her skill in worldly affairs. Her abbacy saw much rebuilding and improvements, not only to the nunnery itself but also to its other property. An admiring chronicler reported that 'she also so conducted herself with regard to exterior affairs that she seemed to have the spirit of a man rather than a woman': to us a dubious compliment, but to a misogynistic medieval religious chronicler, the height of praise. During her period in charge at Wherwell the number of nuns doubled from forty to eighty, and under any circumstances she was a very hard act to follow. Her successor, Mabel de Tichborne, certainly seems to have been faced with legal problems relating to the abbey's estates if she was being summoned before justices in both Somerset and Hampshire at the same time.

Mabel de Tichborne, Abbess of Wherwell, to Walter de Merton, Chancellor, 1263

To a venerable man of discretion and great decency, Sir Walter de Merton, Chancellor of the lord King, Mabel, by divine permission Abbess of Wherwell, greetings in the name of the Lord with honour and increase of glory. By certain reports of your most clear love and friendship we have been led to expound to you certain business of our house, namely that we have recently received a common summons that we should be in person before the justices at Ilchester in county Somerset on the morrow of Low Sunday [first Sunday after Easter] to plead with a plea for certain lands which we hold in the said county, and since it will be difficult and very onerous to come in person to the said place on the said day, because we have to be in person before similar justices on Hock Day [second Tuesday after Easter] in county Hampshire, we ask . . . and request that you procure for us acquittance of the common summons to the said justices at Ilchester, for which, if it please you, we are and always will be . . . May your dearness fare well always in Christ.

(PRO SC 1/7/206; Latin)

One of the burdens that religious institutions had to bear in the thirteenth century was the support of Jewish converts to Christianity. Converts were under the specific protection of the king, who would request a monastery or convent to provide a named convert with a corrody or pension, usually for two years, to help support them while they set themselves up in a new life. In the reign of Henry III there were about 500 converts, and King Henry decided to set up a special house for them in London. There they were housed, educated and helped to set up new businesses. Henry was following the example of other philanthropists; there was already one such house attached to Bermondsey priory and one in Oxford. Winchester was another place that was generous to former Jews and Peter de Roches, Bishop of Winchester, left a bequest of £100 in his will of 1238 to buy more land for the expansion of the London house. Edward I continued his father's generosity, since there were usually more converts than could be placed in the dedicated houses. Alice was one of them and her request for the continuation of a charitable pension suggests that she was elderly and unlikely to be able to earn a living as a Christian. She remained dependent on the priory in Winchester for her support, and she seems to have been there for about twenty years. The priory was not wealthy and was a small house in a city dominated by the Abbey of St Mary, so naturally it hoped for some reimbursement. Alice's letter was probably written at the priory's request and by one of the nuns or their clerk.

Alice 'the convert' of Winchester, to Edward I, 1289

To our lord the king, if it pleases him, Alice 'the convert' of Winchester sets out how she had, with the consent of King

Henry your father (may God have mercy on his soul), charity in the priory of Winchester. And then with the permission which you granted in Gascony where she sent her son when you were in those parts, and there you gave him authority that she should receive the charity on your arrival in England, as she had received it previously at the time when you came to England, may our Lord be praised, she asks you in the name of God and by holy charity, if it pleases you, that you give your authority to the Priory and Convent of Winchester that she should receive the charity as she had previously, for the Priory and the good people of the house greatly wish this.

(PRO SC 1/16/63; Tanquerey, no. 61; French)

Elstow was another of the few nunneries big enough and rich enough to be an abbey. It had been founded soon after the Conquest by Judith, widow of the great Saxon Earl Waltheof and niece of the Conqueror. It is, therefore, not surprising that its abbess in the early fourteenth century should be a member of the aristocratic family of Balliol, whose descent from the Scottish royal family led to their claim to that throne. The issue that Clemence raised with Edward I's chancellor was the apparently minor one of a highway diversion, but it was of considerable importance to the abbey. Elstow lay just south of Bedford and the warden and brethren of St Leonard's hospital had been erecting new buildings on their land on either side of the roadway from Bedford, but finding that they then suffered from the depredations of passers-by, applied to the king to stop the existing road and make another avoiding the hospital, and also the abbey. Edward I ordered an enquiry and St Leonard's produced a case whose findings were that the proposed alteration of his highway would not injure anyone and indeed would be an improvement, since they would make the new road wider than the existing one. This, however, did not suit the abbey, and Abbess Clemence wrote this letter of protest to the chancellor. She argued that the abbey enjoyed royal patronage and the king himself would suffer when the next vacancy for an abbess occurred, because his income from the abbey's temporalities would be much reduced if the new road was in place. Her letter had its effect, because the king

247

ordered a new enquiry by an impartial jury, which found that the new road would indeed lead to financial loss to the abbey, and thus the king, as well as inconvenience to the nuns and local people. In the end the case was carried to Westminster, but although the abbess fought to the bitter end, it was settled in the hospital's favour and the old road was closed.

Clemence de Balliol, Abbess of Elstow, to William Hamilton, Chancellor, 1306

To the very noble and wise William Hamilton, Chancellor of our lord the King of England, if it pleases him, his own Clemence de Balliol, by the grace of God, Abbess of Elstow and the convent of the same place, greets him with honour and reverence.

Very dear lord, because the master of the Hospital of St Leonard of Bedford is carrying out an inquest on your behalf into the disinheritance of our lord the King and of our house of Elstow by the diversion of the king's highway to the great loss of our lord the King and to our house, we ask, if it pleases you, as an act of charity, that you would maintain the rights of our lord the King, as the chief founder of our house (and the matter would result in great loss to him in the time of vacancy of the abbess), and ours; with the result that you would not permit him the authority of our lord the King to the detriment of our lord the King or of our aforementioned house.

Farewell, may God save you in body and soul.

(PRO SC 1/25/185; Tanquerey, no. 88; French)

In contrast to Elstow, Rowney priory in Hertfordshire was one of the smallest and poorest of the nunneries. It had been founded in about 1146 by Conan, Duke of Brittany and Earl of Richmond, but with insufficient endowment. In 1457 it was found to be too poor to continue and was therefore dissolved. Fifty years before that, when an unnamed prioress petitioned the king, however, the need for money was for once not foremost in her mind. A percentage of nuns were in convents unwillingly, often placed there as children and professed because they had no option, others took the veil willingly and then found they had made a terrible mistake. Some nunneries were lax and disorderly enough to keep their discontented inmates within the walls, allowing them to indulge themselves with lovers from both inside and outside the walls.

In the stricter, more spiritual convents, many of those who found the religious life intolerable had no option but to run away. To do so meant becoming apostate, outcast and excommunicated. With no means to earn a living and a family unlikely to take her back, unless an ex-nun had a lover to support her, she usually found that prostitution was one of the few options open to her. Once she had left the convent, the secular arm could, as here, be employed to find her and return her to her vows. The occasions when this happened were few, but clearly Rowney, though small, was not lax, and Joan Adeleshey felt she was left with no alternative but to abscond. The response to the prioress's letter was an order to the sheriffs of London and Middlesex, Essex and Hertfordshire to set men hunting for her. The first order seems to have been unsuccessful because there was a second order a year later in response to another letter from the prioress, but it is not known whether Joan was ever found and returned to the priory. None of the names of the prioresses have survived for Rowney until 1449, just before its dissolution, so the identity of the correspondent is unknown, but in such a poor nunnery, she was likely to have come from the lower ranks of the gentry.

The Prioress of Rowney to Henry IV, 12 November 1400

To the most excellent prince and lord in Christ, lord Henry, by God's grace illustrious King of England and France and Lord of Ireland, his humble and devoted suppliant the Prioress of Rowney sends the divine aid of prayers, with all sorts of reverence and honour.

By the tenor of these presents I certify to your royal highness that the sister Joan Adeleshey, a nun of the order of St Benedict, and publicly professed in the said house, wanders and roams abroad from country to country, in a secular habit, despising her vow of obedience, to the grievous danger of her soul, and manifest scandal of her order, and pernicious example to others. May it therefore please your royal excellency of your royal clemency, hitherto ever gracious, to extend the secular arm for the capture of the said Joanna, to be chastised according to the rule of her order in a case of this kind, lest for want of due chastisement a plant given up to divine culture may thus perish. And may He who gives to all kings to reign preserve your royal highness in prosperity.

Given at Rowney the 12 day of November 1400.

(C 81/1786/30; Wood, I, p. 29; Latin)

Denny abbey in Cambridgeshire belonged to the order of Minoresses, whose main house in London was immensely fashionable as a comfortable retreat from the world for secular women, either for a short stay or on a long-term basis in one of the local houses owned by the order. However, Denny was not quite in the same league. At the time of the Dissolution of the Monasteries in 1535, its net income was £178 a year, while London's was £318, but Denny was popular and housed between thirty-five and forty nuns at any one time. It had been refounded in 1342 by Marie de St Pol, Countess of Pembroke (see chapter 6), who built a new convent at Denny, increased its endowment and arranged for the nuns to move there from their old building at nearby Waterbeach. The abbey owned four manors and lands and properties in about twenty parishes, so it should not have been poor, but between 1452 and 1470, the nuns were engaged in a long legal struggle with Thomas Burgoyne over the abbey's rights in their manor of Histon, which the nuns seem to have bought as an investment of part of the £100 left them under the will of their foundress. Burgoyne, who was a JP, seems to have been successful in his campaign against the abbey during his lifetime. He forbade the sisters' tenants to attend their manorial courts, impounded their cattle, arrested their servants and occupied their fens, and it was not until after his death in 1470 that the abbey reached a compromise with his son. Because of his 'insatiable covetiss', the abbey faced legal expenses of about £200 and damages of about £883 from lack of income from the manor over nearly twenty years. Halfway through the battle, with no end in sight, the abbess made her plea to John Paston for financial help under the will of Sir John Fastolf.

The lack of a Christian name and the misspelling of his surname indicates that the abbess and her clerk did not know Paston and probably did not learn of his executorship until some months after Fastolf's death. The previous abbess, Katherine Sybyle, had succumbed to ill health brought on by the stress of the situation, and Joan seems to have been elected against her own wishes, while the cost of her election and the fees the abbey had to pay merely compounded their financial dificulties. Joan was the sister of William Keteryche, holder of the manor of Bray in Landbeach, Cambridgeshire, and thus from the ranks of the local gentry. She remained in charge at Denny until her death in 1479, and her sister Agnes was also a nun there, as was Elizabeth, daughter of their brother William. This is a good example of a family connection with a local convent among the nuns, which paralleled the continuing patronage of a particular house by generations of a family of benefactors.

Joan Keteryche, Abbess of Denny, to John Paston, 31 January 1462

To the right worshipful gentleman Paiston, executor to Sir John Fastolf.

Reverent and worshipful sir, after due recomendation premised, please it you at the reverence of our spouse Jesu, to whom we be willingly professed, to hear graciously our humble petition, as now compelled either to complain us, or else to suffer our devout place fall and perish in our days, which has been so long time wrongfully oppressed by plea for our best and most substantial livelihood; so that our good and wholesome mother that was Abbess is so wearied and broken with it that she is overthrown with daily sickness, unable to occupy her office, and we compelled against our will, if it might have been otherwise, to choose another, by the which election after our custom we must pay to the Bishop of Lincoln twenty marks and to the Bishop of Norwich as much. And as to the payment to the Bishop of Lincoln we be so straitly bounden that the said lord may distrain our goods of the which we have our necessary sustenance; and not only we be out in this discomfort and heaviness, but also our jewels, which were ordained of our first foundation to array our church and to steer us and provoke others to worship God and to have our benefactors in more fresh remembrance, are now for need laid in mortgage and some lost for ever, and others in haste like to be lost, and thereto our places, beside all this misery, are so far decayed by non-reparation that we may not well repair them again, and so our tenants are the more poor and the worse they may pay to us by duty of their farms.

And, reverend sir, I being full simple and young of age and chosen to be Abbess of this wrongfully oppressed place, God knoweth full much against my will, in my complaint making to God I was put in mind of the goods that been in your hands, and also of your wholesome and good disposition which gave me a great courage to make my petition to you for the recovery of our poor place, beseeching your goodness to consider how we be closed within the stone walls and may not otherwise speak with you but only by writing, and the rather succour us for Our Lord's love with such goods as may continue still the servants of Jesu, and others after us in like wise; the which we would think to us a new foundation. And so in our suffrages we would annex the soul of that worthy knight Sir John Fastolf and such others as you will desire unto the soul of our blessed foundress; and worshipful sir, it is more easy as that to relieve us up again than to build a new place, which I trust verily you would do if you knew the blessed disposition of my well-disposed mothers and sisters; by whose good conversation I trust in Jesu to have of you some succour and comfort at my most heavy beginning. And if Our Lord would move your heart to see our poor place, I trust verily to God we should have you and yours ever after in good remembrance.

The bringer of this simple letter written in great heaviness hath experience of all our importable hurts before rehearsed, the which

252

truly was the cause that he would of his own costs be our messenger. Our blessed Lord reward him therefore, which ever preserve you and yours body and soul in goodness for his great mercy.

Written at Denny the last day of January. Your poor bedewoman Joan Keteryche, Abbess of Denny.

(Paston Letters (Davis), no. 656)

Sources

All previously unpublished letters are in the Public Record Office, class SC 1. They are published by permission of the Controller of Her Majesty's Stationery Office. Each document is given its document reference. Where the current document references of printed letters are known, they are also given.

The printed references to previously published letters are to the following works.

Carpenter, C. (ed.), *Kingsford's Stonor Letters and Papers, 1290–1483*, Cambridge, 1996.

——, *The Armburgh Papers: The Brokholes Inheritance in Warwickshire, Hertfordshire and Essex*, c. 1417–c. 1453, Woodbridge, 1998.

Davis, N. (ed.), *Paston Letters and Papers of the Fifteenth Century*, 2 vols, Oxford, 1971, 1976.

Gairdner, J. (ed.), *The Paston Letters*, 4 vols, reprinted Gloucester, 1983.

Jenkinson, H., 'Mary de Sancto Paulo, Foundress of Pembroke College, Cambridge', *Archaeologia*, 66 (1914).

Kirby, J. (ed.), *The Plumpton Letters and Papers*, Cambridge, 1996.

Moriarty, C. (ed.), *The Voice of the Middle Ages in Personal Letters, 1100–1500*, Oxford, 1989.

Tanquerey, F.J. (ed.), *Recueil de Lettres Anglo-Françaises, 1265–1399*, Paris, 1916.

Waller, W.C., 'An Old Church Chest', *Transactions of the Essex Archaeological Society*, new series, vol. 5 (1895).

Wood, M.A.E. (ed.), *Letters of Royal and Illustrious Ladies of Great Britain*, 3 vols, London, 1846.

Bibliography

Ailes, A., 'Armorial Portrait Seals of Medieval Noblewomen', in *Tribute to an Armorist*, ed. J. Campbell-Kease, London, 2000.

Archer, R.E., 'Rich Old Ladies: The Problem of Late Medieval Dowagers', in *Property and Politics: Essays in Later Medieval English History*, ed. A.J. Pollard, Gloucester, 1984.

——, 'Women as Landholders and Administrators in the Later Middle Ages', in *Woman is a Worthy Wight: Women in English Society c. 1200–1500*, ed. P.J.P. Goldberg, Stroud, 1992.

Bennett, H.S., *The Pastons and their England*, Cambridge, 1968.

Carpenter, C., 'The Stonor Circle in the Fifteenth Century', in *Rulers and Ruled in Late Medieval England: Essays presented to Gerald Harris*, eds R.E. Archer and S. Walker, London, 1995.

Coss, P., *The Lady in Medieval England, 1000–1500*, Stroud, 1998.

Dockray, K., 'The Troubles of the Yorkshire Plumptons in the Wars of the Roses', in *History Today*, xxvii (1977).

——, 'Why Did Fifteenth Century Gentry Marry? Pastons, Plumptons and Stonors Reconsidered', in *Gentry and Lesser Nobility in Late Medieval Europe*, ed. M. Jones, Gloucester, 1986.

Fleming, P., *Family and Household in Medieval England*, Basingstoke, 2001.

Goldberg, P.J.P. (ed.), *Women in England c. 1275–1525*, Manchester, 1995.

Jewell, H., *Women in Medieval England*, Manchester, 1996.

Kirby, J., 'A Fifteenth-Century Family: The Plumptons of Plumpton and their Lawyers, 1461–1515', in *Northern History*, xxv (1989).

Lander, J.R., 'Family, "Friends" and Politics in Fifteenth-Century England', in *Kings and Nobles in the Later Middle Ages*, ed. R.A. Griffiths and J. Sherborne, Gloucester, 1986.

Leongard, J.S., '"Of the Gift of her Husband": English Dower and its Consequences in the Year 1200', in *Women of the Medieval World*, ed. J. Kirshner and S. Wemple, Oxford, 1985.

Leyser, H., *Medieval Women: A Social History of Women in England, 450–1500*, London, 1995.

Mate, M.E., *Women in Medieval English Society*, Cambridge, 1999.

McFarlane, K.B., *The Nobility of Later Medieval England*, Oxford, 1973.

Michalove, S.D., 'The Education of Aristocratic Women in Fifteenth Century England', in *Estrangement, Enterprise and Education in Fifiteenth-Century England*, ed. S.D. Michalove and A. Compton Reeves, Stroud, 1998.

Payling, S., 'The Politics of Marriage: Late Medieval Marriage Contracts', in *The McFarlane Legacy: Studies in Late Medieval Politics and Society*, ed. R.H. Britnell and A.J. Pollard, Stroud, 1995.

Richmond, C., *The Paston Family in the Fifteenth Century: The First Phase*, Cambridge, 1990.

——, *The Paston Family in the Fifteenth Century: Fastolf's Will*, Cambridge, 1996.

——, *The Paston Family in the Fifteenth Century: Endings*, Manchester, 2000.

——, 'The Pastons Revisited: Marriage and the Family in Fifteenth-Century England', in *Bulletin of the Institute of Historical Research*, lviii (1985).

Swabey, F., *Medieval Gentlewoman: Life in a Widow's Household in the Later Middle Ages*, Stroud, 1999.

Taylor, J., 'The Plumpton Letters, 1416–1552', in *Northern History*, x (1975).

Thompson, S., *Women Religious: The Founding of English Nunneries after the Norman Conquest*, Oxford, 1991.

Ward, J.C. (ed.), *English Noblewomen in the Later Middle Ages*, London, 1992.

——, *Women of the English Nobility and Gentry, 1066–1500*, Manchester, 1995.

Waugh, S.L., 'Marriage, Class and Royal Lordship under Henry III', in *Viator*, 16 (1985).

Index

Note: members of the royal family are indexed under their Christian name, women who married into the royal family, by their maiden name; all other women are indexed under the name of their husband, but their maiden name, where known, is given, and the names of former husbands indicated.

Index

Index

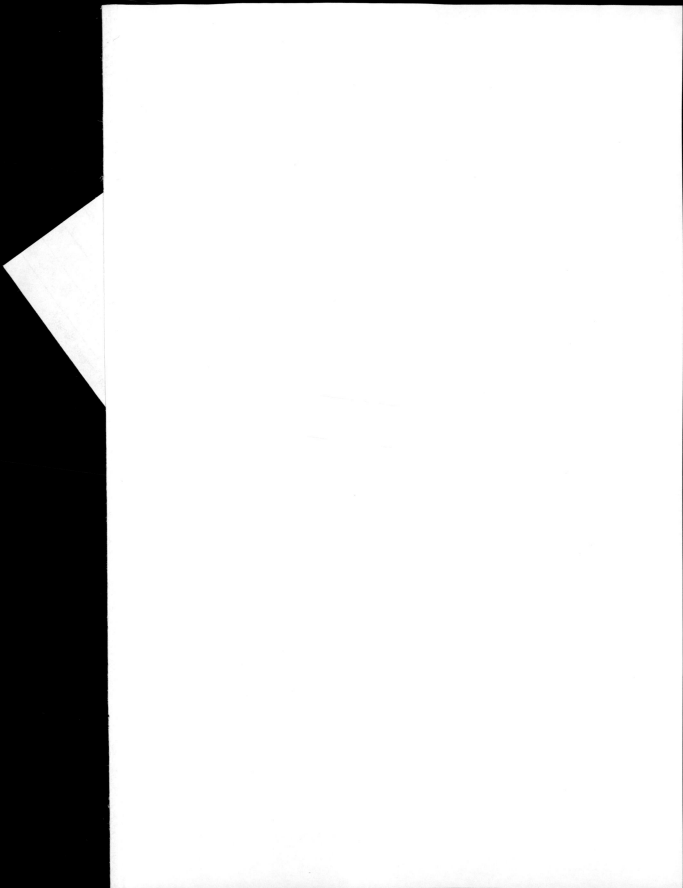

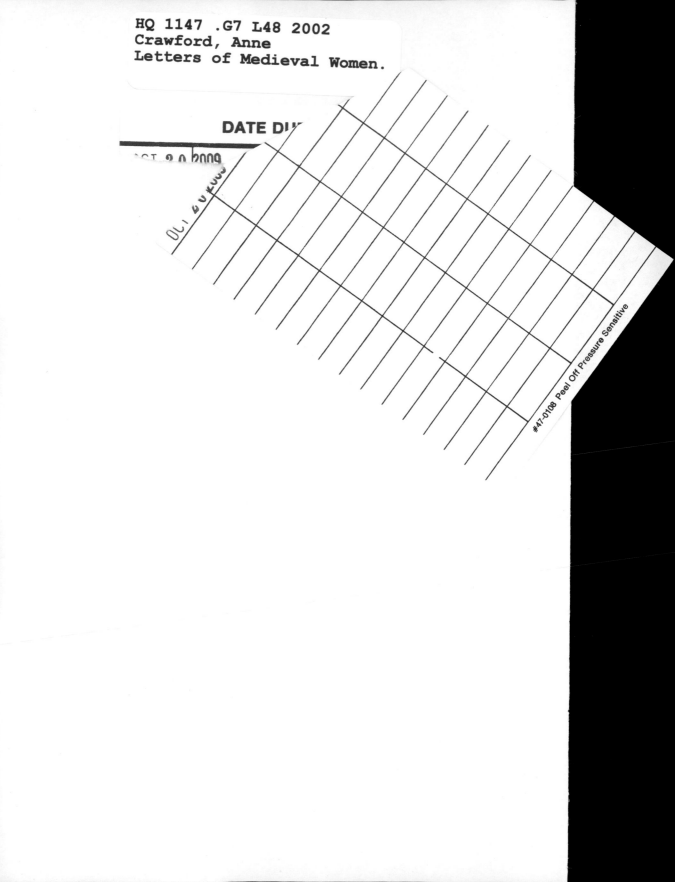